First Person Jewish

VISIBLE EVIDENCE

Michael Renov, Faye Ginsburg, and Jane Gaines, Series Editors

(for additional series titles, see page 204)

VISIBLE EVIDENCE SERIES, VOLUME 22

First Person Jewish

Alisa S. Lebow

 University of Minnesota Press

Minneapolis

London

Portions of chapter 1 were previously published as "Memory Once Removed: Indirect Memory and Transitive Autobiography in Chantal Akerman's *D'Est*," *Camera Obscura* 52 (vol. 18, no. 1) (2003).

Published by the University of Minnesota Press
111 Third Avenue South, Suite 290
Minneapolis, MN 55401-2520
http://www.upress.umn.edu

Library of Congress Cataloging-in-Publication Data

Lebow, Alisa.
    First person Jewish / Alisa S. Lebow.
        p.   cm. — (Visible evidence ; v. 22)
    Includes bibliographical references and index.
    ISBN 978-0-8166-4354-7 (hc : alk. paper) — ISBN 978-0-8166-4355-4
(pb : alk. paper)
    1. Jews in motion pictures.   2. Jewish motion picture producers and direc-
tors.   3. Documentary films—History and criticism.   4. Autobiography.
5. Identity (Psychology) in motion pictures.   6. Stereotypes (Social psychology)
in motion pictures.—I. Title.
    PN1995.9.J46L43 2008
    791.43'6529924—dc22
                                                                2008005308

Printed in the United States of America on acid-free paper

The University of Minnesota is an equal-opportunity educator and employer.

15 14 13 12 11 10 09 08   10 9 8 7 6 5 4 3 2 1

Contents

Acknowledgments

A book that takes the first person as its main focus would seem a likely place for an expansive first person narration. It is the logical choice for an author, to match subject and subjectivity. Yet, surprisingly and perhaps in a misplaced deference to a misbegotten sense of academicism, with the exception of the chapter about my own film *Treyf* I have mostly eschewed, if not the first person grammar, at least the first person account. Even as I aspire to the elegantly agile intellectual acrobatics of "personal criticism" projects such as Nancy K. Miller's *Bequest and Betrayal* and Annette Kuhn's *Family Secrets*—or, for that matter, Roland Barthes's *Camera Lucida*—which effortlessly fuse autobiographical and theoretical reflection, I have not managed to achieve such a dignified balance here. Still, I had such studies in mind as I wrote, and this book owes an intellectual debt to these bold and brilliant forays into what I have come to think of as the "first person critical" tense. And if nothing else, I will avail myself of the first person voice liberally in this admittedly circumscribed prefatory space.

Chantal Akerman has said that a filmmaker doesn't realize what her film is about until it's finished. In my case it has taken much longer than that. This project began, without my quite realizing it, when I set out to make a first person Jewish film with Cynthia Madansky back in 1995. We finished the film *Treyf* in 1998, at which point I began researching more seriously questions of Jewish first person representation. I had to explore the issues raised not only by my film but by many others before beginning to understand even a fraction of the forces at work on these cultural artifacts. This exploration was the basis of a critical study that eventually, after many incarnations (and with the assistance of a grant from the UK Arts and Humanities Research Council and research leave granted by the School of Cultural Studies of the University of the West of England), turned into the book you hold in your hands.

Going from practice to theory requires a conceptual shift. The making of a film, however profound its effect and multidimensional its approach, still allows for only limited theoretical exploration of the concepts it raises. One's concerns are driven by, and limited to expression within, the time-based audiovisual medium. Film may be a thin medium for theory (ask anyone who has attempted to take on dense theoretical issues in a film), but it is an infinitely rewarding object of study for the theorist and one made even more interesting when one wades in unknown territory. When I began writing about Jewish autobiographical documentary, there were no monographs available on any aspect of first person filmmaking, let alone anything so specific as a case study. I had to rely on individual articles by such intrepid film and literary scholars as Michael Renov, Susana Egan, and Jim Lane, as well as on writings by literary critics who had never considered how their theories might (or might not) apply to film, but who had nonetheless made important contributions to autobiography studies (I'm thinking of Sidonie Smith, Philippe Lejeune, James Goodwin, and of course Jacques Derrida). By the time this study developed into a book, there were two books published on first person film—which attests to exactly how long a road this has been. On such a long and circuitous journey, there are inevitably many people to thank, and indeed many unpayable debts of gratitude. Perhaps at least an acknowledgment here of my thanks will go some way to convey my deepest appreciation of the support, advice, assistance, and love I have received.

My greatest debt of gratitude goes to Cynthia Madansky, without whom none of this would have gotten off the ground. Together we made not only a film that I'm still proud of many years later, but much more. No other single individual has had so profound an influence on my thinking and creativity. I hope she is pleased with the result.

The intellectual encouragement of the documentary theorists I most respect, among them Michael Renov, Elizabeth Cowie, and Janet Walker, meant more to me than I can convey here. Chris Straayer, Faye Ginsburg, and Barbara Kirshenblatt-Gimblett never failed to amaze me with their endless generosity, not to mention their brilliance. I thank Faye and Barbara in particular for inviting me into their hotbed of intellectual ferment, the New York University Center for Media and Religion. I had the privilege to present my work to the center's working group on Jews, media, and religion, whose members (especially Jeffrey Shandler) gave me useful feedback. I thank Barbara Abrash and Angela Zito at the Center for inviting me to further benefit from my connection to this community of scholars as a CMR Visiting Fellow in autumn 2005.

Thank you to my stalwart editor at the University of Minnesota

Press, Jason Weidemann, and to the editors of the Visible Evidence series. A special mention goes also to Nancy Sauro, Paula Friedman, and Adam Brunner at the Press. A prize for unshrinking tenacity should go to Senem Aytac, who patiently and laboriously input my barely legible changes to the manuscript; the award for technical support in the way of invaluable video dubs goes to Lauren Steimer. Thanks to the editors of *Camera Obscura,* especially Patty White and Lynne Joyrich, who believed in this project enough to publish two articles originating from it.

Ivone Margulies's encouragement with regard to my work on Akerman was an unexpected pleasure. I thank Bob Stam, who may still be in search of the latent film scholar in me, and Anna McCarthy, who encouraged me to ferret out the not-so-latent links in my analyses to discourses of race and racism—which I have perhaps not done to her satisfaction, or even to mine. Jane Arthurs first suggested I apply for research leave after working at the University of the West of England for barely three months, something I would never had had the chutzpah to do on my own. Her support and mentorship continues to be a precious gift. Other colleagues and friends have given their time and attention to work through sticky ideas or read a passage or chapter. Here I would like to especially mention Sara-Jane Bailes, Jonathan Boyarin, Michael Chanan, Tuna Erdem, Rachel Gabara, and Bülent Somay.

In the process of writing and rewriting this manuscript I have benefited from the close scrutiny of old and new intellectual companions, some of whom, like Michele Aaron and Jeffrey Skoller, really got to know me only through my writing, and with whom I hope to continue a more mutual dialogue in the future. Marcos Becquer and Bliss Lim (whom I also admire deeply) suffered through many early drafts only out of love for the person they already knew. Our dialogues were responsible for advancing my thinking well beyond the limits of my own imagination. To Marcos, I must apologize for at times selfishly privileging the state of my book over the infinitely more important state of his health.

My fellow Bristol Docs First Person Films Symposia Series organizers, Jon Dovey and Tony Dowmunt, made me recognize that there really is strength in numbers. The symposia that we organized helped me to clarify what is most salient about first person filmmaking and to see that there are many others who are interested in developing this particular line of theoretical inquiry. I learned much from the participants of these symposia as well.

Of course, this book could never have been written if not for the filmmakers who made the fascinating films discussed within it. For this reason, I am grateful to Chantal Akerman, Jan Oxenberg, Alan Berliner,

Barbara Myerhoff, Debbie Hoffmann, Gregg Bordowitz, Ruth Novaczek, Abraham Ravett, Jonathan Caouette, and many others. Some of the filmmakers helped more directly by providing copies of their films, stills, interviews, and feedback. I am indebted to them for all they have done to advance Jewish self-representational strategies as well as film language more generally. To paraphrase Sandra Bernhard: without them, this book is nothing.

No one could hope for a more beautiful, quirky, and loving family than mine. I want to acknowledge the incredible and unquestioning support I received from my mother, Gloria Lebow-Green, my sisters, Deena, Deborah, and Beth, my brother-in-law, Rodney Alan Greenblatt, my nieces and nephews, Kim, Cleo, Matthew, and Joshua, and my aunt Selma. May you all *shep'n nakhes* from this book, despite its flaws and failures.

I will abide by the time-honored custom of saving the sweetest for last: the lover's coda. I never imagined a more engaged and joyful writing environment than the one I had when revising my manuscript in New York, writing side by side, taking breaks, making life-sustaining meals, and generally thriving on the love, intellect, and wisdom of the beautiful soul who is Basak Ertür.

Introduction:

Reading First Person Documentary

I am the other of me.
:: Edmond Jabès

First person documentary entails a range of practices, techniques, and temporalities: it can document a moment or event in the filmmaker's life; it can be a diary of thoughts and feelings; it can be a memorial for a relative, friend, or lover; it can be a testimony or a poem, an essay or a diatribe; it can be a rant, a romp, or a drone; it can be framed in the present, past, future, or even subjunctive tense. Some first person documentaries fit the more common autobiographical mold by giving a chronological account of the narrator's history. Others fulfill Walter Benjamin's ideal of fruitless searching and nonnarrative fragments that "yield only to the most meticulous examination."[1] Many make little or no effort to explore the past at all, entering a story in medias res, giving the impression of events unfolding before the camera, perhaps even for the camera's sake.

Despite this range and diversity, there are two distinguishing features of the first person documentary: subjectivity and relationality. All such documentaries, with their first person address, signal a subjectivity that was once, not very long ago, actively suppressed in documentary films. And, with the arguable exception of some video diary work, these first person works also share an aspect of relationality, involving many others in the project of constructing the self on screen. Filmmaking, auto-biographical or otherwise, is not generally a solitary pursuit. With the exception of some video diaries, the films of this study are not made by a single individual sitting alone in a room as does the writer pensively penning her/his autobiography. Not only do films require crews (however skeletal), they also generally require subjects, someone to put in front of the lens. The first person filmmaker may well put herself before the camera, but this then requires someone to operate it from behind. More commonly, autobiographical filmmakers frame their familiar or familial others in the participatory project that is filmic self-representation. It is the very personal relationship between filmmaker and subject that subtends the gaze and indeed defines the work. As autobiography scholar Susanna Egan has noted, "film may enable autobiographers to define and represent subjectivity not as singular or solipsistic but as multiple and as revealed in relationship."[2]

If there can be said to be a grammar of the filmic autobiography, that grammar is surely film in the first person but it is not the first person singular. Autobiographical film implicates others in its quest to represent a self, implicitly constructing a subject always already in-relation—that is, in the first person plural. As psychoanalysis teaches, and as others such as Emmanuel Levinas and Judith Butler have argued, the self is always a relational matter, never conceivable in isolation.[3] First person film merely literalizes and makes apparent the fact that self-narration—not to mention autobiography—is never the sole property of the speaking self. It properly belongs to larger collectivities without which the maker would be unrecognizable to herself, and effectively would have no story to tell. This study further emphasizes the relationality of the autobiographical subject by recognizing its cultural imbrications. The first person in the title and in the films in question is modified by a very particular plurality, Jewishness.

Avant-garde filmmakers discovered the first person well before documentarists.[4] The artist's vision could be foregrounded, at a time when the documentarians had to be suppressed. The emergence of the subject in documentary has long been hampered by the burden of disinterested objectivity, an impossible ideal that required innumerable evasions and repressions to effect.[5] A genealogical study of that which has been repressed in documentary's drive toward maintaining the illusion of objectivity would reveal whole storehouses of subjective interventions lying on the proverbial cutting room floor, omissions required to sustain the impression of an unmediated flow straight from "reality" to the viewer. No such unmediated (automatic) stream carries the first person film. The filmmaker's subjectivity is not only brought back into frame, it permanently ruptures the illusion of objectivity so long maintained in documentary practice and reception. These films, which have proliferated for the last quarter of a century, expose the inherent instability of the documentary as well as the autobiography, and pose a challenge to the conceptual framework of the documentary field.[6] Michael Renov credits "the new autobiography" with the "construction of subjectivity as a site of instability—flux, drift, perpetual revision—rather than coherence," and claims that filmic autobiography's transgressive status can be found partly in that it "posits a subject never exclusive of its other-in-history. In so doing, it challenges certain of our staunchest aesthetic and epistemological preconceptions."[7] Thus, ironically, the rise of the author in first person films (something not conceived of as a particularly radical proposition in its literary counterpart) has been a most effective tool in derailing the ill-fated quest for objectivity, so long the quixotic dream of documentary.

There were sprinklings of first person films in the 1970s, an increase in their production in the 1980s, and a virtual explosion in the 1990s, showing no sign of abatement today.[8] As documentary has found its way onto the big screen and into the public imaginary, with unprecedented commercial success in the beginning of this century, one cannot help but notice that many documentaries speak in the first person. Michael Moore, of course, led the way, with his inimitable obstreperous style, but many more have followed suit. Of the early-twenty-first-century "block-buster docs" (as they have come to be known), several were first person films, and a disproportionate number were made by Jewish filmmakers: *Supersize Me* (Morgan Spurlock 2003), *My Architect* (Nathaniel Kahn 2003), *Tarnation* (Jonathan Caouette 2004), to name but three of the biggest. Although I will not be analyzing all three in-depth, the very fact of their popularity spurs me on, considering that when I began my inquiry into Jewish first person films several years ago, few people had any idea what I might be going on about. I can now point to any one of these examples with some assurance that people may have at least heard of it. My hope is that, by the end of this book, the reader will be familiar with quite a few more and will also have an animated sense of what is most compelling about them and of the ways they enliven debates about the representation of (specifically Jewish) subjectivity in documentary film.

The films I choose to focus on in this study are not blockbusters, nor are they "popular" (or even widely seen). Quite the opposite, in fact, since one of my objectives as a film scholar is to write about lesser-known works that I believe deserve critical attention not only for their artistic merit and sensibility but for their near-seismographic sensitivity to cultural shifts and tremors. As Renov claims and as I intend to demonstrate, "it is in this domain of artistic practice—at the margins and interstices—that one can begin to take the measure of a culture, to discover its latencies and phobias as well as dismantle its preconceptions."[9] The films that permit me to take that measure, and which comprise the core of this study, are: *D'Est* (1993) by Chantal Akerman; *Everything's for You* (1989) by Abraham Ravett; *Thank You and Goodnight* (1991) by Jan Oxenberg; *Fast Trip, Long Drop* (1993) by Gregg Bordowitz; *Rootless*

Cosmopolitans (1990) and *Cheap Philosophy* (1993) by Ruth Novaczek; *Complaints of a Dutiful Daughter* (1994) by Deborah Hoffmann; *Nobody's Business* (1997) by Alan Berliner; *Daughter Rite* (1979) by Michelle Citron; *Tarnation* (2004) by Jonathan Caouette; *Phantom Limb* (2005) by Jay Rosenblatt; *In Her Own Time* (1985) by Barbara Myerhoff and Lynne Littman; and my own film *Treyf* (1998), made in collaboration with Cynthia Madansky.[10]

I make no claim, nor have I any intention, to conduct a comprehensive survey of all first person films made by Jewish filmmakers, in part because I do not have much faith in studies that pretend to be exhaustive, and in part because I lack the requisite archivist's compulsion. Instead, this study is a selective sampling of Jewish first person films that treat the question of subjectivity in particularly challenging and innovative ways, and which raise interesting questions about Jewish identity and cultural production. That is to say, it is an idiosyncratic look at complex strategies of self-representation in contemporary Jewish first person documentaries.

Many of these independently produced films construct a second or a fictionalized "self" that severs the autoenunciative lead character from the author of the text. Others detour through family or geography in their representation of self. Still others feature multiple authors. These films invent alter egos, present prior work as synecdoche for self, substitute other's memories as the filmmaker's own, and swap identities between characters. In this process of self-fictionalization, they wittingly or unwittingly contribute to the historicization of a postmodern Jewish subject.

Rather than constituting a separate genre, the use of experimental and fictional techniques in recent Jewish first person films is in line with larger, synchronous developments cross-culturally in contemporary autobiographical documentaries, also known as the "new autobiography."[11] The forces of identity politics and related academic fields (queer studies, ethnic studies, etc.) have played a significant role in the increased production of Jewish first person films (along with that of much other ethnic and identity-based first person filmmaking) and also in the critics', curators', and scholars' interest in such filmmaking.[12] An emphasis on cultural specificity and the politics of location—the place from which one speaks—has demanded that filmmakers (and artists more generally) attempt to evaluate their own situatedness and consider ways in which that positionality impacts one's work, worldview, and relations with others.

I have found that many of the Jewish first person films in this study fall well in line with contemporary theoretical concerns, including those of documentary studies itself. The films deploy the so-called new, postmodern documentary strategies to ultimately reenact and update a number of the struggles, conflicts, and concerns of earlier Jewish intellectual and cultural work. The modernist concerns of Ashkenazi diasporic culture that perturbed the early twentieth century's newly emancipated Jew—anti-Semitism, assimilationism, secularism vs. traditionalism, Marxism vs. Zionism, Hebrew vs. Yiddish—have found their way, in somewhat altered but still recognizable forms, into the creative lexicon of contemporary Jewish self-imagining.[13]

These films are examples of the autoethnographic impulse, wherein cultural concerns are explored or displayed through the representation of the self. The term *autoethnography* was coined in opposition to the colonialist ethnography, signaling the subaltern's appropriation and arrogation of the colonizer's gaze.[14] As such, it has constituted a critical intervention in the history of anthropology, representing a radical break with that discipline's checkered colonialist past. It has also, ingeniously (and indispensably for my purposes), been applied to autobiographical work that can best be analyzed in and through the paradigm of culture. Catherine Russell asserts that "[a]utobiography becomes auto-ethnography at the point where the film- or videomaker understands his or her personal history to be implicated in larger social formations and historical processes."[15] I would modify this claim, shifting the emphasis onto the act of reception rather than the intentionality of the filmmaker. Thus, for me, autobiography becomes autoethnography at the point where the critic or viewer understands the film to be implicated in larger social formations and historical processes—which is to say, any autobiographical or, indeed, first person film can be productively read as an autoethnography. And this, in brief, is my preferred reading strategy.

The subject has been subjected to severe scrutiny in the last half century and what we have been left with is a famously fragmented, divided, multiple, refracting, incoherent muddle. Along with the dismantling of the subject comes the dismantling of reading subjectivity exclusively as the expression of an autonomous, isolated individual. Not only is every utterance social in the Bakhtinian sense, but every autobiography engages the embodied knowledge, memory, history, and identity of much larger entities than the self. One encounters a lively, interactive communicative process with history in these films. To paraphrase Bakhtin: "each [auto-biographical utterance] tastes of the context and contexts in which it has lived its socially charged life; all words and forms are populated by intentions."[16] It is these intentions, traces, and resonances (which are not always intentional on the part of the filmmaker) that I will tease out through an exploration of contemporary Jewish self-representation in film. First person film is a fluctuating and variable, yet infinitely generative, indicator of cultural horizons well beyond the narcissistic concerns of the individual subject and, as such, is an apposite if anomalous site for the study of cultural production. Thus we begin our journey of a collectivity spoken in the first person and the first person spoken in and through a collectivity (or several collectivities). The individual subject is neither subsumed nor wholly separate, but rather is as much a part of the process of collectivization as she or he is its product. To paraphrase a worthy locution, the subject in autobiography "must always belong—at some level—to a body politic."[17]

The process of producing a self onscreen engages typologies and tropes drawn from distinct, though multiple, cultural histories, and in turn contributes to the iconic representations of those histories. For all of the ontological difficulties that the terms *culture* and *history* present, this emphasis on cultural and historical context can, I believe, alter the expectations placed on autobiography that ordinarily (and problematically) assume a unified self within a singular, linear narrative—instead positing a constructed, culturally inscribed, fragmentary, and incomplete narrative that is neither the sole invention of an ideologically autonomous author, nor the collectively overdetermined product of a monolithic *culture*,[18] but rather is some admixture of these two impossible positions, made even more impossible (or exciting) by the fact that the cultural context is highly heterogeneous and always at some measure of remove.[19] In negotiating a similarly paradoxical set of relations, Chon Noriega proposed a third position for, in his case, Chicano testimonio videos, a position that he calls, following Doris Sommer, a "plural self," wherein the individual is not only multiple in and of herself/himself but is always understood as a set of relations to a larger collectivity. This *plural self* is my analytical reference point for the Jewish first person films of this study.[20]

As will become apparent, this book identifies a distinct tendency in Jewish autobiographical documentary film: the use of self-fictionalization strategies to define a multifaceted, nonessentialist, contemporary "Jewishness" while dialogically engaging tropes of Jewish cultural identity originating in the pre- and post-Enlightenment eras. Questions of Jewish identity and cultural production suddenly fit quite strikingly with larger multicultural concerns, serving as a theoretical magnet where the politics of race, sexuality, gender, cultural and ethnic difference, political polarization, assimilation, tradition, and a host of other cultural determinants are all drawn together in one very dense, historically loaded, cultural location: *Jewishness*.[21] Jewishness is, of course, itself a manifold and polysemous cultural site. Better known for its unsituatedness or disaggregatedness (otherwise known as the Diaspora), Jewishness provides dynamic and variegated vantage points from which to explore the range of concerns related to contemporary autobiographical film.

I want to say a word about my cultural object choice. It is not enough to simply claim uncritical affiliation as the motivation behind the choice to write specifically about Jewish work. I am conscious of the fact that Jews and Jewishness stand at the citational center of twentieth century trauma studies, as the paradigmatic modernist metaphor for suffering and victimhood, and, for that matter, as a potent contemporary political symbol of the return of the repressed. I do not wish to contribute further to an already overstated sense of exceptionalism. "The Jew" and "the Jews" have been allegorized, hyperbolized, metaphorized, and abstracted to such an extent that we could easily forget that we are not the model for all studies of identity, power, victimhood, witnessing, survival, diaspora, and of course trauma and memory.[22] Certainly the Holocaust has been cast by countless theorists and artists alike as the singular event that predicated the crisis of Western modernity, revealing the murderous underbelly of Enlightenment rationalism. By this, I do not mean in any way to refute the profound and horrific facts or effects of the Holocaust or to minimize its relevance. Surely it ranks as one of the most gruesome, nefarious, and pre-meditated genocidal catastrophes in history, and its tortuous ramifications will continue to play themselves out for some time to come. However, it is also true that scholars and artists in the West have a tendency to privilege that cataclysmic event to the near eclipse of all other massacres, genocides, wars, coups, revolutions, epidemics, or other man-made or natural disasters. Books, films, and museums about the Shoah are so numerous there are claims that they constitute an industry unto themselves. Jewish historians, sociologists, psychologists, and others are busy compiling stacks of video testimonies from survivors of the Shoah that would take the average human being multiple lifetimes to view. There is a protuberance to this archive that is somehow disquieting. It places Jews, and their peripatetic histories, at the eye of a cultural vortex in ways that would seem to need no further elaboration from the likes of me; if anything, a sense of scale might be in order. Yet it is precisely the force of these overarching narratives—and their concomitant metaphors and tropes—that make the films of this study so engaging. Indeed, this very lack of proportion may go some way to explain the proliferation of Jewish first person films in the last quarter of a century, giving me an uncommonly rich and varied object of study. That said, I do not intend to claim a special place for Jews in history, or even in the history of first person filmmaking. Importantly, I view the Jewish "I" in this book as an opportunity, not an exception; Jews are not the Chosen People here, they are simply a chosen focus for a case study of an ethnically charged subjectivity as it has been elaborated and articulated in an ever growing and diverse body of films. In addition, there is some value in pursuing a study on the representation of subjectivity from one's own situated subjectivity. In this study, I start from my own first person perspective as a Jewish filmmaker who has made a first person Jewish film, and as a film scholar advocating for a culturally and historically situated study of first person films.

▶ ───

Old Tropes, New (Con)texts: Auto-Jewish Reappropriations

In the process of self-representation, the autobiographer inevitably encounters a profusion of cultural tropes that must be negotiated. It has been suggested that this is all the more true for film, considering its tendency to "typify" characters.[23] Autobiography, then, has the unenviable task of confronting, confounding, and even confirming the assumptions, impressions, and (mis)conceptions about the author's or filmmaker's identificatory positionings. We might even say, following Foucault and Butler, that it is in the process of negotiating and articulating these perceptions that the autobiography generates the self, which may then be (mis)apprehended as having existed prior to these mediations. In other words, it is only through this process of naming and imag(in)ing that the subject is constituted, and this naming always emerges out of a history of names that have been called. This name-calling is of course the process through which knowledge is attained and power is gained and claimed. Naming may not always necessarily be pejorative but it certainly can and has been a zone of danger, as in the case of the mentally ill, the queer, the nonwhite, and the Jew, among others. Names are not neutral, and the histories they carry take on a life of their own. As Judith Butler has argued in relation to queer identification, terms may be "redeployed, twisted, queered from prior usage and in the direction of urgent and expanding political purposes" but they are "never fully owned" or controlled by the enunciator.

Names—and, I want to add, stereotypes and tropes—have a history that cannot be contained in the reappropriative gesture, no matter how important and strategic the intervention might be. Yet it is also crucial to appreciate the power and relevance of reappropriation, even if it is never conceived of as the final answer, the last word on the names we've been called. Reappropriation is a risky game that can easily backfire, but it also has the potential to disrupt earlier meanings that may never regain their former implications and influence, due specifically to the syntagmatic shift that has occurred. The reappropriative maneuver involves precisely the unauthorized arrogation of "properly" held power (the power to name or to subjugate), a typically destabilizing tactic. The question of whether a stereotype can ultimately be effectively reappropriated, reinterpreted, resituated, or repudiated is not easily resolved. History may persist in the trope, above and beyond the author's intentions, but that does not mean that these sometimes tortured twistings of type cannot also be themselves torqued, altering both their form and their impact.

> The expectation of self-determination that self-naming arouses is paradoxically contested by the historicity of the name itself: by the history of the usages that one never controlled, but that constrain the very usage that now emblematizes autonomy; by the future efforts to deploy the term against the grain of the current ones, and that will exceed the control of those who seek to set the course of the terms in the present.[24]

Butler remains unconvinced of the radical resignifiability of names, although she recognizes the provisional value of the strategy.

In the process of discussing several of the works in this study, I will consider the ways in which these contemporary filmmakers attempt to remold inherited stereotypes and their various (and varied) successes in reshaping the representation of their "selves" as Jews, among other identifications, through a manipulation of the terms of the stereotypes themselves.[25] The types of characters that fill the screens and who stand in for the autobiographical subject in many of these films include several by now well-worn Jewish cultural stereotypes: the chameleon, the charlatan, the rootless cosmopolitan, the pathological or sickly Jew, the wandering Jew. The slippery, contradictory, image of the Jew formerly found in the lexicon of the anti-Semite has come to yield a new meaning in the context of postmodern identity, basking in the cultural approbation of a currently sanctioned discourse. In this redemptive, culturally affirming shift, traditional Jewish stereotypes drawn from a vast antipathetic cultural cache have been transformed into a positive conception: the self as open-ended figure.

Let me briefly recount but a few of the recycled tropes that appear in the films of this study. The very title of Ruth Novaczek's *Rootless Cosmopolitans* refers to a derogatory image of the Jew as a suspicious, shifty-eyed, urban byproduct. Novaczek also delights in parading loud, pushy, neurotic, typically Semitic-looking women across her screen. In *Cheap Philosophy,* her multiple characters and costume changes harken back to the image of the Jewish chameleon. Chantal Akerman fairly epitomizes the wandering Jew in *D'Est* and several of her other films. In Gregg Bordowitz's *Fast Trip, Long Drop* we see a reemergence of the stereotype of the sickly, neurotic, and pathological Jew. In each of these films the stereotypes are transformed by their new context. The opposite also occurs in some films—the absence of Jewish markers (including stereotypes) in some leads us to question our own normative typecasting assumptions, such as happens when the white lower middle-class Texan family of Jonathan Caouette's *Tarnation* leaves critics such as Stuart Klawans scratching their heads and proclaiming the film a "demolisher of stereotypes."[26]

▶───────────────────────────────────────

Unruly Corpus

Given my skepticism as to the inherent usefulness of overarching categories, and a distinct indisposition toward defining limits and borders of categories, it is not surprising that the films I have selected for this study prove relatively difficult to characterize, let alone categorize. I do not intend to create an airtight category of Jewish first person films that resists all conceptual leakage. The films of this study are exemplary of the crisis of definition and categorization that plagues documentary, autobiography and identity, in that they call attention to the necessary impurities of genres and categories to which they are nonetheless ascribed.

Nevertheless, it is possible to delineate five key criteria used in selecting these films. They are:

1. Independent films. As noted earlier, I am particularly interested in looking at noncommercial films, where a certain degree of autonomy can be assumed, and where it is virtually ensured that the films have not been considered in as much critical depth as they deserve.

2. Documentaries. Not unrelatedly, I focus on documentary and experimental films rather than fiction films. I might well have chosen to include autobiographical feature films, such as many of Woody Allen's or Barry Levinson's films, but I have decided to limit my discussion to those films, including the experimental variety, whose truth claims overlap in more directly troubling ways with documentary. In other words, the majority of films in this book partake of fictional and/or experimental strategies calling attention to the limits of documentary while still operating within identifiable documentary conventions. These "hybrid-docs" are more *about* flouting conventions and categorizations than properly constituting a coherent category in and of themselves.

3. Autobiographical. Even though I use an expanded definition of autobiography that includes many possible detours to the self, the films have nonetheless to be made by the person who was also in some sense

the central figure in the text. That is to say, the film had to be about some aspect of the filmmaker's own life.

4. Made by diasporic Jewish filmmakers. The films have to be made by diasporic Jewish filmmakers. Although there are many "new" auto-biographical documentaries made by Israeli Jews, most notably and inter-estingly by maverick mockumentarist Avi Mograbi, I have chosen not to include a discussion of them here since I believe the conditions that have produced Israeli Jewish identities are too radically distinct from those forming their diasporic counterparts to be collapsed into one study. It was difficult enough to negotiate the *Jewish* criterion, which required that the filmmakers could somehow be identified or identify themselves as Jewish, though not necessarily in their films. Of course, this is a highly problematic criterion, not least because of the essentialist assumptions that subtend it (what makes a Jew—descent, ascent, or both? who gets to self-identify as a Jew? if one isn't self-identified as Jewish, but is born Jewish, can one still be identified by others as Jewish?). One quickly finds oneself in deterministic quicksand, with the ominous overtones of the Nuremburg laws lurking a bit too close for comfort. Would I have excluded, for in-stance, an autobiographical film made by a non-Jew who finds out belat-edly that her paternal grandmother was Jewish, making her Jewish enough to be sent to the gas chambers but not Jewish according to rabbinical law? Of course I would include it, due precisely to the troubling issues it raises about identity and identification in relation to Jewishness.[27] However, any move on my part to finally determine Jewishness as a fixed criterion is doomed to repeat an unreflective essentialism that leads to myriad pitfalls, none of which would augment the value or the rigor of this study.

5. Aesthetically innovative. Crucially, any film that I have chosen to discuss in any depth has had to approach the autobiographical subject in innovative and multifaceted ways. This means that I have not included discussions in any detail of the most common Jewish autobiographical documentary: the artless, sincere, direct-address video that makes no attempt to deconstruct the subject or allow the subjectivity of the film its full range of complexity. These films do have their merit and their audi-ences, and much can be said about them, but inventiveness and creativity is not their strong point. The films in this study generally attend to the aesthetic dimensions of filmmaking in ways that make them particularly intriguing and rewarding from both a thematic and a formal point of view. This last criteria also seems to have had a determinative effect on the content of the films, especially with regard to the issue of traditional Judaism. It is not a coincidence, I believe, that films that defy or expand traditional documentary aesthetics and pose challenges to any simple or

unified conception of the self, such as those discussed in this book, tend to refrain from negotiating the question of religious tradition head on. They are by definition rebellious texts.[28]

Beyond these five general criteria, other factors emerged, quite apart from my own determination. For instance, all but one of the filmmakers (Barbara Myerhoff) were born after World War II. In addition, and to my dismay, there are no films here by Sephardic or Mizrahi Jews—that is, Jews of non-European origins—with the exception of Alan Berliner's work. Berliner is half-Sephardic; however, the film I focus on here, *Nobody's Business,* is mainly preoccupied with his Ashkenazi father and his father's side of the family.[29] I hesitate to speculate as to why so few first person films have been made by Sephardic and Mizrahi Jews in the Diaspora, but I am gratified to know that more are in the process of being made.[30] In all other ways, the attributes of the filmmakers are surprisingly diverse; the films are made by men and women, straight and gay, American and European, of differing ages, socioeconomic backgrounds, formal and aesthetic inclinations, trainings, and points of view.

To return for a moment to the problem of the Jewish criterion, permit me to pose a few further questions. Is it enough to insist that the filmmaker is Jewish? Without explicit Jewish thematics, how can I justify including a film depending merely on highly suspect and unreliable essentialist categories? To insist that a film is Jewish because its filmmaker *may be* is to position myself as a gatekeeper of dubious authority. This book is meant to be a protracted consideration of a set of films that speak to contemporary cultural issues of Jewishness as elaborated through sites of subjectivity. And although by default I do stick fairly close to a notion of Jewish descent, almost exclusively including films made by people born into Jewish families, this is not a meaningful criterion in and of itself. Nor is a filmmaker's own exploration or explanation of his or her Jewishness. Many films in this study do not engage Jewishness directly or forthrightly as might be expected. There is even a tendency toward crypto-Jewish expression in some of these films, as with Deborah Hoffmann's understated, nearly undetectable, Jewish references in *Complaints of a Dutiful Daughter,* the perfect American family stock footage in *Phantom Limb,* or the Converso confusion when Jonathan Caouette's mother sings a gospel song in the opening of *Tarnation.* Still, these light imprints and even erasures are important Jewish representational strategies, difficult as they may be to discern, and having sometimes to be read against the grain.

Regardless of how the filmmaker wants to position a given film in relation to Jewish identity, I discuss each film with regard to a set of reading practices. In practical terms, this means that the Jewishness of the film may inhere more in my reading of it than in the film's or filmmaker's own insistence. Barbara Kirshenblatt-Gimblett has ingeniously claimed that "Jewish film is what happens when it encounters an audience."[31] This makes Jewishness in film an event—a happening that occurs in the encounter, not necessarily in the encoding. Intentionality of the filmmaker is secondary at best, and it is for this reason, in line with Kirshenblatt-Gimblett's insight, that I eschew any extended consideration of intentionality (with the admitted exception of the discussion of my own film) and rather emphasize modes of reception—listening, observing, perceiving, filtering—that can be conceived of as "watching Jewishly." This reception can entail seeking out or being attuned to (or even distracted by) the "Jewish moments" in a film, to use Jon Stratton's term,[32] or it can mean analyzing the film precisely for the ways it effaces the trace of its own Jewishness. There is no one way to watch Jewishly, and in the course of this book I hope to propose several alternative approaches to the encounter.

▶───────────────────────────────

Precursors and Prototypes

It is important to situate Jewish first person films within a history of first person documentary and experimental filmmaking generally. The personal documentary has developed as a form only in the last thirty years. Its insistent subjectivity flies in the face of documentary's unspoken dual dicta of objectivity and mastery. It does away with third person omniscient narration, and pirates documentary's legendary authority for personal use. As soon as a filmmaker declares "I think" or "I feel" in a film, the illusion of documentary disinterestedness disintegrates. First person film poses a challenge to the journalistic approach as well as to empiricist (scientific) and imperialist (ethnographic) models of filmmaking. The move toward first person filmmaking can be seen in part as a combining of the artisanal filmmaking techniques made popular by the lightweight sync-sound equipment developed in the late 1950s, and the rejection of the tenets of observational cinema that had become the documentary norm, especially in anglophone countries (notably the United States, the United Kingdom, and Canada), by the end of the 1960s. American avant-garde filmmakers Kenneth Anger, Jonas Mekas, Stan Brakhage, and others made early use of the first person in film, though we do see evidence of it much earlier, for instance in the very personal and intimate *Rain* by Joris Ivens (1929) or Dziga Vertov's *The Man with a Movie Camera* (1929). Although Vertov is nowhere pictured in the film frame, he posits his family (his brother Mikhail and his wife Elizaveta Svilova) as his surrogate filmmaking selves.[33] Self-reflexivity combined with a sense of personal stake was a strategy pursued by both Jean Rouch and Chris Marker in the 1960s and increasingly by the more critical ethnographic filmmakers beginning in the 1970s, who experimented with revealing the investments and positionalities of the filmmaker as she or he pursued the ethnographic object of study.

An early rebellion against the hegemony of observational cinema in the United States is the film *David Holzman's Diary* (1967), by Jim McBride. I mention this film because it signaled a break from the increasingly dominant Direct Cinema movement that touted fly-on-the-wall filming techniques—revealing the voyeuristic invasiveness of those very techniques while introducing the then unwelcome specter of the filmmaker's point of view. I mention this film also because it somehow seemed logical to McBride and his audience to make the protagonist—a self-absorbed, camera-wielding, Columbia University student obsessed with documenting every moment of his life—Jewish. His Jewishness goes completely un(re)marked in the film except for the obvious clue of his name. Why is the protagonist Jewish? What makes sense—in an unarticulated, self-evident way—about this choice?

I would argue that beyond the by now obvious tropes of the self-involved hyper-intellectual, Upper West Side Jew (not yet made internationally famous by Woody Allen at the time of *David Holzman*'s release, but nonetheless a stock New York character) is the tacit recognition of a cultural proclivity, relative to its WASP counterpart, to break down barriers between personal and social, formal and informal, that subtend the distance required to maintain the illusion of objectivity in observational film.[34] Jewish culture has a deeply hermeneutical tradition, one where interpretation and argumentation are privileged over dispassionate engagement. The quip "two Jews, three opinions" playfully encapsulates the value of the situated relation to issues of the world that is characteristic of Ashkenazi Jewish culture. Personal opinion, in a word, matters. And it is this value, among others, that lends itself to the personal, subjective approach.

Again, in the United States, feminist filmmaking of the early 1970s was the first identifiable movement that hailed the personal film as an important medium through which to explore cultural and political issues; think only of the famous incantation "the personal is political" and you can imagine why this would be. One of the very first autobiographical films from that movement was a film called *Joyce at 34* (1972), by Joyce Chopra in collaboration with Claudia Weill, two Jewish women who went on to direct feature films. Chopra was originally known for her film collaboration with one of the founders of the Direct Cinema movement, Richard Leacock.[35] *Joyce at 34* has become a classic feminist film and has come to represent (for better or worse) the white, middle-class, professional agenda associated with that movement. Chopra's Jewishness is effaced in all commentary on the film (despite the Passover seder that signifies "extended family" within the film), and instead it is her class and race (and, of course, her gender) that have been foregrounded.

Six years after Joyce Chopra's groundbreaking autobiographical film came out, Michelle Citron made one of the early feminist theory films,[36] *Daughter Rite* (1978). Citron's film received very similar critical acclaim, reception, and even derision as *Joyce at 34,* again without any mention of the filmmaker's Jewishness. *Daughter Rite* is a fake documentary that combines optically step-printed home movies and first person voice-over with a verité style narrative of two adult sisters who visit the house they grew up in while their mother lies ill in the hospital. Both narratives—the diaristic home movie footage narrated by a flat-toned disembodied female voice, and the fictional one of two sisters in their childhood home— represent what I took to be the lives, thoughts, emotions, and attitudes of non-Jewish, working-class, Midwestern women in their twenties. That the film was made by a working-class woman in her twenties, who may or may not have been the voice we heard in the voice-over sound track, seemed plausible. What was not at all apparent (at least to me) in the text, metatext, or even subtext, until Citron's autobiographical book came out in 1999, was that the film was made by, and to some extent about, a working-class Jewish lesbian from Boston.[37] Regardless of motivation or circumstances of production, the Jewish (and lesbian) content of Citron's own biography was suppressed in her semiautobiographical film, which has since become a classic of feminist film history.[38]

▶──

Why Now?

There has been a striking increase in Jewish autobiographical films in the last two decades, accelerating in quantity, and also transforming conceptually and aesthetically in the last ten years. This rise is directly in line with the increase of autobiographical film production generally, not exceptional to it, but the proportion of Jewish autobiographical films in relation to the proportion of Jews is quite high. It is worth considering why Jews in particular have gravitated toward the autobiographical film at this juncture in history. As I have already suggested, the extensive focus on Jewish history and experience does create an encouraging environment for such explorations, but this does not guarantee its emergence. On the practical level, one might be tempted to surmise that the advent of affordable, accessible video equipment has enabled this work, as it has for so many other communities, yet only two of the dozen or so films treated here were actually shot on video, and both of these (*Fast Trip, Long Drop* and *Complaints of a Dutiful Daughter*) were blown up to film at considerable expense. What seems like a plausible explanation, one that indeed may go a long way to explain, for instance, the popularity of the video diary, turns out to be inadequate to describe this wave of films.

One may wonder what would make someone turn to such an unwieldy and expensive medium as film to create their autobiographical work, especially at a juncture when funding is by no means assured—as it was not, for most of the films considered here. Most films in this study were, in fact, made before there was any single funding source that specialized in or prioritized Jewish documentary. The funding sources vary from film to film, and, at least in the United States, funding for independent documentary became much scarcer by the mid-1990s than before, so there is little basis to deduce that the material conditions were ripe for this efflorescence of Jewish autobiographical filmmaking. The resources were by no means secure or steady and, at the time, there was no foundation or funder spurring the work on.[39] In terms of exhibition, though, there has been, beginning in 1981, a lively Jewish film festival circuit in the United States and Canada, and to a lesser extent in Europe and elsewhere, virtually ensuring that films with even the vaguest Jewish content have an outlet to reach (mostly) Jewish audiences. Speaking as one of the Jewish autobiographical filmmakers in this study, one of my primary motivations for making *Treyf* was precisely this opportunity to engage in direct dialogue with Jewish audiences internationally, specifically on questions of Jewish identity and politics, which I, along with codirector Cynthia Madansky, felt was in considerable need of new perspectives and alternative political/ideological paradigms.

There are also historical reasons for this outpouring of Jewish autobiographical films. In addition to the pervasive sense that Western culture is increasingly "characterized by surface homogenization, by the erosion of public enactments of tradition, by the loss of ritual and historical rootedness," as anthropologist Michael M. J. Fischer has persuasively argued, there are more particular contemporary Jewish cultural anxieties.[40] As the experiences of migration and genocide recede from the province of personal memory, filmmakers have begun to construct images to depict that which remains or can be reclaimed in the formulation of contemporary Jewish identity.

I want to suggest that this moment in history marks a key transition for Jews. As the immigrant and the survivor generations pass on, younger Jews, born well after World War II, have been searching for ways to articulate Jewishness in their own terms while at times clinging to, or at least drawing from, representations of Jewishness from the past. As in a palimpsest, layers of histories resonate in the imagery, iconography, and thematics of these films. They are far more than accounts of individual histories. The films can be seen as examples of the Benjaminian flashes and bursts of history that erupt at a moment of danger and that reflect the "constellation which [their] own era has formed with a definite earlier one."[41] What that moment of danger is may differ in each case, though some distinct themes do emerge. Half a century after the Holocaust, the most fearsome danger point of reference for any contemporary Ashkenazi Jew, the generations of Jews who personally experienced prewar Jewish life (either in Europe or elsewhere), or who survived/lived during the war, are aging if not already gone. The connection to an already fragile and endangered history is receding, and several of the autobiographies of this study have seized the moment to render the constellation visible between this present, post-Holocaust era and that definitive earlier one.

Those of us coming of age in the latter quarter of the twentieth century bear the burden of inventing Jewish identity anew, albeit with flashes of the past shocking us at moments. For the secular Jewish filmmakers of this study, there comes, along with a generational remove from what we might call "embodied Judaism" or *yidishkayt,* a lack of clarity and assurance as to the precise elements constituting a contemporary, secular, Jewish identity. Yet the films enact the very Jewishness that eludes their filmmakers; in this sense, the quest is the reward. Writing about Jewish ethnographic film in a way that also pertains to Jewish autobiographical film, Faye Ginsburg quite accurately asserts that these films play an important role in the figuration of Jewish identity and in the revitalization of Jewish life in new contexts. They are "part of, [and] even create, the phenomenon they document." As such, she suggests, they would be "better understood . . . as part of 'participatory' or indigenous media, an emerging practice in which the subjects of the film are engaged as both makers and audience, so that the works are simultaneously about and part of the culture they depict." She continues, "they are not simply filmic texts, but are *mediating* documents, part of the process of the re-invention(s) of contemporary Jewish identity."[42] Borrowing Ginsburg's insights, Jewish autobiographical film allows for identity construction and transmission in ways that engage emotional and sensory as much as intellectual perception. As Ginsburg aptly suggests, "these filmmakers forge meaning and definition from fragments of past and current Jewish experience, creating works that both mark and are part of the process of cultural transformation that challenges and inspires the present generation."[43]

Moving from Singular to Plural

This book is organized into two broad sections, each section comprising two chapters. The first chapter in a section entails an in-depth analysis of an individual film; the second analyzes multiple films that can be said to share the section's common theme.

The first section thematizes first person films generated through some aspect of familial association and identification. If this sounds like a circumspect way to describe what could easily be called "family autobiography," there is a reason for my awkward phrasing. Although it is true that the family figures in many if not most autobiographical films, Jewish or otherwise, it often does so in unexpectedly complex and indirect ways, as seen especially in my analysis of Chantal Akerman's film *D'Est* in chapter 1. These first two chapters consider the multiple ways the family inspires, conspires, or indeed desires, in a range of first person Jewish films.

The second section focuses on a set of queer Jewish first person films, and the myriad issues raised in this dynamic conjuncture between two not entirely harmonious identity configurations.

Chapter 1 explores the relationship between history, memory, nostalgia and loss in the very dense and elliptical Jewish autobiographical film *D'Est*. This chapter explores Akerman's indirect autobiographical style, where the countless anonymous faces she encounters on her journey to Eastern Europe serve as surrogates for her own. Akerman returns to the terrain of her family's evacuation during World War II, reversing the east–west path of forced Jewish migration while enacting a very personal displacement of her own—that of the self. Akerman's oblique autobiographical style not only transposes others' faces for her own, but, equally uncannily, substitutes other's memories, particularly her mother's, for her own. Akerman imagines a past she never experienced, a past of exile and evacuation, her mother's memory transmogrifying into her own in a poignant rendition of what Marianne Hirsch calls "postmemory."

This form of indirect, displaced autobiography searches for traces of the past in the landscape of the present, where they erupt and disappear mysteriously. Walter Benjamin shadows Akerman in my analysis, echoing and prefiguring her movement eastward in his *Moscow Diary*. I examine the two texts and indeed the two assimilated Jewish thinkers' work in relation to their treatment of the "East," their shared corporeal representation of it and their refusal to make a political judgment or determination about it. Benjamin's own era becomes one important flashpoint of Akerman's vision as she searches faces for resemblances to, and hints of, a Jewish presence that has all but been effaced. A telescopic sense of time and a compulsion to remember mark this film as a Jewish text. In traditional Jewish culture, memory is an obligation and history contracts in an impossible millennial collapse where the catastrophes of each epoch come to exist palimpsestically in every present moment. *D'Est* exemplifies this Jewish form of remembering and constructs a Jewish self, that of the invisible filmmaker, as constituted through it. The film is a most elaborate detour to the self, opening the borders of autobiography to an expansive definition of an historical subjectivity.

The films addressed in chapter 2 also take a detour to the self, albeit one closer to home. Whereas Akerman's family may haunt her text, these films all construct their autobiographical subject explicitly through and in relation to the family. In doing so, these "domestic ethnographies" insist, in effect, on the heterogeneous nature of self-representation.[44] The films considered in detail in this chapter are: *Nobody's Business, Thank You and Goodnight, Everything's for You, Complaints of a Dutiful Daughter,* and *Phantom Limb,* though others, including *Daughter Rite, Tarnation,* and *Orders of Love,* are also addressed. The chapter begins by briefly analyzing the representation of the mainstream Jewish family, especially with regard to depictions of the Jewish mother and the Jewish grandmother, and considers the recasting of these codified types and roles in the films under consideration. The offspring (the filmmakers themselves) reveal themselves as perpetual children in relation to the family, even as the adult filmmakers display mastery of their craft. A child's triumphalism is effected, whether in recutting home movie footage or revisioning dominant family narratives.

In several of the films, access to family and to ancestral history and/or Jewish heritage is held at a frustrating remove. The knowledge may seem easily available, yet it remains ultimately locked in or lost to memory, making it inaccessible to the filmmaker. A recalcitrant father nearly refuses to remember or even care to remember the family lineage, in *Nobody's Business.* A dying grandmother no longer has the strength to transmit her "kitchen Judaism" to her granddaughter, in *Thank You and Goodnight.*[45] A noncommunicative father dies before he can disclose the details of his prewar life, populated as it was with another wife and two mysterious children, in *Everything's for You.* And in *Complaints of a Dutiful Daughter,* cultural, familial, and personal identity are on the verge of collapse with the loss of a mother's memory from Alzheimer's disease. Loss is repeatedly thematized as death haunts these family "autobiothanatoheterographies," with dead siblings, parents, grandparents, and ancestors continually resuscitated at twenty-four frames per second, all vying for space in the frame of self-construction.[46]

Although it seems that one's sense of Jewish identity is never constructed entirely outside the bounds of family, these films reveal the family to also be an impediment to any full or complete constitutive rendering of one's self as a subject in history (a quest already illusory and elusive). In these Jewish autobiographical films, the family becomes both necessary fiction and incomplete fantasy, simultaneously enabling and inhibiting any coherent semblance of cultural subjectivity. The films appear as attempts to improve upon or repair family narratives—a preliminary, personal step toward the Jewish mandate of *Tikkun Ha'Olam* (repair of the world), a step we might call *Tikkun Ha'Mishpakhah* (repair of the family).

Chapter 3 performs an autocritique of my autobiographical film, *Treyf,* made in collaboration with Cynthia Madansky. This chapter entails a close analysis of not only the film but the process of performing an autocritique, in what may be seen as a treyf—that is to say, unkosher—mixing of criticism and production. I avail myself of the opportunity to analyze my own film critically as a segue into a broader consideration of Jewish autobiographical film. The chapter raises questions, regarding the constitution and representation of self in first person film, that are central to this study. These questions are complicated, in regard to *Treyf,* by the differing rhetorical positions occupied by the autobiographical *I* and the autocritical *I*; by the discrepant registers of the filmic and the written; and by the double-voicedness (indeed the multivocality) of a coauthored autobiography. The analysis of this film elaborates the volume's discussions about problems of authenticity, nostalgia, tradition, identification, ambivalence, visibility, and dissent, all of which are taken up in various guises in the chapter that follows. Analyzing my own film allows me to consider these issues from a first person position, anatomizing my choices and strategies that bear on my understanding of other first person films in this study. Indeed, my interest and investment in the films studied here come from a deeply engaged relationship, the result of struggling with many of the issues, and inventing my own solutions to the conundra, raised in the making of contemporary Jewish autoethnography.

In this chapter, the concept of treyf, a Judaic proscription, becomes a metaphor for the liminal space claimed both within the film and in the process of autocritique. In the film, our characters stand in dynamic tension with the religious and Zionist traditions in which we were raised. Made in part to advance a dialogue within the American Jewish community on the ethical dilemma of the Israeli occupation of Palestine, the film attempts to construct a credible Jewish "insider" to maximize its political effectivity, for we know full well that many factors, not least our queerness and our political perspective, contribute to our outsider status. We resemble Trinh T. Minh-ha's "deceptive insider/deceptive outsider"; that is to say, our position questions the rightful attribution of insider/outsider ("who gets to say what's treyf? who's treyf?" the film asks) and posits our characters as never fully insider nor ultimately outsider to the parameters that molded and shaped our oppositional yet engaged stance.[47] The insider/outsider logic also marks my act of autocritique, as I endeavor to analyze at some measure of distance a text and a tradition in which I am inevitably implicated.

Treyf is a queer film that takes its queerness for granted, preferring to interrogate notions of Jewishness from a queer perspective. Yet it does not entirely manage to portray both identities in dynamic relation. Rather, it reveals the difficulty of so doing. Chapter 4 looks at a range of queer Jewish first person films, which, like *Treyf,* fail, to one degree or another, to filmically integrate the two identities. This chapter considers the double movement of queer Jewish first person films that seem to assert their desire for queer and/or Jewish visibility while at the same time retreating into a haze of ambivalence and ambiguity. This queer/Jewish pairing is not arbitrarily chosen. Many of the filmmakers in this study identify or can be identified as queer, whether or not they treat sexuality thematically in their work. In addition, the two identities, homosexual and Jewish, have interrelated histories, making the pairing particularly intriguing. The films treated in this chapter are: *Cheap Philosophy, Rootless Cosmopolitans, Thank You and Goodnight, Treyf, Tarnation, Complaints of a Dutiful Daughter,* and *Fast Trip, Long Drop.* Surprisingly but undeniably, in many of these films, queerness and Jewishness coexist uncomfortably in the frame. The pressures of visibility politics so prevalent in the Western gay rights movements since the 1970s do not translate directly into a clear queer Jewish aesthetic. There is a noticeable reticence on the part of some of these filmmakers to explore or even to reveal these identities explicitly in these films. For instance, both Akerman and Oxenberg are so circumspect about their sexuality in the films, that recourse to extratextual information is necessary. Others, like Hoffmann, are so subtle in reference to their Jewishness that I am prompted to analyze their silences on the subject symptomatically. Ambiguity and ambivalence, in terms of queer and/or Jewish articulations, become the common elements defining the films in this chapter.

Ambivalence is theorized in this chapter through sociologist Zygmunt Bauman's definition of Jews as modernity's ambivalent *other*. Bauman contends that, in modernity's ordering compulsion, the Jews have come to signify disorder and alterity by exceeding all national, racial, and class limits, the very categories that have obsessed modernity.[48] Similarly heterogeneous, though never mentioned by Bauman, queers are another of Western culture's consummate *others*. But, if Jews and queers can signify the excess of Western modernity, that which cannot be contained, classified, or bureaucratically regulated, then the ambivalence of self-representation witnessed in these films merely extends these claims. The queer Jewish filmmakers of this study often reproduce this state of ambivalence through a formal or thematic ambiguity that remains ultimately unresolved.

Identifying yet another ambivalence, the chapter makes connections between nineteenth-century tropes of the homosexual and of the Jew, and explores the risky reappropriation of the sickly, pathological nineteenth-century Jew in the contemporary first person film by queer, HIV-positive, Jewish filmmaker Gregg Bordowitz. Bordowitz refuses the by-now bankrupt "positive images" strategy in favor of a defiantly sardonic "HIV-positive" one. Beneath his youthful good looks and strong, healthy demeanor is a sickly, sexually suspect Jewish man, dying to come out, as it were. Bordowitz, through his onscreen alter ego, Alter Allesman, reclaims the stereotype of the diseased and perverted Jew, and in doing so flies in the face of Jewish survival strategies of the last one hundred years. In Allesman's ethical rebelliousness, Bordowitz instantiates no trope so closely as the character who, when caught between the two ineluctable and unsavory poles of pariah or parvenu (available both to the nineteenth-century Jew and to the invert in the salons of Saint Germain), chooses the third option of the moral gadfly, Hannah Arendt's "conscious pariah."[49]

In concluding this volume, I look at a film that epitomizes some themes of this study yet takes them a step further. Barbara Myerhoff's *In Her Own Time* is ostensibly an ethnographic film about the Hasidic community in the Fairfax section of downtown Los Angeles, framed in the reflexive ethnographic practices that she helped to develop. The film, however, exceeds its rhetorical context and passes from the strategic reflexivity it deploys—meant to illuminate the practices and beliefs of the ethnographic subject—to a full-fledged autobiographical film, wherein the central focus shifts from the community to the filmmaker. This film, however, even exceeds the terms of traditional autobiographical film, since an implicit requirement of the genre is that the filmmaker survive at least as long as it takes to finish the film. A filmmaker may foreshadow or foretell her or his own death; she or he may even stage it as Gregg Bordowitz does (stepping out into traffic in front of a bus), providing she or he lives to tell of the staging. In Myerhoff's case, the film was finished posthumously (by the only credited director of the film, Lynne Littman), making it in effect a communiqué from the grave. This is a clear instance of what Michael Renov in an unpublished paper has termed "assisted autobiography,"[50] yet I am captivated by the spirit of the film, which haunts like a revenant, a dybbuk who speaks to us from the other side through a figure who both is and is not the film's author. Jacques Derrida and Paul de Man have each theorized autobiography as thanatography, an epitaph and a death mask foreshadowing the imminent demise of the autobiographic subject, and this film literalizes that demise.[51]

Further, the film, with its head-on collision of secular and orthodox Jewish culture, stages a discomfiting reconciliation between what function for many contemporary Jews, and certainly for the filmmakers in this study, as opposing and irreconcilable forces. Not content to evoke Jewish tropes to create or affirm a bond with Jewishness, Myerhoff actually (if somewhat skeptically) invokes Jewish prayer and ritual. This film goes beyond articulating Jewishness autobiographically and attempts to embrace Judaism *halakhically*, as a way not only to preserve a tradition and a faith (the ethnographic salvage impulse to which Myerhoff, along with many others, was susceptible) but to preserve a self. This is Jewish autobiography *as* self-preservation, made as if her life depended on it. As lung cancer advances, Myerhoff turns in desperation to Jewish rites and rituals such as mikvah ritual purification and re-naming ceremonies to ward off the Malakh Hamavet (the Angel of Death). This particular Jewish autobiography has raised the stakes of Jewish self-representation literally to a matter of life and death.

The forms that these ethnoautobiographical films take, and the stories that they narrate, for the most part reveal a dynamic and ever adaptable subject-in-relation, continually negotiating the not always compatible forces of tradition, Jewish specificity, and (post)modern identity. What comes across in the collectivity of these films is the inventiveness of the filmmakers as they attempt, each in their own way, to represent Jewishness in the first person.

Memory Once Removed: Indirect Memory and Transitive Autobiography in Chantal Akerman's D'Est

In *The Imaginary Jew*, contemporary French philosopher Alain Finkielkraut laments that, although his Jewishness furnished him with the deepest, most precious aspects of his identity, it was, upon closer examination, not an identity conferred on him by his parents but rather one lived *through* them.[1] He fears that with their passing the substance of his Jewish identity would also pass, for it was through their memories and lived knowledge of the customs and languages of the culture that he experienced Jewishness. Having been secularly educated in assimilationist postwar France, he was without direct experience of a larger Jewish community, one beyond the boundaries of his home. He realizes with astonishment and a great sense of loss that his parents, Eastern European Holocaust survivors who relocated to France after the war, embodied *yidishkayt*, or Jewishness, for him and that with their bodies would go *yidishkayt*. The bridge between the thriving prewar Jewish culture of Eastern Europe that his parents held in their memories and the postwar Western European context in which he was raised was illusory. He even found himself nostalgic for the victimization experienced by the Jews of his parents' generation. In short, his (imaginary) Jewish identity was located at a generational remove.

Questions of displaced memory and indirect Jewish identity raised by Finkielkraut lie at the core of Chantal Akerman's 1996 film *D'Est* (Belgium/France/Portugal). The Holocaust created a distinct periodization, a traumatic before and after, for generations of post-Holocaust Jews that heightens the experience of loss and rupture (cultural, historical) already inherent in the passing of time. The effect for Ashkenazi Jews of Eastern European descent is that "the old country" becomes a sign without referent, an imaginary construct with no actual, geographical correlate. Akerman's *D'Est* approaches this historical chasm in a particularly striking way, attempting to reach across this divide while simultaneously conceding the futility of the gesture. In *D'Est,* Akerman goes "back" to Eastern Europe, the region in which her parents lived until World War II. This quasi-voyage of return could easily be mistaken for what Akerman herself derisively calls a "'back to my roots' kind of film," except that in the film she never specifies any personal markers or indicates her investment in the terrain.[2] She eschews iconographic Jewish or Holocaust images (there are no synagogues, no cemeteries, no crematoria) and avoids interviews and narration that might concretize her position. She even bypasses the specific town from which her family came. Akerman seems convinced of the impossibility of finding any meaningful remnants of the past. Her camera glides on the surface of present-day Eastern Europe with an implacable resolve, surveying the prosaic details of life lived in the interstices of bus stops, bread queues, and train station waiting rooms. Yet even in her resolute refusal to penetrate this façade, the very history she seems assiduously to ignore nonetheless protrudes. For her there seems no eluding the imprint of the past: it is written on the impassive faces and spaces she records.

Walter Benjamin wrote that "an image is that in which the Then *(das Gewesene)* and the Now *(das Jetzt)* come into constellation like a flash of lightening."[3] It is this constellation that the images of *D'Est* conjure. Akerman maps images of today's Eastern Europe onto the memories of a prior time, using the camera as a peripatetic time machine. Time, however,

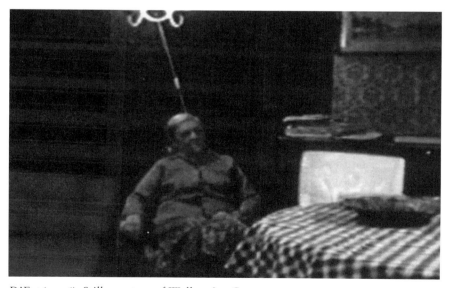

D'Est (1996). Still courtesy of Walker Art Center.

and history more specifically, is not conceived linearly here, but rather as akin to the flashes and ruptures that Benjamin proposes. With only a scant nod toward narrativity (the film follows the seasons and the journey from West to East, East Germany to Russia), Ackerman privileges the incidental detail over the descriptive, the random over the intentional—a woman listening to television, another applying lipstick, a man eating lunch. *D'Est* is a Benjaminian-style autobiography in that Akerman is more concerned with "space, moments, and discontinuities" than with what Benjamin describes as traditional autobiographical concerns: "having to do with time, with sequence, and what makes up the continuous flow of life."[4] She seeks the resonances of the past indirectly, utilizing a methodology favored by Benjamin where "fruitless searching . . . [is] as much a part of [the process] as succeeding."[5]

I find provocative parallels between Akerman's film and Benjamin's approach to time, history, the East, the body, and autobiography, as found specifically in his "Theses for a Philosophy of History," "N," "A Berlin Chronicle," and *Moscow Diary*.[6] Benjamin's insights and idiosyncratic philosophy of history and politics inform my analysis of *D'Est* in ways both explicit and implicit. When Benjamin claims: "what for others are deviations, for me are data by which I set my course," I see a kindred spirit, even an inadvertent disciple, to him in Akerman.[7] Benjamin and Akerman share an oxymoronic methodology of acute indirectness that astounds in its ability to communicate more nuanced and suggestive resonances between history and the present than could any forthright approach toward the subject.

One key difference between Benjamin and Akerman, however, is that not only is Akerman's method indirect but her memory is as well. Like Finkielkraut, Akerman identifies her Jewishness and her roots through the mother, and in effect it is her mother's memory (specifically, in this case, of evacuation from home and internment in the camps) that weighs on Akerman as if it were her own. With this appropriation of another's memory, there is an extended sense of self at work that challenges commonly held conceptualizations of individual memory as well as narrow definitions of autobiography.

In Akerman's process of "return," a self-(re)discovery occurs, and by the end of the film the filmmaker eventually does find herself, not in the landscape or the faces represented, per se, but instead in the revisitation of a recurrent theme (her primal scene) that runs, unwittingly yet consistently, throughout her work. Akerman's oeuvre is marked by a set of tropes—rootlessness, obsessiveness, the quotidian, the body, repetition—all of which appear in *D'Est*.[8] These tropes, along with her exploration of duration and prevarication, compose the formalist tools with which she creates work of intense personal (though often, as in the case of *D'Est*, indirect) revelation. Her work is infused with a particular type of Jewishness, one that retains a strong cultural affinity though it negotiates Jewish terms at a remove.[9] Like the great-grandson in the famous Baal Shem Tov parable, who knows neither the forest and tree nor the words to the prayer that his religious great-grandfather used to say, but nevertheless has the intention to pray and is still heard by God, Akerman is the Jewish descendant who still identifies with and operates in relation to a vague but ubiquitous sense of Jewishness, without the benefit of intimate or intricate knowledge and experience.[10] Whether reciting Jewish jokes and fables directly to camera in a setting that bears no traces of home or even of the familiar (*American Stories*, 1988), citing Jewish laws only to implicitly transgress them (most notably the Second Commandment, which finds its way into several of Akerman's films), or obliquely making reference to the Jewishness of her characters (*Meetings with Anna*, 1978), Akerman often places Jewishness at the heart of her films, while infusing that Jewishness with an alienation that speaks to her attraction/repulsion regarding traditional Jewish law, and also to her particular identification with the trope of the Wandering Jew. In other words, Jewishness, like memory, is treated with much circumspection in Akerman's work. In effect, Akerman perambulates (that is, wanders) around her Jewishness.

Not surprisingly, the figure of the wandering Jew is a trope latently identifiable in *D'Est*, as it is in other Akerman films.[11] In fact, *D'Est* is a wandering Jewish road movie in search of its autobiographical subject. With regard to the autobiographical aspect of Akerman's Jewish nomadism, Janet Bergstrom quotes an interview with Akerman in *Cahiers du Cinéma* in which Akerman states: "In fact, [nomadism is about] finding your place, and I don't know if you ever find your place . . . I think that goes back to my Jewish origin. As far as I'm concerned, I don't have a relationship with any place."[12] It may even be said that the only place with which Akerman is fully identified is a textual one, the site of her own work. In a brilliant solipsistic gesture, which implicitly acknowledges the autobiographical nature of her films while also suggestively situating the self as a product of the work (and not prior to it), Akerman chooses to represent herself in the autobiographical *Chantal Akerman by Chantal Akerman* (1996) through reediting clips of all her films into a new pattern. For Akerman, it can be said that her work elliptically narrates her life. I take as my premise in this chapter that "Akerman's cinema is autobiographical, whether directly . . . or indirectly," and I will read her particular detours to the self (as a daughter, as a Jew, as a filmmaker) in a series of detours of my own.[13]

Through an analysis of Akerman's use of time, her focus on faces,

Bordering on fiction: Chantal Akerman's *D'Est* installation, chamber 2. Still courtesy of Walker Art Center.

and her references to what she calls her "primal scene" (which for her is composed of images of evacuation), I develop a theory of her indirect autobiographical style in *D'Est*—the transitive autobiography—as an elaboration of her (and her generation's) post-Holocaust Jewish identity. I begin with the full text of her monologue, written about the process of conceptualizing *D'Est,* that concludes the museum installation of which this film is a central component.

The feature film *D'Est* was made as an autonomous piece, but its idea originated as part of a multimedia museum installation, which it eventually also became. As an installation, titled "Bordering on Fiction: Chantal Akerman's *D'Est*," the piece was first seen at the Walker Museum in Minneapolis. It then traveled to the New York Jewish Museum (where I saw it). The installation consists of three chambers. The first chamber is set up as a small screening room with rows of chairs, where *D'Est* plays continually and visitors generally sit for a time, though rarely for the entire 107 minutes of the film. The second chamber consists of "eight 'triptychs' of video monitors on which twenty-four sequences from the film are shown simultaneously." The experience is one of mild cacophony, where one's attention is pulled in several directions at once, no single image or monitor taking priority or monopolizing the gaze. The images are all culled from *D'Est*. In the third and final chamber, the spectator is confronted with a single video monitor and the voice of Akerman reciting two texts: the Second Commandment, in Hebrew and English, and "a selection from her own writing on the film," both reproduced in this volume.[14] I refer to this text frequently in the following discussion.

▶──

(Dis)Embodied Memory as History in *D'Est*

Presented over a series of abstract images of street lights against the night sky, the monologue transcribed below essentially forms the aural epilogue to the "Bordering on Fiction" museum installation. It functions as a commentary on the images seen in the two other chambers of the installation, as the stand-alone film playing continually in the first chamber includes no voice-over. Although my analysis here is based on the film, I find this detached transcribed epilogue indispensable for deciphering the film, even though the spoken text is often an allusive riddle. However, at moments it gives more than hints as to how the film can be read, and can serve as an oblique guide to the viewing of the film. The text deserves considerable reflection, which it has not been properly accorded by the handful of writers and reviewers of the work. The monologue begins with the partial recitation of the Second Commandment in Hebrew, then in English:

> "Thou shalt not make unto thee any graven image or any likeness of anything that is in heaven above or that is in the earth beneath, or that is in the water that is underneath the earth; . . . Thou shalt not bow down thyself to them, nor serve them, for I, the Lord thy God, am a jealous God, visiting the iniquity of the fathers upon the children unto the third and fourth generation of them that hate me; . . . And showing mercy unto those of them that love me and keep my commandments."
>
> To write a film before knowing it. To write in order to close. To write a letter to the father from Kazimirz on the Vistula.
>
> I went, then I wrote. Without understanding. Visions in passing. Dazzled by the summer. Travels by East Germany and by Poland. On the way I still passed the town where my mother comes from. Didn't see it, didn't look. At the border summer faded away to make room for autumn. The muted white autumn covered in a bank of fog. In the countryside men and women seemed to be lying on the black Ukrainian soil, blending in with it as they dig up beets. Not far from them the road broken up by rickety trucks constantly passing by, their exhaust fumes covering soil and faces with black smoke. And it is white winter and the vast sky and a few silhouettes walking toward Moscow where the film will draw together and hint at something of this world in disarray as if after a war, where getting through each day seems a victory.
>
> This may seem terrifying and insignificant but in the midst of this I will show faces which as soon as they are isolated from the masses express something still untouched and often the opposite of this uniformity which strikes you sometimes in the crowds, marching off-ward. The opposite of

our uniformity, too. Without getting too sentimental I would say that there are still faces that offer themselves, occasionally effacing a feeling of loss, of a world poised on the edge of the abyss, which sometimes takes hold of you when you cross "the East" as I have just done it.

You must always write when you want to make a film, although you know nothing of the film you want to make. Yet, you already know everything about it. But you don't realize this. Fortunately, I would say. Only when it is confronted with the act of making will it reveal itself. Groping along sputtering in a state of blind and limping hesitation. Sometimes in a flash of self-evidence. And slowly we all realize that it is always the same thing that is revealed. A little like the primal scene. And the primal scene for me, although I fight against it and end up in a rage, I have to face facts. It is far behind or always in front of all images barely covered by other, more luminous or even radiant ones. All images of evacuation, of walking in the snow with packages toward an unknown place, of faces and bodies placed one next to the other, of faces flickering between robust life and the possibility of a death which would strike them down without their having asked for anything. And it is always like that. Yesterday, today and tomorrow, there were, there will be, there are at this very moment people whom history (which no longer even has a capital *H*), whom history has struck down. People who were waiting there, packed together, to be killed, beaten or starved or who walk without knowing where they are going, in groups or alone. There is nothing to do. It is obsessive and I am obsessed. Despite the cello, despite cinema.

Once the film is finished I said to myself, "So, that's what it was: that again."

In this poetic monologue, Akerman's language is oddly evocative, calling attention to unexpected details like "men and women [blending in with the] black Ukrainian soil" or faces "effacing a feeling of loss" in the crowd. We are told that one knows one's film before one makes it, but one is as yet unaware of that knowledge. That is to say, we know and yet we repress that knowing. She then proceeds to tell us that one writes before making a film ("[one] writes in order to close"), and then effectively contradicts herself by describing a filmmaking process that utterly resists closure. Rather, to her, filmmaking seems more akin to acting out than to working through (to phrase this in psychoanalytic terms); one simply revisits and rehearses one's own repressed narratives (which Akerman tellingly refers to as her "primal scene"). Far from closure, she tells us resignedly, "there is nothing to do. It is obsessive and I am obsessed." The recurrent reference in this film to the face (an inscrutable referent par excellence) demands elaboration, as does her mention of the obsessively repressed yet recurrent primal scene. The invocation of the Second Commandment, as we shall see, is not a gratuitous warning against presenting graven images (which of course she would flagrantly defy in the film) but an integral methodological guide to the film's indirect and transitive representational strategies.

Potato pickers in *D'Est*. Still courtesy of Walker Art Center.

Landscape of a Portrait: Facing East

"Landscape," Simon Schama has proclaimed, "may indeed be a text on which generations write their recurring obsessions."[15] This statement most certainly rings true in the case of *D'Est*. In what we will come to see as typical of Chantal Akerman's chiasmic logic, *D'Est* is a portrait of a landscape and a landscape of many portraits. First and foremost, though somewhat covertly, it is a landscape autobiography of Akerman herself. The title *D'Est* (From the East) can be read to suggest not only that the film frames images from the East but, in autobiographical self-referentiality, that the filmmaker herself hails "from the East." Akerman transports herself and her viewers to Eastern Europe in a reenactment, in reverse, of displacement, a homecoming to a land that she herself never called home. She remains displaced in the very heart of her ancestral home, a home that signifies (and exemplifies) the colossal displacement of the Jewish Diaspora.

   D'Est is an abstract portrait[16] of Eastern Europe at a key moment in history, seen from a particular distance (not too close, not too far),[17] and it is a film that details the features of the faces of the people who populate the land. As is well known, Akerman is a keen observer of the everyday. In *D'Est*, we see scenes from people's daily lives: seemingly random people, often in transit, some in crowds, as in the scenes of train station waiting rooms or bus stops, some in their homes or at social gatherings such as a concert or a dinner dance. We learn the identity of no one; names, occupations, beliefs, religions, strategies for survival are all beyond the scope of this film. We learn nothing of the political system, the economic hardship, the way of life of the people, except as all this can be inferred by the expressions on their faces or the clothes on their backs. In general, Akerman asks nothing of the people she is filming except permission to capture their image on celluloid—and perhaps she does not even ask that of most of the people in the film, caught (unawares) as they seem in the act of performing the rituals of their daily existence, much like those caught by Vertov some sixty-five years earlier. Akerman is up at the crack of dawn, scanning the bus stops for early commuters. She shoots at dusk as people leave work, catching them waiting for the bus home. Indeed, there are endless lines of people waiting indefinitely for the bus or train that never seems to come. Some take note of the camera, curiously or with indifference; others ignore it completely, continuing their conversations or contemplations. A handful demonstrate their annoyance by looking the other way, covering their faces, or even shouting aggressively at the camera. Meanwhile, Akerman's relentless dolly shot presses on, unperturbed, its unceasing lateral movement propelled as if by an unknown force.

Faces captured by Chantal Akerman's camera in *D'Est*. Still courtesy of Walker Art Center.

The film has its own way of looking, not only in terms of aesthetics (the way it looks as a film) but in respect to the active engagement of its visual subjects (the way it looks at its subject). The look *in* the film (as opposed to the look *of* the film) is more penetrating than a glance, less entranced than a gaze.[18] There is an intensity in the manner of looking, but at the same time there is a sense of looking beyond what one sees. Except in a handful of fixed shots, the camera moves inexorably past its subject, searching steadily but without an explicit destination. Akerman's camera moves on, that is, even as it continues to look, like Benjamin's Angel of History moving "away from something [s]he is fixedly contemplating."[19] Perhaps, like the description of that angel, Akerman's "look" is a stare, but, if so, it is neither impolite nor inordinately invasive. If it is a stare at all, it is like a stare of the recently awakened: mind still half in dreamtime, eyes searching to decipher meaning in a world that one expects to be more familiar than it actually is. Or less familiar. Either way, one looks harder, more intently, to try to make sense out of the haze. Dreams of the past pervade the air, and it is not entirely clear where the dream ends and the waking present begins. Seen through the metaphor of awakening, *D'Est* is almost a surrealist work, as it engages time in a way that pertains to our daily experience yet is not of that time. Benjamin describes the moment of awakening as "identical to the 'Now of recognizability,' in which things put on their true—surrealistic—face."[20]

For Benjamin, the true face of things is not a self-evident truth that can be simply apprehended and preserved. Geoffrey Hartman sums it up: "[for Benjamin] naked truth is on the side of excessive hope and can only be attained by not being attained."[21] Truth, for Benjamin as for Akerman, is always elusive, partly hallucinatory and utterly surreal. Akerman is not in search of some grounded notion of the *truth* of Eastern Europe, at this moment in history, as she trains her camera on the faces and landscapes of that somber terrain. It is the traces, the hints, and the inferences to the past that she is particularly (though not exclusively) concerned with in this present moment. As Akerman has said, "Our imaginary is charged with Eastern Europe. At each face I felt a history . . . the camps, Stalin, denunciation . . ."[22] I think it is fair to assume that this is not an ascriptive imposition on Akerman's part, in which each face attests to a particular individual's relation to history, but a description of Akerman's own historical associations prompted by the sight of "each face." As associative indicators, I want to suggest, for her it is not only the Soviet Gulag, Stalinist purges, and denunciations that are prefigured in the history of each face. What draws Akerman inexorably eastward is the history of pogroms, concentration camps, denunciations of Jews. She says as much in her monologue when she acknowledges that for her this landscape evokes the forced evacuations and death marches of World War II. Even though others writing about D'Est have tended to downplay the Jewish aspect of this film, I believe it is the Holocaust and the legendary anti-Semitism of the East, more than anything specific to the Soviet Union, that attracts Akerman's attention and haunts her film.[23] It is this sense of the past that comes into view with the "Now of recognizability." Here, Akerman becomes a historian of a Jewish imaginary inscribed in her personal history, as she "grasps the constellation which [her] own era has formed with a definite earlier one."[24] As Ivone Margulies has said in a recent article, "Her affinity with this geography is directly related to her own history, her parents having moved from Poland to Belgium in the thirties."[25] In fact, Margulies has gone as far as to assert, as I too am attempting to establish in some detail, that D'Est's "underlying motif . . . might be a gaze at the traces of a history shared by Akerman's parents."[26] This landscape and these faces are compelling to Akerman almost entirely as they relate to her own history, or to that of her mother (which in this case seems to have been conflated with her own). In this respect, the film is a transitive autobiography of a past life, lived vicariously through her mother's memories and revealed indirectly through the face(s) of others. The face of the other, it turns out, may indeed stand in for the face of the mother, who in turn stands in for Akerman.

Akerman has subsequently reconfirmed this transitive autobiographical strategy. In a gallery installation, "Self Portrait/Autobiography: a work in progress," at the Sean Kelly Gallery in New York City in spring 1998, Akerman speaks in the autobiographical first person, but from the perspective of her mother. As Amy Taubin says in a review of the show, "The text would be purely autobiographical except that the first-person narrator is not Akerman but her mother."[27] More accurately, the voice seamlessly and almost imperceptibly vacillates between the mother's persona and what would seem to be Akerman's own. There is no attempt to differentiate between the two characters' first-person personae, creating a slippage that is perilously unmarked. The visual images one sees as one hears the disembodied words in voice-over are drawn from four of Akerman's films: D'Est, Jeanne Dielman (1975), Hotel Monterrey (1972), and Toute une Nuit (1982); the first two films in particular are so closely linked to an identification with her mother that the distinction between the daughter's and the mother's autobiographical voice becomes nearly impossible to discern.

Marianne Hirsch refers to this transferential identification between children (in particular, Holocaust survivors' children) and their parents as postmemory. She explains that she uses this term:

to describe the relationship of children of survivors of cultural or collective trauma to the experiences of their parents, experiences that they "remember" only as the stories and images with which they grew up, but that are so powerful, so monumental, as to constitute memories in their own right. The term is meant to convey its temporal and qualitative difference from survivor memory, its secondary or second-generation memory quality, its basis in displacement, its belatedness. Postmemory is a powerful form of memory precisely because its connection to its object or source is mediated not through recollection but through projection, investment, and creation.[28]

Hirsch defines postmemory as "a form of heteropathic memory in which the self and the other are more closely connected through familial or group relation" than conceived by Kaja Silverman, who originally defined heteropathic memory as an empathic form of identification with another. Postmemory occurs not with a random other, but specifically with family members from the previous generation, a fact that significantly "implies a temporal distance between the self and other."[29] With postmemory, there is a particular way this temporal element is both recognized and disavowed. Clearly, unless the subject is delusional, the distances between the experience, the memory, and the re-presentation of the (handed down) memory are understood to be insurmountable. Yet, with postmemory, there is a constant movement toward a collapse of the temporal divide, for, through an intimate identification, the fantasy of overcoming that gap and properly acquiring the memory as one's own persists.

Postmemory is a useful characterization of the transitive autobiographical aspect of Akerman's *D'Est*. Retracing in reverse the path of her mother's evacuation "from the East," Akerman binds herself to a memory not her own yet integral to the formation of her own identity. "Postmemory characterizes," Hirsch states, "the experience of those who grow up dominated by narratives that preceded their birth, whose own belated stories are displaced by the stories of the previous generation, shaped by traumatic events that they can neither understand nor recreate."[30]

In spite of this backward movement through memory, *D'Est* is shot in the present tense. In the film, we approach present-day Eastern Europe as it phenomenologically presents itself. Its daily face is all we see. There is no attempt to probe under the facade; the film accepts, as it were at face value, the conditions of the present. There is the conspicuous absence of archival footage that would aspire to literalize the past by anchoring it to definite imagery and lending it an illusory presence.[31] Yet, without any attempt to penetrate the contemporary facade or to put an historical face on memories through the use of archival footage, there still seems no way to see this present represented outside of, or independently from, the past that echoes within it. In fact, *D'Est* derives much of its emotional resonance and iconic power from that which it *refrains* from showing. There is a pointed contrast between the absence of the past in visual terms and its undeniable weight in aural terms. Given the complete absence of archival footage in the film, the voice-over monologue of the installation takes on added weight, haunting the film with its very personal impression of the past (creating, that is, memory effects of its own). Since the film proceeds with only the memory of the voice (even if the viewer is familiar with the installation), the sense of history, of the past, remains at a distinct yet perceptible remove—merely a trace, unseen yet persisting in its effects. When we see people trudging through deep snow, single file, holding their small bags or briefcases, the image in itself holds limited interest. However, it gains resonance in its interarticulation with an historical imaginary, redirecting our attention away from these contemporary specificities toward the collective memory of prior, forced frozen marches.

The present is thus rendered dependent on and in part intelligible through a perception of a very specific past. In other words, for all of its immediacy, *D'Est* is never fully in the present. In essence, Akerman's postmemory drives this return to the East. As she suggests in the installation monologue, these memories are hiding behind (or in front of, or just beneath) every image she records. The present shows itself as a surface on which to stage or reflect a past that refuses to be ignored, yet this past is ephemeral and unpredictable, flaring up in an unexpected moment and evanescing just as quickly. The stage of the present is similarly unstable, like the surface of a body of water that gives way to ripples and distortions at the least disruption. In the faces of the East, Akerman seeks, finds, and also loses the reflections of the past in the visage of the present.

▶━━━━━━━━━━━━━━━━━━━━━━━━━━━━━━━━━━━━━━

Present as Palimpsest

Understanding Benjamin's notion of "the Now of recognizability" is critical to begin to unravel the sense of time, history, and memory as seen in the faces scoured in Akerman's film. The present moment, history in the making, comes into the realm of "the Now" only as it relates to a prior era, the "Then" of a powerful imaginary field. For Benjamin, it is always in a between-time that truth (that is, the decipherability of the past) emerges. "The past can be seized only as an image which flashes up at the instant when it can be recognized and is never seen again."[32] These flashes are likeliest to occur in moments of transition or at borders of consciousness. The truth about history can be found fleetingly and only in the intervals—between sleep and wakefulness, between the present and the past, at a historical instant of transition—when the future's uncertainty is the only certainty. For Benjamin, one will not find truth in statistics, facts, pronouncements, or positive assertions. That which is positively articulated and held to be self-evident contains only clues to a truth that, nevertheless, is to be found elsewhere. With the past no longer accessible and the present largely unreadable outside of its relation to the past, we must find our truths in the interstices.

"The Now of recognizability" does not just come and go randomly, nor does it appear predictably at every interstitial moment. Akerman says in her epilogue that sometimes one only realizes the subject of one's inquiry (in her case, her film) in a "flash of self-evidence." I believe this is the same flash that Benjamin speaks of when he tells us that articulating the past as history means "to seize hold of a memory as it flashes up at a moment of danger."[33] In fact, there is a perceived moment of danger for Akerman in shooting *D'Est*—not a physical danger per se, but the political and historical one of a world on the brink. She tells us that she wants to shoot Eastern Europe "while there's still time,"[34] to see what there is of these countries "that have shared a common history since the [W]ar, and are still deeply marked by that history."[35] There is the sense that this shared history is unraveling—to the point where, in a very short time, the commonalities with the past will dissolve into an era of indecipherability: the past she is haunted by will no longer be readable on the faces of the present. She perceives that, beneath the laughter of some of these faces, "you get a sense of impending disaster." She realizes that this sense of impending doom is perhaps a delayed reflex, as the disaster is already present, like Benjamin's state of emergency that is not the exception but the rule. "It is impending from week to week but never comes—quite simply perhaps because it is already there."[36] Yet, also like Benjamin, she sees a linkage with the past and some hope for the future, though not necessarily a messianic one, in the "faces that offer themselves, occasionally effacing a feeling of loss, of a world poised on the edge of the abyss, which sometimes takes hold of you when you cross the East as I have just done it." The loss or the disaster she references is, of course, in part what many feared would be a slippery slide into either economic and political chaos or full-tilt capitalism, a process unfolding steadily if unpredictably since at least the fall of the Berlin Wall, thus predating the making of the film by several years.

However, since Akerman's concerns exceed any limited economistic notion of the *political*, there must be another disaster enabling this flash of historical recognition. Indeed, that disaster would be the loss of decipherability of a painful but constitutive past that may no longer be legible on the faces inhabiting a radically altered national body. Although some might argue that a loss of such a negative and unresolved memory might be conducive to a healing process, such a salvific discourse is anathema to most Jewish conceptions of history. Traditionally, Jewish memory is not necessarily invoked to heal old wounds but (in religious invocations of Jewish memory) in order to reconfirm survival against all odds and theologically recommit to the God who has intervened on the Jews' behalf. It is considered crucial to Jewish continuity to remember these moments of historical struggle and to incorporate them into present conceptualizations of what it means to be a Jew. The grave risk of losing signs of a memory vitally constitutive for Ashkenazi Jewry is palpable in this transitional moment.

Akerman is clearly aware of the political and economic conditions that constitute the elements of the present crisis, yet in a film purportedly about faces, she decides not to face these conditions head on. When answering what amounts to a rhetorical question, "Why make this trip to Eastern Europe?" Akerman replies:

> There are the obvious historical, social, and political reasons, reasons that underlie so many documentaries and news reports—and that rarely indulge a calm and attentive gaze. But although these are significant, they are not the only reasons. I will not attempt to show the disintegration of a system, nor the difficulties of entering into another one, because she who seeks shall find, find all too well, and end up clouding her vision with her own preconceptions.

She adds, tellingly, "This undoubtedly will happen anyway; it can't be helped. But it will happen *indirectly*.[37] Her indirect route entails a detour through an historical imaginary. The present is only glimpsed through its past (and vice-versa), a past written on these faces displayed so prominently. An example of this interplay can be seen in the panning shot of the Russian train station's waiting room. Akerman has her camera perform a subtle, almost imperceptible, circular pan of the room; it takes some time and considerable attention to notice that we've (just) seen these faces before. There is a return, a revisitation, enacted within this shot that stands in metaphorically for the cyclical reemergence of the faces of a prior age in the visage of the present. Here Akerman evinces a desire to turn the present into a palimpsest.

As I have stated, the feeling of loss that Akerman both registers and evokes in *D'Est* concerns not simply the present time, the loss of idealism, the fall of Communism, the "impending" invasion of the West.[38] There is the constant, nagging sense of losses accrued over time, accumulating as at the feet of the Angelus Novus. The victims of Stalin are piled upon the corpses of the Holocaust, who rest uneasily upon the raped and pillaged shtetl villagers of the czarist pogroms. Akerman is not interested in the present only for the present's sake. If not for the past, in which her family's history is directly implicated, there would be no *D'Est*. As Margulies has noted:

> Akerman's interest in this moment of the break up of the Soviet bloc, triggered initially by her desire to make a film on the poet Anna Akhmatova, further connects Jewish and Eastern European themes: the Pale of Settlement, where most Jews were living at the turn of the century, and from where the greatest migrations to America took place, was located in Poland, at that point a Russian Province.[39]

There is an imbrication of time, the past and present each threatening to eclipse the other at moments, yet both partially discernible at all times. Although she only uses prime lenses, the perceptual and chronotopical effect is akin to looking through a telephoto lens, where that which is distant in time appears close, and that which is close and immediate is on the verge of falling out of focus altogether. Yet the present never does fully fall out of focus. We see the faces and landscapes of present-day Eastern Europe, with its buildings, stores, fashions, cars, streetlights, smokestacks, and fields. There are instances when the present is indistinguishable from the past, as when we see fields with no structures or machinery to indicate a given historical period. Most shots include some apparatus or sign that could bring us up to date, but a billowing smokestack in what could be East Germany or a procession of people trudging through the snow down a rural road in what might be Poland inevitably recalls images from a not so distant and none too bucolic past. The landscape itself is imbued with the reverberating presence of an historical imaginary, and it might be argued that the topography only exists for us through the tropology. As Simon Schama has so eloquently observed, "Before it can ever be a repose for the senses, landscape is the work of the mind. Its scenery is built up as much from strata of memory as from layers of rock."[40]

My suggestion that Akerman has overlaid the present and the past might lead one to expect a cinematic equivalent of this temporal palimpsest, in *D'Est*. One can imagine superimposing archival and contemporary images, or simply intercutting the old with the new.[41] Yet Akerman resorts to neither of these more predictable strategies. Willing to risk the appearance of superficiality, she stakes her bets that the history she is obsessed with is an open secret, written on the faces and terrain of this oblique land: she merely has to train her camera and look. It is as if Akerman has invented a cinema verité of intersticiality, where, if one looks long enough, the pressure of the stare is enough to trouble the surface in meaningful ways.

The Enlightenment conception of the linearity of time is here replaced with a moiré pattern; the separation of past and present becomes an optical illusion that never ultimately resolves. This inventive and ultimately antihistoricist approach to time has antecedents in Jewish culture. Although Judaism has long been associated with linear time (rather than Greek cyclical time),[42] it is true that in Jewish tradition, flagrant liberties have always been taken with time, beginning with the life spans and chronologies in the book of Genesis (e.g., Sarah conceiving Isaac when in her nineties, Isaac studying Mosaic law though it would not be revealed until ten generations after his birth).[43] Jewish historian Yosef Yerushalmi argues that the rabbis, commenting on the Torah, "seem to play with time as though with an accordion, expanding and collapsing it at will." Also, in the Talmudic dialogics, scholars from vastly different historical periods enter into lively debate as if the temporal plane of the Talmud transcends historical constraints.[44] In Jewish tradition, then, time is telescoped.[45] The Jewish injunction to remember creates a relationship with the past where the present, lived reality is perpetually filtered through the selective memories of the past. There are specific stories and events that are (re)invoked, generation after generation, to form the central tropes of the Jewish people. The stories are told and retold, usually in abbreviated form, in ways meant to have direct implications on how one is to live in the present.[46]

Over time, some of these stories become intertwined, as if what happens in one generation reiterates what has happened to past generations, to the point where there is the impression of one overarching tragedy that has befallen the Jewish people—a tragedy called by different names in different times and places, not unlike the Benjaminian angel of history's "one single catastrophe." This homologization of variegated events is explained by Yerushalmi in part as a rabbinical "resistance to novelty in history."[47] Yerushalmi tells of the preponderance of "second Purims" observed in medieval Jewish communities "to commemorate a deliverance from some danger or persecution."[48] He also recounts the story of one fast day (the twentieth day of the Jewish month of Sivan) commemorating a Jewish tragedy in twelfth-century France, which was adopted to commemorate a different tragedy occurring in the seventeenth-century Ukraine and Poland. About this "typological equation," a seventeenth-century rabbi, Yom Tob Lipman Heller, wrote, "What has occurred now is similar to the persecutions of old, and all that happened to the forefathers has happened to their descendants. . . . *It is all one.*"[49]

Of course, the most recent catastrophe to be integrated into this radiating jeremiad of sacrifice, loss, and destruction that has shaped the landscape of Jewish memory over thousands of years is the mass extermination of millions of Jews under Nazism. Even the names of these monuments of loss are interchanged with those of the past. Most arrestingly, in recent nomenclature the event is referred to as the Holocaust, the Shoah, and, by some Yiddish speakers, as *Der Khurbn* (the Destruction). The latter two names contain profound resonances with the legendary destruction of the Second Temple (the Western Wall of which stands in Jerusalem as Judaism's holiest site), an event that traditionally marks the beginning of the Jewish Diaspora.[50] With the invocation of a single formative event, millennia are telescoped, and certain very select tropes are renewed and imbued with the weight and import of a rabbinically sanctioned history.[51]

Akerman does not implicitly reference the entire range of Jewish losses throughout history in her imagery, but, in her palimpsestic overlay of present-day Eastern Europe onto the setting of what she calls her primal scene, she does invoke the potency of such a telescopic method, through which the present moment is suffused with the force of specific and overwhelming tragedies of the past in a way that lends added gravity to the scene. In so doing, she borrows the rabbinical mode of representing moments of memory and history as fully intricated with the present. Benjamin also advocates this type of "telescoping of the past through the present."[52] Further, this is not the first time Akerman has been associated with a condensed historical presentation. In Margulies's essay on *Meetings with Anna*, the author refers to a monologue by a German character named Heinrich, in which he recites the recent events in German history as a litany, connected by the synopsizing phrase "and then"; Margulies calls this style of delivery "the telescoped historical references" of the text.[53]

Jews have often been called "the people of remembrance." In fact, in the Jewish religion, it is considered every Jewish male's duty to be the repository of sanctioned Jewish memory. In Benjamin's final thesis on the philosophy of history, he states: "The Torah and the prayers instruct [Jews] in remembrance."[54] Yerushalmi singles out the Jews in this respect: "Only in Israel and nowhere else is the injunction to remember felt as a religious imperative to an entire people."[55] Jews are instructed not only to remember, but on *what* to remember. Harold Bloom reminds us that Jews are "urged by their tradition to *remember*," yet are urged to remember "very selectively."[56] Yerushalmi states this as "memory is, by its nature, selective, and the demand that Israel remember is no exception."[57] In other words, it is not all events that deserve recounting, and even those recounted are to be done so only selectively or partially. The stories to be remembered become encapsulated homilies that, in the (post) modern era, approach the status of cliché, a form at which Akerman is quite adept.[58] Akerman's Jewish memories of living in the East, which are not personally experienced memories but the inherited memories of her parents and her people, pervade the text as if ordained by tradition. Akerman's maternal postmemory is overlaid with a broader, indirectly experienced, Jewish ancestral postmemory. What Margulies refers to as "Akerman's minimalist writing of a Jewish European history"[59] based on her own family's wartime trajectory, actually borrows heavily from a long tradition of selective and telescopic Jewish remembering.[60]

▶

Moscow Diaries

As noted previously, *D'Est* makes no attempt at reportage. It doesn't even begin to document or theorize the state of politics, economics, or living conditions in the former Soviet Union. When we compare this to Walter Benjamin's autobiographical journey eastward, we see interesting resemblances in methodology, as well as methodical avoidances of standard documentary, historiographic, and autobiographical practices, in the two works.[61] Like Benjamin in his foray into the East seventy years earlier, Akerman resists grand pronouncements or political prognostications. Benjamin wrote to Martin Buber, his commissioning editor for what ultimately became known as *Moscow Diary:* "My presentation will be devoid of all theory. In this fashion I hope to succeed in allowing the creatural to speak for itself." Here the body, as well as what is related to it, is expected to cede enough information to obviate the need for analysis. He continues: "I want to write a description of Moscow at the present moment in which 'all factuality is already theory' and thereby refrain from any deductive abstraction, from any prognostication, and even within certain limits from any judgment."[62] The Moscow that Benjamin encounters in 1926–27 is just settling in to the implications of the Russian Revolution, the success of which Benjamin believes is still too early to assess. Akerman encounters Moscow after the demise of that revolution, the two "diaries" bracketing it like two ends of a frame inside which is a portrait, or landscape, of an unfolding scene that refuses to be (exhaustively) interpreted.[63] The indeterminate aspect of both projects is presumably an effect not only of the two artists' interests in ambiguity per se, but also of their similar approaches toward this subject. They share the disarray and precipitous quality encountered in the East, that sense of "a world poised on the edge of the abyss." Neither Benjamin nor Akerman is particularly optimistic about what they have seen, yet both refrain from elaborating an interpretation. It is tempting to attribute this mutual interpretive aversion, especially given the subject, to some latent orientalism on their parts, some concept of an inscrutability and irrationality of the East.

It is important to recognize the relevance and power of this all-too-prevalent trope among Western European Jews toward Eastern Jews. Yet I do not believe it accounts fully for Akerman's or Benjamin's hermeneutical abstention, though of course both look to the East from the vantage point of the West, with that inbuilt sense of superiority no doubt having an effect on their readings. In a time when the Eastern Judeophobia among Western European Jews was at an all-time high, Benjamin was nonetheless visiting to some extent as a student (of Marxism and revolution, not to mention love). For this reason, I think he would have been disinclined to cast a jaundiced eye on his revolutionary "betters" or, of course, on his beloved Asja Lacis.[64] For Akerman, identification with the West seems as tenuous and problematic as with the East; she seems never to have fully assimilated (at least in her own mind) with the rhythms and values of the West. I do not mean to suggest by this that either Benjamin's or Akerman's forays to the East are somehow miraculously free of orientalism or have escaped the pervasive attitudes of Western Jewry toward "Ostjuden" (the pejorative name used by Western Jewry for Eastern Jews).[65] I do assert, however, that Akerman's and Benjamin's interpretive restraint cannot be reduced to a mere prejudice.

Ultimately, Benjamin is quite disillusioned by what he sees, yet he studiously refuses to publicly anticipate the upheavals and betrayals that lay immediately ahead. He merely indicates that the future is unclear, that events could go in any number of directions, not all of them grave. In his words: "Moscow as it appears at the present reveals a full range of possibilities in schematic form: above all, the possibility that the Revolution might fail or succeed. In either case, something unforeseeable will result and this picture will be far different from any programmatic sketch one might draw of the future. The outlines of this are at present brutally and distinctly visible among the people and their environment."[66]

This could easily have been an account of Akerman's trip, minus the success or failure of the Revolution, the failures of which the readers of *Moscow Diary* would have been well aware, since the full diary was not published until after Asja Lacis's death in 1979, by which time Stalinist purges and continued political and intellectual repressions had long been confirmed. What resounds from Benjamin's description in Akerman's work is the absence of political prognostication or direct engagement. Due to the timing of both *D'Est* and *Moscow Diary*, it is politics one expects to learn about and politics one is explicitly deprived of. In *Moscow Diary,* Benjamin never writes about the power struggle being waged between Trotsky and Stalin, which occurs precisely during the time of his visit. Similarly, Akerman never portrays the politicians or bosses, nor does she attempt to uncover the corruption or scandals allegedly rampant in this moment of transition. Benjamin and Akerman enter into these politically fraught scenarios and resolutely look elsewhere for their material, intentionally frustrating audience expectations and revealing a preference for a more somatic view of the land. It is through faces and bodies that we will get to know this terrain, and we will know it on the surface, as a facade thick with the underlayers of an irrepressible history.[67]

Although Benjamin is the more explicitly politically engaged of the two, the work of both can be characterized by an unaligned and unalignable political perspective. Benjamin famously flirted with, then rejected, the idea of joining the Communist Party. His theories resist simple appropriation or utilization for political purposes, to the point where it has been asserted that his are a politics of inutility.[68] In his resistance to the inexorable rise of National Socialism, he developed his theories to reflect the paradoxical complexity of life that was in no way accounted for in the reductive politics of fascism. Akerman is by no means working at a moment of such a palpable threat as National Socialism, nor with the heady potential of a recent Revolution so near at hand. As a result she has not encountered the same pressures to articulate a political position. Nonetheless, perhaps as an indirect consequence of Benjamin having forged the path, she unwittingly chooses her preferred mode of (dis)engagement in his image. It is through faces, not words, that she searches for meaning, and the meanings are never simple or direct, just as they never were for Benjamin. So it is that, indirectly, one imprint of the past to protrude on Akerman's eastern text comes from Benjamin's work. Although *Moscow Diary* and *D'Est* differ considerably in style, the sympathies between their makers are clear. They share an agnostic disdain for direct political engagement and reportage, a personal and autobiographical dimension in (some of) their work, and a distinctive concern and attention for the human form, more specifically the face, as the privileged site of the (in)decipherability of history.

▶ ─────────────────────────────

The Facade of the Face

The face figures prominently in both Akerman's description of her project and in her visual representations. There are countless dolly shots of people, shot at eye level, standing and waiting, or working, or sleeping; we are rarely given a close-up, though it is people's faces Akerman says she wants to engage. She tells us in her monologue that, in the midst of images of "visions in passing," of seasonal shifts and the "vast sky" of the Eastern European landscape, she will "show faces." Her concern with faces is predominant. These faces are meant to break through the mask of conformity, to give life and meaning to the landscapes represented; these faces are presented as signs of hope, evidence of humanity in this otherwise desolate and depersonalized environment. Yet the faces, though they may mitigate the monotony of the moment, mask meanings of their own.

What is Akerman hoping to show us with her focus on the face? What is it we see when we face another, when we look into another's face? How is it that a face can efface anything, let alone, as she states, "a feeling of loss," which is the very feeling that lingers around the periphery of every face and every image seen in this film? The face, as a conduit of meaning about the present and the past, is both remarkably nuanced and decidedly unreliable. Even as it can be read in a register that is both personal and cultural, individual and collective, as a testimonial to aspects of both memory and history, it is a mask or facade that conceals as much as it reveals. The face does not yield its secrets plainly or unambiguously. As one knows well from searching the faces of one's own world, or indeed one's own face, the past leaves its imprint, yet its expression is only partially and occasionally legible (to oneself or to others). By declaring her intention to show faces that stand out from the crowd, Akerman claims to be offering an antidote to uniformity ("theirs as well as ours"). In fact, the faces themselves are meant to offer some semblance of hope for a new and completely different order than the one that has come before—one that might now allow for the individual, idiosyncratic expression of the face.

Yet it is hard to decipher this supposed revelation of the face. I have to disagree with Margulies when she asserts that there is evidence of "the surprising interest of each person and face" in *D'Est*.[69] In spite of Akerman's, or indeed Margulies's, enthusiasm, I am not convinced that the image that stands out for us is not still one of uniformity and indistinctness. Very few faces in the crowds strike us at the moment of watching, and fewer remain in the memory once the film has concluded. Akerman faces the crowds but is unable to efface the effect of years of anti-individualist socialization and a deep suspicion toward the uninvited camera.

In Akerman's scanning pans, the people are treated as landscape, part of the scenery as the camera rolls past. As such, the landscape becomes human; it adopts a corporeal form. It is this embodied landscape that reveals aspects of its face to us, at first appearing homogeneous, presented as unspecified terrain. Then, as the long takes unfold,[70] this living landscape yields an expressiveness more commonly associated with the portrait than with the landscape. It is thus the same to say (as mentioned earlier) that *D'Est* is a portrait of a landscape and a landscape of a portrait. The face is at once depersonalized—that is, taken out of the context of an individual subjectivity—and then reparticularized as a landscape that does eventually, through the persistent and attentive gaze of the camera, yield hints of the intimate, subjective, human secrets it contains, not through the interest of each person, as Margulies suggests, but through the interest of an embodied and living terrain.

Yet, however it is manifest, as landscape or portrait, distinct or indistinct, individual or en masse, the human face (in its Eastern European variations) is undeniably a central point of attraction in this film. Akerman has commented on the surprising familiarity she felt when traveling in Eastern Europe. Akerman goes East to find familiar faces, to find her likeness in the crowd. Never having been there before, not knowing the language or the terrain, she claims to have felt strangely that it was "almost like home or close enough."[71] When Akerman tells us (in her written essay that accompanies the installation) that, amid all strangeness and indecipherability of the East, there was also an impossible familiarity, as if she had been there before, she is in some ways enacting a homecoming, which (judging by the expressions of annoyance and fear on some of those faces), is also in part, a return of the repressed. Though we never see Akerman in this film, it is perhaps she, not history, who embodies the repressed: a revenant, coming back to haunt these people, who are after all looking at her face as she stares at theirs. We do see faces that resemble hers in the dark intensity of their stare.[72] What constitutes this resemblance? Certainly it cannot be reduced to something as race-based as phylogeny, yet it is not so predictable as presentational style. The familiarity she discovers is in part framed by desire, a narcissistic one, without a doubt, the desire to see herself reflected. In this case, and against her better judgment, she seeks and finds "all too well," an overdetermined strategy that Akerman claims to want to avoid.[73] She looks for herself in others' faces and sees presumably what she wants to see, but also something more.

Such a surplus is implicit in face-to-face interactions, where we inevitably encounter that which is both familiar and beyond ourselves. According to Emanuel Levinas, the other is never fully knowable or containable in our experience or understanding; therefore the face of the other represents infinite possibility. As Levinas states, "such a situation is the gleam of exteriority or of transcendence in the face of the Other."[74] This is the potential that the face of the other represents for us, but only if we understand that face as completely outside ourselves, as the face of extreme exteriority. This is not entirely the case in *D'Est,* since the representation of the face here may be read as, in part, a narcissistic projection, precisely the opposite of extreme exteriority.

Elsewhere, Levinas suggests that in the face-to-face encounter, "we are uprooted from history."[75] Whereas I have interpreted the face-to-face interaction in *D'Est* as being mired in history, Levinas would have us believe that Akerman might blast out of history, beyond the clutches of the past, into a transcendent realm of infinite possibility. There is certainly the hope on Akerman's part that something emerge through these encounters that may escape the constraints of time. She believes that there are moments of such transcendence (flashes) amid and against the monotony. However, it is not Levinas's *infinite possibility* that she attains; the flashes correspond more closely to Benjaminian notions of historical materialism blasting out of the continuum of time. Benjamin's interdictory moment points simultaneously in two directions, the past and the future, whereas Levinas's looks strictly forward. If the representation of faces in *D'Est* represents an historical rupture at all, it does so regarding the past. We are not uprooted from history per se, only from its continuum. The faces root us firmly in time as trees or mountains might, transcending the present by the past, not by some deracinated future. The past inheres in the present, undermining any straightforward sequential chronology.

Another theorist of the face, Paul de Man, suggests that faces seen in autobiographical work are masks, or prosopopeia (*prosopon* means literally to confer a mask or a face), of the past: portraits of the dead, resurrected by the living in a conversation with "an absent, deceased, or voiceless entity."[76] De Man writes specifically of the face of the autobiographical subject as if she or he is proleptically writing her or his own epitaph, but it is also possible to read the presence of prosopopeia in the faces represented in any autobiography, or perhaps in any documentary or nonfiction work, that maintains what de Man calls "the illusion of reference."[77] With that illusion comes the illusion of presence, which hides or disavows the unattainability of that subject, like reaching for a shadow from the grave. The cinematic image is a shadowy figure or mask standing in for true presence, which nonetheless always remains substantively elusive. In the prosopopeia of *D'Est,* Akerman is engaged in a conversation with the dead, both with her own imaginary death as a victim of Nazi persecution (in this, she has perhaps committed Dominick LaCapra's ultimate sin of overidentification with the victim) and with the all too real death of the faces *not* seen in the crowd. She glides (cinematically) past the living, a shadowy figure herself.

Prosopopeia also means personification, wherein the inanimate embodies the properties of the animate (and human)—for instance, a landscape formed by a portrait in which people's faces and bodies make up the aspect of a landscape, not reducing them to the passive plane but rather animating the landscape to the realm of conscious, interactive subjectivity. There is a tension in *D'Est* between the dead and the living, the animate and the inanimate, absence and presence, and Akerman keeps this tension taut on each side of the binary. De Man is aware of such peregrinations in a way that applies directly to the subtleties in Akerman's work. Quoting Milton, he states, "the gradual transformations occur in such a way that 'feelings [that] seem opposite to each other have another and finer connection than that of contrast.'"[78] Like a holographic image, the faces in Akerman's film are alternatingly visages from a (filmic) present and visions from beyond the grave, and they never fully resolve themselves into either.

We may believe that a face threatens to reveal that which lies beneath it, yet the true form, underneath the mask, is formlessness, or what Rilke called "the non-face." As Richter notes, "Rilke's non-face signals the advent of what cannot be contained by the positing of a face as a figure of identification and hermeneutic closure." The threat of peering underneath the facade is terrifying, a prospect that would disturb "the logic of the face altogether."[79] By remaining so resolutely on the surface of these faces, Akerman paradoxically holds out the threat of the ultimate defacement, skinning rather than skimming the surface of the face, turning the image inside out. Writing about the installation as a whole (rather than only the feature film), Catherine David has noted that, at its most abstract (as in the footage of streetlights and fog with which Akerman accompanies her monologue), the work does indeed efface, or de-face, the image almost entirely. David asserts, "It's as if the film had been turned inside out to exhibit henceforth its reverse side, the hidden face of the images, the origin and end of representation, the 'primal scene.'"[80] Leaving aside for now the question of the primal scene, it is clear that Akerman's interest in the landscape of faces is that of both familiarity (representation) and unrecognizability (David's "end of representation"). Time both is and is not of the essence in these images, as they exist within some measurable chronology while resisting a final resting place. The dead live on in the faces of the living even as time passes, languorously, in the present. In a paradoxical manner typical of Akerman, time is condensed in a telescopic contraction even as it elongates via seemingly eternal long takes measured in increments of viewers' patience. Hence, in the zero sum game of temporality, Akerman performs an antipodal balancing act, leaving us with no more and no less than the infinite and enduring facade of the present with which to contend.

Time and Timeliness

In *D'Est,* Akerman's slow, measured tracking shots are interspersed with static camera shots, creating a lilting, erratic, rhythm all its own. There are painterly shots of city landscapes in winter's dusk or dawn that expressively thematize space passing in time. There are also "still-lifes" which thematize time passing in space, their duration a testament to the loving attention Akerman confers on the quotidian event. These tableaux are always indoor, generally of people in their homes performing remarkably Akermanesque tasks. One woman puts a record on an old turntable, lifting and replacing the needle hesitantly, and she is seen in the next shot, music bridging the cut, in her kitchen diligently and overdramatically slicing salami and bread as if she were auditioning for a part in *Je tu il elle.* Another man heartily eats his dinner while sitting at his kitchen table, the camera immovable in the doorway, reminding us of its placement in other Akerman films, notably *Jeanne Dielman.*[81] There is a deliberateness and a self-consciousness in evidence, on the part of the performers and of the filmmaker, that is not the usual fare of documentary. The images ride the border between the real and the hyperreal, between naturalistic and staged: this is documentary, as Akerman says, "bordering on fiction."[82] For me, there is no doubt that the majority of these indoor scenes are staged, and yet, as if Akerman were an adherent of the filmmaking style of ethnographic provocateur Jean Rouch, there is an unquestioned faith on her part in the expressivity of the image whether caught unaware or by design.

Then there are what one might take to be the more traditional documentary shots—the driving shots, cityscapes, shots of people going to and from work—which nonetheless manage to defy documentary convention. Principally, it is Akerman's sense of time and timing that distinguishes her from other documentarians (as well as narrative filmmakers). A shot, whether moving or static, is always allowed to run its course, to come to its own conclusion (or inconclusion), rather than having to conform to the utilitarian demands of narrative or of (limited) audience attention. In this, *D'Est* conforms more to the tradition of the avant-garde—or at least to that of the avant-garde of observational cinema, such as the work of Michael Snow or Andy Warhol (two of Akerman's acknowledged influences). She displays absolute confidence that the accretion of shots, each in its own time, will ultimately accomplish what no amount of staccato editing can. Akerman takes her time, and time, in turn, repays her (and our) patience by allowing its multiple layers and levels to be registered.

For all the ambling slowness, time is of the essence. Certainly the piece was made in a timely manner, with some concern for its historical timeliness. *D'Est* was notably not made at a random moment, nor was it made at a leisurely pace. Funding was available for the piece at an important historical transition, and Akerman is not unaware of the interest that this juncture holds for her audience. That Akerman does not always satisfy the viewers' curiosity, or any presumed hunger for news, inclines me to conclude that she has her own interpretation of the yields of time, one that cannot be pressed into the compulsory service of the journalistic imperative. The story she wants to tell cannot be encapsulated and narrated on demand. In fact, the story that appears so new that we eagerly await the novelty of its telling turns out to be an old one with a few new twists, and it takes time to notice the contours of the familiar tale. Only after the film is made and each shot accedes to the demands of its own internal time does the filmmaker note, in belated understanding, that she has, yet again, retold the central narrative of her own identity, what she refers to as her primal scene. "That, again," she tells herself knowingly, as if hearing the refrain of a familiar, but emotionally fraught, tune.

Still, as I have indicated, *D'Est* is not a film that could have been made at any point. Its power resides in the complex interconnectedness between the "present" rupture and the infamous, cataclysmic rupture of half a century earlier. Time, its passing and its effects, is a central trope of *D'Est*. Akerman evinces a tremendous respect for time, the frailty of individuals and the silence of the dead, in her ability to take account of time's passing. She evinces this respect by remaining sagaciously silent and watching. By this, I do not mean to suggest that Akerman is mute or uncommunicative; she is something of a neophenomenologist for whom observation yields not things in their essence but things (concepts, ideas, people, landscapes) in their ambiguity and complexity.

Here it might be useful to contrast *D'Est* with two very different films, Ruth Beckermann's *Paper Bridge* (1987) and Claude Lanzmann's *Shoah*. Ruth Beckermann is a Jewish filmmaker, raised by Romanian Jewish Holocaust survivors who settled in Vienna after the war. *Paper Bridge* is an autobiographical film about the filmmaker's sudden and apparently unplanned sojourn into Eastern Europe. She finds herself in her parents' hometown in Romania, among the mostly elderly Jews of the town, exploring graveyards and the one town synagogue. Her unnamed search continues in Czechoslovakia, where she films Jews acting the part of victims for a Hollywood production shot in Theresienstadt, and she wends her way, via long takes of breakers in icy waters, back to Vienna to interview her parents. Some images resemble Akerman's, like the long take of a peasant emerging out of the deep mist driving a horse-drawn carriage—an image that in fact prefigures Akerman's by a few years. Both filmmakers favor the long take and seem to place their faith in the unfolding mysteries of landscape shots. However, the questions that remain subterranean in Akerman are made manifest in Beckermann's film via interviews and voice-over. For instance, over the opening shot of an attic (a barely concealed metaphor for memory), Beckermann questions her obsession with her Jewish past, asking herself as much as her audience, "Remembrance to what end?" Soon thereafter, having undertaken her journey and begun to introduce us to both her history and the town of Radautz in northern Romania, she tells us that she doesn't know why she had traveled east that winter: "I think I was just curious to know whether there was still any resemblance to the stories I grew up with." There it is, point-blank. Beckermann's journey is motivated by a desire to find references in the present of a past she had only heard about. She seeks concrete validation of her postmemory, a validation that time mischievously withholds. Her voice-over, though pointedly direct at times, is always thoughtful and poetic, and she has a gift for knowing when to let the images speak for themselves. In contrast with Akerman's indirectness, it is almost a relief to be released from the formalist constraints of *not* telling. Beckermann simply tells us that the quest is perhaps a bit aimless and the timing not entirely justified, but the desire to find traces of the past in the faces of the present has motivated this journey.

For all its obliqueness, *D'Est* tells us something similar, however wordlessly. Actually, Akerman's words in her voice-over from the installation do say as much, when she tells us of her primal scene, which is undeniably at the core of her return. The difference is that in the feature film Akerman then allows the images to do their work with only the enhancement or disruption of the sync sound to affect meaning.

Having set out on a personal journey with no concern for the timeliness of her subject, Beckermann is not burdened with the expectation that her film will address the present political dimensions of life in the East. Her objectives are more modest, her pretensions less grand, and as a result, at least for the first half of the film, which deals with Romania, she succeeds in creating a poetic engagement with her displaced postmemory as it holds up (or disintegrates) in the encounter with the present. The present is scavenged for remains of the past and what is seized, ironically, is a considerable dose of life in the present. We learn of people's plans to emigrate to Israel; we meet the rabbi of the town, the only rabbi in the region, who performs everything from daily services to the ritual slaughtering of chickens, from circumcisions to cantorial duties. In Beckermann's search for signs of the past, we learn more about the day-to-day life of the people she encounters than we ever do in Akerman's *D'Est,* a film that purports to be about the present. *D'Est,* however, is more successful than *Paper Bridge* at evoking images of the past, letting the hints of the shadows of what has receded from full view to emerge in the absence of voice-over. In *D'Est,* the unseen (of history, of memory, of the dead) can be felt in the unsaid.

My comparison between *D'Est* and *Shoah* has less to do with timeliness than with time itself. In *Shoah,* Lanzmann has a completely different strategy of historical engagement. His is a direct, investigative, even combative strategy. Lanzmann goes (back) to Poland (and to some extent Germany) to interview survivors and to interrogate former low-level Nazi officials, kapos, Polish peasants, and anyone else who will talk to him about what they did or failed to do during the war. His style is aggressive, he takes no prisoners, lets no one off the hook, and yet, after nine-and-a-half obsessive hours, one realizes that no amount of questioning will ever satisfy our unquenchable thirst for answers. The answers are simply inadequate and the unfulfilled (and unfulfillable) need for resolution and closure too deep. The Nazis and the local collaborators he interrogates are ailing and inconsequential at this point, and one is left with a hollow sense that there is no one left to blame.

Shoah engages time as a central thematic in relation to the Eastern European history of the Holocaust. Both filmmakers stretch the limits of time and of the viewers' patience, though, for Akerman, the time taken is an accounting of the time that has passed, whereas Lanzmann seems to want to muscle his way through time, back to a moment when answers to his questions might still have had some redeeming value. Lanzmann himself has said that his film "is the abolition of all distance between the past and the present; I relived this history in the present."[83] For Lanzmann, it is as if the past can be relived fully in the present, through sheer force of will and the desire to restimulate and reanimate the traumatic event(s). Whereas Akerman acknowledges the distance between the present and the past tense, while simultaneously registering their mutual imbrication, Lanzmann disallows the possibility of the passing of time and insists that in his film he successfully managed to eradicate the space between past and present.[84] It is impressive to see the extent to which Lanzmann believes in his ultimate victory over time. Akerman makes no such claims. It is precisely this possibility of full presence that her work, like Benjamin's, denies.

The issue of time, in terms of the duration of shots and the unusual length of the film as a whole, is a signature Akerman statement, in *D'Est* no less than in her other films. The long takes of scenery or machinery in which nothing out of the ordinary happens are a trademark that has lent itself to extensive commentary on her work. In *D'Est,* Akerman meditates on images of the landscape as a bridge for memory. She bears witness to the work of time, whether of healing or covering over, neither trying to arrest it nor trying to avow its allegedly progressive flow. Its march may not necessarily be progressive, but it does nevertheless change its scenery. As in Akerman's landscapes of faces, we scan the imagery for evidence of change and remnants of the past. The past never reveals itself in full, and what it does show, it shows indirectly.

▶───

Indirect Address of Memory

Akerman begins the direct address monologue of the installation, speaking in a strongly accented and sometimes stumbling Hebrew, as she gravely recites the Jewish dictum concerning graven images, the Second Commandment. The voice-over continues in English, again in Akerman's heavily accented voice, with the translation of the commandment.

The Second Commandment is the gravest commandment of all. As W. J. T. Mitchell asserts:

> Breaking the Second Commandment, the prohibition against idolatry, is the most serious sin a believer in the Bible can commit. God spends more time explaining, emphasizing, and repeating himself with this commandment than with any other. Simple moral commandments—against killing, adultery, stealing, and lying—concerned with the relations of people to one another are clearly negotiable. All of them will be justified, even encouraged or commanded by God, sooner or later, given the right circumstances. But idolatry is the one sin God will not forgive under any circumstances. It is the absolute crime, not a sin against other people, but against God himself, and the idolater must be stoned to death for his violation of the stony law.[85]

Why does Akerman choose to frame *D'Est* with this prohibition? Is it a gesture of rebellion? The comprehensive language of the prohibition would seem to extend to all likenesses, including the filmic image. Certainly that is how this commandment has been interpreted in modern times, and such would likely be the interpretation that Akerman has accepted and, albeit ruefully, defied. It has been suggested that the Bible finds its way around this prohibition by describing how things are made, rather than how they look. Others have argued compellingly that the biblical injunction found in Exodus 20:4 only applies to representational and iconographic depictions of God. Intellectual historian Kalman Bland compellingly argues that there never was, nor is there now, any Jewish prohibition against visual representations tout court.[86] Undoubtedly, visual representation is, according to Jewish law, restricted, but, despite commonly held beliefs and many erudite arguments to the contrary, the ban on representational images is *not* comprehensive. Nonetheless, as Bland cogently explains, various forces have aligned, from the time of the emancipation of European Jewry, to create the conditions in which total belief in Jewish aniconism has tended to prevail.[87] In other words, whether or not a comprehensive ban was ever rabbinically sanctioned, by the eighteenth century it was firmly believed to exist. Most Jewish visual artists from that time onward have believed, rightly or wrongly, that they were acting in defiance of the injunction. In this regard, Akerman is no exception.

Harold Bloom contends that the purpose of the Second Commandment is to "compel us to an extreme interiority" leading to thoughtful meditation, of the kind that Akerman promotes in *D'Est*.[88] Half a century earlier, Hermann Cohen, a German Jewish neo-Kantian, affirmed the belief in Jewish aniconism suggesting (as had a few before him) that poetry, rather than the visual arts, was the preferred artistic expression of the Jews, for it "is able to make spiritual thoughts more inward than can the visual arts."[89] However, it is not poetry but film that Akerman makes, and we do see images the likeness of which exist "on the earth beneath." Some of her images are quite abstract and it has been contended that abstract art is a valid circumvention of the commandment, and that artists such as Mark Rothko and Barnett Newman made the only truly distinctively Jewish art.[90] Yet Akerman is not, strictly speaking, an abstract artist. Most of her imagery is figurative and quite recognizable, even though her meanings can be relatively abstract. Given what we can safely assume is Akerman's (mis)understanding of the Second Commandment, she clearly believes herself in direct violation of the law.[91] She tells Godard, in an interview from 1979, that "Jews have a big problem with the image: you do not have the right to make images, you are transgressing when you do, because images are linked to idolatry."[92] I want to suggest, however, that her defiance (however misinformed) is itself superficial and incomplete. On the ontological level, she remains in full compliance. Even though Akerman's images tend toward the representational, her meanings, at least in *D'Est*, tend toward the abstract and indeterminate, complying in essence if not in form with the commandment's (misperceived) injunction. But there is another way in which Akerman is working with, rather than against, the commandment.

I shall return to this question of the Second Commandment via a detour. Akerman tells us, "you must always write when you want to make a film." This statement takes the form of a "vorschrift," what Richter calls a "'pre-scription,' or 'pre-writing,'; a 'pretext' that is always already written and in place from the outset."[93] Writing precedes action—in this case, as Akerman asserts, the "act of making [a film]" that then reveals precisely what one knew all along. But why, one wonders, write, or make anything at all, if what one writes and then makes is always already known? Perhaps this is a talmudic question, since the rabbis have always returned to the same passages again and again. The famous phrase in the Babylonian Talmud, attributed to the sage Ben Bag Bag in reference to the Torah, is "turn it and turn it, for everything is in it." As Bloom reminds us, paraphrasing Yerushalmi, rabbinical memory "insists that all meanings are present already in the Bible, in its normative commentaries, and in the oral law represented in each generation by the interpreters who stand centrally in the tradition."[94] In Jewish tradition, all meaning is always already available, and it only remains for us to find it. For Akerman, much as for Freud, it is as if we know ourselves and are ignorant of that knowledge (that is, *forget ourselves*) at the same time. Creation (the act of making things) for the artist, like study for the rabbis, is a process of revealing what we knew but would not let ourselves admit we knew. It might seem akin to the process of *working through,* in the psychoanalytic sense, wherein we overcome our disavowal, and the need to repeat a scene ad nauseam, by letting ourselves be cognizant of that which is already known but has been repressed. Filmmaking thus becomes a vehicle for the process of mourning, of healing historical wounds, of closing a chapter. However, Akerman contradicts herself tellingly when she admits that closure is ultimately elusive, that there is "nothing to do. It is obsessive and I am obsessed." That is to say, one will repeatedly go over this terrain of one's primal scene, endlessly and, significantly, without working it through.[95] Once Akerman finishes writing one script and making one film, she goes on to the next, ultimately rehearsing the same scenario. "Once the film is finished I said to myself, 'So, that's what it was. That again.'" Condemned to repeat one's obsessions ad infinitum. This of course transforms normative, finite mourning into its more intransigent twin, melancholia: the process short circuits any effective working through.

There are resemblances between Akerman's repetition compulsion and the repetitions and revisitations that inhere in many Jewish religious and cultural practices. The Torah scroll is read year after year, from beginning to end and then from the beginning again. Yerushalmi tells us that "any [biblical] event can be retold and reinterpreted [by the rabbis], sometimes simultaneously, in several different ways."[96] The stories are meant to be told repeatedly, to remind each successive generation of what has been done to the Jewish people: enslaved in Egypt; exiled from Spain; scapegoated in Russia; victimized by genocidal policies in the Holocaust. "Never forget"—yet Jews do not necessarily remember so as to avoid the recurrence of oppression in the future. Santayana's famous admonition, "those who cannot remember the past are condemned to repeat it," is not in the spirit of Jewish remembering. As I have said, memory is constitutive of (Jewish) identity, but a biblical Jewish understanding of the past necessarily involves recognizing repetition—that of history itself. Think only of the quote from Ecclesiastes, "What has been, already exists, and what is still to be has already been and God always seeks to repeat the past."[97] To go back to an earlier point, healing or working through are not necessarily historically Jewish motivations for remembering. It may be more "Jewish" to simply obsess, as does Akerman.

It is important to note that it is not only remembering that Akerman highlights here, but also merciful or timely forgetting, as when she says that, even though one knows all about the film one is making, "you don't realize this. Fortunately, I would say." Nietzsche's *On the Uses and Abuses of History* has made it impossible to address the subject of memory without considering its corollary, forgetting. Although Yerushalmi denies that forgetting has a place in Jewish history, others, such as Harold Bloom (who incidentally wrote the introduction to Yerushalmi's *Zakhor: Jewish History and Jewish Memory*), claim that forgetting is an inherently Jewish act.[98] Akerman's remembering and forgetting is uncannily close to Freud's model of repression. Freud, in his discussion of the uncanny, tells us that once an emotional impulse (perhaps generated by a memory) is repressed, it is transformed into anxiety and as such recurs continually.[99] Freud calls this recurrent anxiety the uncanny or *unheimlich*—the not home (which can be seen also as a form of nostalgia, the pain of not being home). Freud states: "The uncanny is in reality nothing new or alien, but something which is familiar and old—established in the mind, and which has become alienated from it only through the process of repression."[100] Akerman tells us that she knew her film before she made it but "fortunately" didn't know she knew (i.e., she forgot) until she made it. In other words, she repressed knowing something that was familiar and old, the return to which felt almost (but not quite) like going home. And that which she ultimately knows about this film (and all her others, it seems), but repeatedly represses from consciousness, is that it is ultimately about her primal scene: (the fear of) evacuation. As Bloom notes, "Freud speculated that what we first forget, and only subsequently remember, is the most important element in a dream, or perhaps in any other representation of our desires."[101] This speculation would place Akerman's primal scene at the core of this film in a way that those writing about the film seem to have themselves repressed. No vague hint or trace, the scene is present on every face and in every waiting room, each dawn and dusk, the cold and the snow, all conditions of and for evacuation. Akerman's reference to the Second Commandment may become less ambiguous in this context, too, if Bloom is correct in asserting that "the Second Commandment, in our time, is called Primal Repression,"[102] where that which is not seen, or cannot be depicted outright, is nevertheless a presence felt at every turn.

Seeing the Second Commandment as primal repression of, in this case, the primal scene of evacuation leads us to better understand the indirectness of Akerman's path. For while her camera never shrinks from looking directly into people's faces, there are ways in which her gaze is indirect. I have already described her particular mode of looking past what is in front of her in the present. We learn from her monologue that at a critical moment she even averts her eyes from what is available to be seen. She passes by her mother's home town and, she tells us, "didn't see it, didn't look." Why this sudden and total aversion to the site of evacuation? As I have suggested, she is certainly capable of looking directly and *not* seeing, yet here she refuses to even look. Why are the ancestral roots not to be gazed upon directly, but only sought indirectly in strange faces and scenarios, which are, nonetheless, strangely (that is to say, uncannily) familiar? Is it the miasmic, presymbolic *Real* that she somehow knows to avoid? Slavoj Žižek reminds us that "the Real" cannot be apprehended with a direct gaze, but must be seen indirectly, by "looking awry."[103] One may look elsewhere and even find "hints," but, just as one may not regard a direct representation of the Holiest on high, one may not, and indeed cannot, look squarely into the abyss—or the "Real"—of one's own family's evacuation.[104]

Another, nonpsychoanalytic, interpretation of this willful aversion is linked to notions of *truth* rather than of *the real*. Here we might argue that Akerman's resistance to direct representation of the actual site of the personal family memory and trauma is related to the Benjaminian proposition that "nothing is more miserable than a truth expressed as it was thought." In Benjaminian terms, when one looks for the truth directly, it—much like the *Real*, in fact—inevitably eludes. What appears instead is an impoverished version that may pass for truth to the undiscerning, but does not begin to reveal the complexity of its meanings. Truth is a recalcitrant subject, "facing the lens of writing while we crouch under the black cloth, [refusing] to keep still and look amiable."[105] The only access we can hope to have is via indirection.

Akerman has turned this indirectness into a dictum: "She who seeks shall find all too well and end up clouding her vision with her own preconceptions. This undoubtedly will happen anyway"; she continues, "it can't be helped. But it will happen *indirectly*."[106] She is purportedly concerned with the problem of overdetermined readings and discoveries. Better to look elsewhere, just off axis, to see what can be revealed. Yet the history that she seeks indirectly via the contemporary facade of Eastern Europe is, as we have seen, itself overdetermined. This history does not need to be stated explicitly. It demands no direct engagement. It simply exists, persists in its potential to overwhelm all other images laid before us, as does Akerman's own primal scene.

Akerman essentially admits, "though [she] fight[s] against it and end[s] up in a rage," this film is ultimately about her self and her attendant obsessions. It is perhaps the most indirect of autobiographies, detouring through thousands of kilometers of faces yet always hinting at the possibility of revealing her face as the face that was (nearly) effaced by history. This is Akerman's scenario, adapted from the story of her mother, passed down from generation to generation (as the Bible dictates: *l'dor v'dor*). It is known that her mother never actually told her this story. Like many children of Holocaust survivors, Akerman lived with the effects and symptoms left by the war without learning the specifics until much later. Yet, the story, however wordlessly, was indelibly passed on, to the point of becoming Akerman's own. It becomes her burden to represent, as well. The Second Commandment foreshadows such intergenerational implication when it states that the Lord will visit "the iniquities of the fathers [sic] upon the children unto the third and forth generation." Just as the children are to be held accountable for their "father's" deeds, here the child is to be held in thrall to the mother's memories. As the mother's story, this film is an autobiography of another, a self displaced through time, telescoped intergenerationally, beyond the limits of the filmmaker's experience—a "post-autobiography," if you will. *D'Est* is more a hallucination of a memory than a narrative per se, if narrative (at its most basic and attenuated) is to be understood, as Roberta Culbertson has said, "as simply an accounting in time of events in time."[107] There is no recounting, no proper chronological ordering of historical events. The film is a nonlinear eruption, a flash, in search of an elusive truth. If it is a story at all, it is the story of an evacuated present, of a displaced, transgenerational self traversing a landscape transformed into a chronotype caught indefinitely between past and present.

[**2**] *Reframing the Jewish Family*

Unlike *D'Est,* the films of this chapter *appear* to take a direct route home, tracing memory, tradition, and history to the psychological ground zero of modern identity construction: the nuclear family. This apparent directness may be no more than a wish, illusory in its fulfillment. The memories, however personal, are nonetheless filtered through family narratives the telling of which involves a multiplicity of perspectives and a liberal dispersion of the self. Inextricably bound to personal identity as such family narratives are, they may well reveal the displaced nature of memory itself, there being, finally, no direct route to the home of the self. What unites the films of this chapter is that family relations are the chosen mode of autoreferentiality.[1] The questions that find their way into these family dramas are still, as in the previous chapter, ultimately about history, memory, nostalgia, and loss, but their detours to the self occur in the most familiar personal setting. In these films, the only history that seems to matter is that which can be traced through ancestral lineage or gleaned from the faulty and erratic memory of living relatives. In other words, history in these texts is not only the solipsistic construction that Barthes once wryly quipped constituted "the time when my mother was alive before me," but is subject to the vicissitudes of memory, which as Janet Walker observes, is by definition, "friable, fallible, and frail."[2] The family itself is often a delicate construct and the edited image is the glue, or, better, the "tape," that can splice the fragmented pieces back together. These Jewish "domestic ethnographies" (a term coined by Michael Renov) tend to add a restorative dimension to the family narrative, attempting to filmically repair ruptures endured within the family fold.

As Michael Renov suggests in his essay "Domestic Ethnography and the Construction of the 'Other' Self," the family is a complex and "co(i)mplicated" site of identity formation, and as such a critical nexus of exploration for many autobiographical filmmakers.³ It is in and through the family that countless filmmakers choose to represent themselves. Michelle Citron goes so far as to insist that "most autobiographical films and videos are about the family."⁴ In the case of the Jewish first person films of this study, this generalization does not fully hold, at least not in a literal sense (*Treyf* makes mention of the filmmaker's families but does not feature them, and neither *Rootless Cosmopolitans* nor *In Her Own Time* is directly about the filmmaker's family), yet in a figurative sense family is surely an overriding theme. *D'Est* is perhaps the most circuitous domestic ethnography, yet is no less about the filmmaker's Jewish family than are the key films of this chapter: *Thank You and Goodnight, Nobody's Business, Everything's for You, Complaints of a Dutiful Daughter,* or *Phantom Limb,* all of which place the family center frame, very nearly as the filmmaker's synecdochic self.

The family is a particularly fecund field of exploration within the context of filmic self-representation. A filmmaker growing up within the past half century, at least in the United States, is likely to find a treasure trove of home movies, videos, and family photos waiting to be raided and reedited into a newly reconfigured family film. It is by no means uncommon for an autobiographical filmmaker to feed at the home movie trough. In fact, the majority of films discussed in detail in this study (with the exception of *D'Est, Thank You and Goodnight, Orders of Love,* and *Rootless Cosmopolitans*) include archival images of the filmmaker's family, often in the form of reedited home movies. The familiar (in both senses) narratives of those earlier films are in essence rewritten in the process, with the filmmaker inevitably situated at the center of the story.

Additionally, the filmmaker, in these retrospective films, sees himself or herself multiply, as the child she or he once was and as the adult child she or he has become, in what Bachelard has plurally referred to as "states of childhood."⁵ There are temporal conjunctions that imply an impossible union, merging the child and adult self in ways that the passage of time would otherwise foreclose. Thus, in revisiting one's childhood, one is and is not one's self. The integrity of the self is challenged by the presence of multiple selves and competing narratives, at the same moment that one's existence is affirmed by these same shared stories. In family autobiography, the most privileged mode of autobiographical filmmaking, the subject is always necessarily a divided subject, infinitely split by the reflections of others, the refractions of time, and the multiple tenses (not to mention tensions) of one's simultaneous existence(s).

The image that these reflections suggest is none other than the Lacanian mirror phase, where the child's perspective frames the looking but a double image is seen: that of the child (albeit an idealized version) and that of the entity holding the child up to the mirror—the (m)other or a mechanical "prop."[6] It is a moment of differentiation from the (m)other even as the image visually reinscribes dependency on the (m)other. The child is, after all, being held by the (m)other and doesn't begin to have the autonomy or mastery that she or he imagines her or his idealized image to have. In other words, the autonomy and mastery that the child sees reflected back is an illusion, a fantasy, much like the autonomy of the autobiographical subject in these films. She or he is figuratively being held, or propped up, by the family and it is through reimaging and reimagining the family on film (another screen surface) that the adult child asserts a triumphant (Lacan says "jubilant") stance. There are ample signs of the child's triumphalism in these films, as we shall soon see.

We may also think of the mechanical prop that Lacan references as the filmmaking apparatus, a mechanized prosthesis that enables a projection of the self (and the family, for that matter) that fits the measure of the filmmaker's fantasy. Just as the infant imagines himself or herself to have greater powers than she or he actually has, these filmmakers (as perpetual children) do the same, performing almost miraculous feats that unite long lost family members, revive the dead, or (re)introduce a harmony that may or may not have existed in their families. The act of going back, if not to the physical childhood home, then to its filmic figuration, enables the filmmaker to reconceive the space and ontology of home. This process of remapping enables the filmmaker to conjure his or her preferred version of the family narrative. Such a reconceptualization is often undertaken in an effort to repair certain ruptures or disunities of the filmmaker's identity, as conceived in and through the context of the family.

The self is clearly conceived, in these domestic autobiographies, not only in relation to the family but as only imaginable, in some sense, through the family. The autobiography is dependent upon these others in the frame, seemingly inconceivable and unrecountable without them. It is this integral dependency that interests me here, both in the way it complicates any simple notion of autobiography (which is revealed to concern many selves) and in the way it allows the cultural implications of autobiography, in this case Jewish filmic autobiography, to be more fully considered. I will explore the terms of Jewish cultural expression and identification in and through these selected autobiographical representations of the family, a primary site of socialization and cultural inculcation. I particularly appreciate Renov's term *domestic ethnography,* in that it embraces the anthropological relevance and resonance of these works. Culture as manifest in the microcosm of the family provides the context for the autobiographical representations to be staged.

Families serve not only as the context but actually as the pretext for many autobiographical explorations, filmic and otherwise, to the extent that most domestic ethnographies appear as much biographies of family members as autobiographies. *Nobody's Business, Everything's for You,* and, to a lesser extent, Pearl Gluck's *Divan* are about intractable fathers; *Complaints of a Dutiful Daughter* and *Tarnation* are about mentally ill mothers; *Thank You and Goodnight* is structured around the maternal grandmother's death from cancer. Each of these films refracts the auto-biographical subject through the prism of another's biography, privileging neither *auto* nor *bio* in this intricated double gesture. Feminist literary critic Nancy K. Miller writes, in her essay on memoirs and mourning, of the multiple biographies implied in family autobiography. She is concerned with the others in the story when she asks "Whose story is it?" suggesting that when writing a memoir that involves the family, one's autobiography drifts in and out of others' biographies.[7] Her point is well taken, in that autobiography is inextricably bound to biography, nowhere more so than in family autobiographies. But rather than ask about the others in the story, as Miller does, I want to ask about the ways the others serve as an integral part of self-representation, and indeed about the other-ness of self in the story. The others in the story do not so much emerge as whole and separate beings in their own right, but rather as extensions of the autobiographical narrative. This is not something peculiar to Jewish domestic ethnographies, so much as a general rule. In *Nobody's Business,* Alan Berliner self-indulgently asks his parents what traits of theirs they see in him. "I see brains, I see smartness, in a way your personality is a lot like mine," says the father with some pride. "I've given you a little bit of artistry, I think, a good outlook on life, poise, intelligence, a nice way of dealing with people," says his elegant mother. Jonathan Caouette, in *Tarnation,* less ingratiatingly and much more hauntingly realizes, as he huddles in the bathroom, desperate for psychic space, there's no escaping his mother, "She lives inside me. She's in my hair, she's behind my eyes, she's under my skin, she's . . . downstairs." The interpenetration is nearly complete.

The family is a central locus of socialization and acculturation, hence for our purposes a key site for the inculcation of Jewishness—which, it should be said, does not necessarily entail Jewish religious practices. In this handful of Jewish autobiographies whose exploration of self detours through the (Jewish) family, I have looked for ways in which Jewishness is or is not explicitly expressed, and ways in which it might be celebrated, mourned, lamented, pursued, or even assiduously avoided. In other words, one recurring theme in this chapter has to do with how the Jewish self is constituted through these family narratives—and, indeed, what , if anything, makes these films (and these families) Jewish. These are not necessarily questions the filmmakers ask themselves, nor necessarily ones to which they should be held accountable. Rather, these are externally imposed questions, designed to examine not only contemporary representation of the Jewish family but also the way that family representations intersect with Jewish self-representation.

Jewishness comes to the fore as more a mystery than a question in many of these family films, since it is not always clear how it is transmitted, in these nearly unanimously secular settings, or what exactly constitutes Jewishness. Some Jewish family autobiographies are particularly concerned with lineage *(Nobody's Business, Orders of Love)*, locating Jewishness consanguineously as much as culturally. Others trace it through food *(Thank You and Goodnight)*, and still others make almost no reference to Jewishness *(Complaints of a Dutiful Daughter, Tarnation)*, or none at all *(Daughter Rite)*. To some extent, the concept of Jewishness is at issue here. If Jewishness is strictly a matter of descent, then lineage is the sole means of tracing its effects. The problem of essentialism obviously weighs heavily on all communal identifications, but on none so much as on those dependent on bloodlines and genetics for definition.[8] If one is born Jewish does that mean one cannot meaningfully disidentify or dissent?[9] Barbara Kirshenblatt-Gimblett has written about dissent (as opposed, in her terms, to descent or consent) as a meaningful contemporary mode of Jewish expression for many young "New Jews," thus reinscribing the act *as* affirmatively Jewish.[10] Dissent can be seen as a way to "[have] your rebellion and your *hemshekh*" (continuity), too.[11] Can a Jew never meaningfully and *conclusively* disidentify? Conversely, if one is not born Jewish, can one never, short of religious conversion, consider oneself Jewish? In other words, can Jewishness never be strictly a matter of assent, but be always ultimately reducible to a matter of descent?[12] In the past—and even now, within many traditional orthodox communities—Jewish identity rests on descent and is augmented or supported by assent. However, this has changed significantly for many in the organized Jewish communities, and certainly for those Jews who identify as secular.[13] Philosopher Michael Krausz contends (and I concur) that any meaningful discussion about Jewish identity should depend not on essentialist conceptions of Jewishness but rather on culturally constructed and historically fluctuating definitions of what it means to be Jewish. Dissent from traditional Jewishness, in what Kirshenblatt-Gimblett refers to as "edge," often entails the celebration of difficult, embarrassing, stigmatized, or disturbing aspects of Jewishness, irreverently calling attention to what Jews in the past may have tried to avoid.[14]

A critic must also be able to read a film against its own grain, regardless of the individual filmmaker's identificatory allegiances. This enables, for instance, a way to contend with texts that make only the most oblique references (or none) to Jewishness. Such a film may be otherwise unreadable in Jewish cultural terms, yet it may still contribute a great deal to an analysis of contemporary Jewish cultural expression, since everything from irreverence to erasure has its ethnographic valences, marking a potential "Jewish strategy" in a given time and place. I have decided, to include discussions of such films (specifically *Daughter Rite* and *Tarnation*) in this study because of the salient issues that such strategies raise—and not as an insistence or imposition of a Jewishness the films would otherwise seem to disavow.[15]

This chapter is made up of distinct parts. I first look at the ways two filmmakers in particular (Michelle Citron and Alan Berliner) use home movies to reenvision their family narratives, replacing the father's point of view with the child's, and the ways in which that gendered child might identify or disidentify with the dominant patriarchal narrative inscribed in the family films. This discussion leads me to consider the representation of the stereotypical "Jewish mother," since, beginning with Berliner's film and moving on to any of the others in this chapter, she has gone missing. Absent in all of these films (at least in the guise of the mother) is the food-pushing, doting, sometimes overbearing, self-sacrificing stereotype made famous in Hollywood films *(The Jazz Singer, Portnoy's Complaint, Goodbye Columbus)* and in American television programs like *The Goldbergs, Rhoda,* and *Seinfeld.* We find her figure one generation back, though in much gentler form, having grayed and mellowed considerably, in the role of the grandmother, or the *bobe* (Yiddish for grandmother), in a spate of Jewish autobiographical films beginning in the 1990s, most notably in *Thank You and Goodnight.* The bobe becomes the embodiment of *yidishkayt* and the films betray a salvage impulse that is cultural as much as personal. Who and what is being salvaged appears prescribed by a set of expectations. Those bobes who do not fit the mould are almost unanimously excluded from the frame.

I then return the discussion to the children, the filmmakers themselves, who may disappoint their parents and bobes in some predictable ways (Berliner's father wants him to find "respectable" work, Oxenberg's grandmother wants her to marry), but who nonetheless take center stage in ways both admired and otherwise indulged by the parents. The child is never gone completely in these allegedly adult narratives, as is shown to us through the use of archival material and in the sentiments expressed. If the refractions of family multiply the self innumerably, the recognition of the simultaneous adult filmmaker as child adds yet another split. This is most elaborately conveyed in Oxenberg's *Thank You and Goodnight,* with the advent of her two-dimensional cartoon character alter ego, who is the quintessential perpetual child, inhering in the adult yet able to express thoughts and sentiments usually considered unbecoming in someone Oxenberg's age.

Further unbecoming residuals come to the fore: Oxenberg is just one of several Jewish autobiographical filmmakers to betray family secrets and speak the unspeakable by recounting the death of a sibling. The loss of a sibling is also thematized in Jay Rosenblatt's film *Phantom Limb* and in several of Abraham Ravett's films. These films are haunted by ghosts, who hover around the edges of the frame, unbidden and insistent, like the living dead. In their fixation with the dead, these films perhaps too thoroughly instantiate the thanatographic impulse of autobiography that Jacques Derrida and Paul de Man ascribed to it. In fact, in the films' heterogeneous subjectivity (filtered and funneled variously through parents', grandparents', and siblings' subjectivities), and in their obsession with death, they most closely approximate Derrida's awkward designation for autobiography, "autobiothanatoheterographies."[16] As autobiothanatoheterographies go, Ravett's film *Everything's for You* is veritably overpopulated with the souls of the dead, the filmmaker's very existence being predicated upon them in ways only the cruelest of histories could construct. I will explore the implications of this tormented history in some depth, looking at the hysterical historical recountings and the symptomatic repetition compulsion found in the film. As the child of two Holocaust survivors, Ravett is of course under the weight of millions pressing down, but in this domestic autobiography the family's personal losses are what preoccupy the filmmaker, in particular (in this film) his father's prewar family, about which Ravett knew nothing as a child but nonetheless felt palpably. In a sense, this film becomes an occult medium, allowing a communion with the dead that brings generations of siblings together in one frame who could never otherwise meet. In this complex and tightly woven film, the effects of repressed family trauma are everywhere evident: in the obsessive repetition of words; in the insistent quest for answers to relentlessly asked, impossible questions; in the affectless tone of the filmmaker's voice masking an unendingly burdened soul. As with Akerman, the silences surrounding the parents' traumatic history imprinted themselves on the filmmaker's psyche, though in Ravett's instance it was the pain more than the memory that was transmitted.

Jewishness may not be at issue in Ravett's film, but in several of the other family films it is. I take up this theme in relation to *Thank You and Goodnight,* a suburban American family tale. One must read the Jewishness in the details and in the affect, which is faint and seemingly fading, like the life force in Jan's grandmother. Jan's character's inability to accept the death of her grandmother can be seen here as evidence of a fear of a much greater loss. As beloved as the grandmother, Mae Joffe, may have been, her death symbolizes the death of the last remaining signs of *yidishkayt* in the family, and Oxenberg has difficulty reconciling herself to that loss. What the filmmaker cannot see is the Jewishness that she and her family display and express through humor, through food, through argument, discussion, and even something as ephemeral as timing and delivery. Rather than religious Judaism, or even the "kitchen Judaism" of the grandmother, what the film evinces are "Jewish moments" and Jewish affect.

Since affect is ephemeral, I then turn the discussion to something apparently more concrete: genealogy. In *Nobody's Business,* Alan Berliner is desperate to make links through the generations, tirelessly researching his family tree through informal mechanisms (telephone directories, word of mouth) and formal mechanisms (the Family History Library in Utah). His way of coping with the secular terror of losing his Jewish specificity is to document his lineage. He attempts to elicit the help of his father in reconstructing the family ties, but his obstinate father refuses (or pretends to), seeing the whole endeavor as fruitless. The father's refusal to remember or recount much about his lived family past stands as a direct obstacle to the son's quest for a history (and hence a place in it). The narrative the son is able to piece together with marriage licenses, passports, maps, old photographs and letters, rich as it is, is full of gaping holes. Firsthand memory is needed even to partially fill in the details, and it proves highly unstable and unreliable. But where Berliner meets resistance, Deborah Hoffmann faces a complete blank. In *Complaints of a Dutiful Daughter,* the final film discussed in this chapter, Hoffmann bravely confronts the chilling prospect of a mother without memory. As Doris Hoffmann's memory cedes to the ravages of Alzheimer's, the daughter is left to grope her way toward a recognition of self and (m)other without the benefit of their shared memory. What is left in the wake of memory is akin to an identity crisis, indicating the heavy dependence of identity on memory, frail and friable as it is. Without memory, we begin to operate on a generic level, "down to basics," as Hoffmann says in the film, a level with the appearance of being without culture, without history, without specificity—but is it really to be seen as such?

▶ _____

Family Autobiographies

Family autobiographies have a distinct tendency toward self-absorption. Presumably the filmmaker assumes that the microcosm of his or her family portrait may elicit universal identifications. Very few filmmakers endeavor to explore these wider connections, but most rather expect that if one has ever had a parent, a sibling, or a grandparent, identification must not be far behind. In general, the historical framework and cultural and political implications of these narratives is left to the viewer to account for and assess.[17] To be sure, there are Jewish family autobiographies that do little to illuminate subjectivity, the (Jewish) family, or its filmic figuration,[18] yet there are a surprising number of films that offer a great deal more than self-indulgence. Within the context of family narratives, the films discussed here innovate new approaches to a subject (or subjects) that seem otherwise hopelessly familiar. These films are, as Citron suggests, all about the family, but they all rework and restructure these complex and co(i)mplicated relationships in particularly ingenious ways. In other words, these films perform a remapping of the family terrain. *Everything's for You* does this by interjecting lost siblings into the filmmaker's family narrative, adding points of demarcation heretofore unmarked in the family diagram. *Thank You and Goodnight* introduces a new family member: a cardboard cutout alter ego, deployed as commentator on emotion-laden family scenes. Through this alter ego, family relations are reconsidered and an unusual type of *kheshbon hanefesh* (spiritual accounting) is performed. In *Complaints of a Dutiful Daughter,* the cinematographer/lover is suddenly admitted into the family fold after years of homophobic rejection, an opening that is in part due to her ubiquitousness during the filming and the film's function as a family project. *Nobody's Business* rewrites the family narratives as inscribed in the filmmaker's father's home movies, intercutting stock footage to comment on or reimage, hence reimagine, a family scene.

▶ _____

Revisioning the Family: The Child's-Eye View

Home movies, along with family snapshots, often stand in for family memory. We may remember little about events surrounding the image; once recorded, the image takes over. The lifelike animation of video and film tends to make the memory seem all the more true, even though inevitably it has been overlaid with family lore. The collective viewing practices of families (though changed from Super 8 to video viewing) often serve to consolidate versions of the family narrative so that the story told during screening becomes the shared "memory" even at the expense of individual experiences. An embarrassing memory for one family member may become a hilarious shared memory upon group viewing, and a disturbing emotional moment may be obfuscated by a happy wave to the camera. In general, these images serve (not unproblematically) to anchor the narrator's past—separate from, yet informative of, the narrator's adult self. They can perform a corroborative, almost Cartesian, authenticating function: the film exists, proof that my childhood happened; therefore I exist. Home movies, then, are often used to give evidence of a personal historical trajectory otherwise elusive, left to the vicissitudes of memory or the frozen moment of the snapshot.

When filmmakers bring their prodigious editing skills to the corpus, or body, of home movies, they are literally performing an operation, a creative surgery on the material, at times to excise a memory, at times to adjust it to the order of personal rather than collective memory, and at times to reconstruct the memory entirely. In revisiting and reediting archival footage from the family's past, the child/filmmaker attempts to wrest control of the gaze, if not literally (the child cannot go back and reshoot the parent's footage) then syntagmatically, rearranging the shots and creating new juxtapositions that alter the meanings of the original images. As Nancy K. Miller suggests, these recontextualizations signal "the triumph of the child's view of the past."[19]

I want to briefly invoke Michelle Citron's use of home movie footage in her (by now legendary) film *Daughter Rite,* in part because this serves as such a pointed contrast to Alan Berliner's use of home movies in *Nobody's Business,* and in part because she does such gentle and elegant violence to the image of the home movie.[20] Both filmmakers recut footage shot by their amateur-photographer fathers. Both filmmakers take pains to analyze and revise the dominant family narratives and, most important, both filmmakers attempt, though in different ways, to reappropriate the patriarchal gaze. The point of view of the home movie camera is generally, in both cases (as in most cases), that of the father.[21] The power of the gaze, interrogated by Citron, taken for granted by Berliner, would seem to demand to be subverted. The child's perspective wants to take precedence, even though shot, exposed, and processed to the father's specifications, and indelibly marked by his vision. Clearly there is an oedipal coup waiting to be staged. Yet, ironically, it may only be the woman, in this odd pair of filmmakers, who is committed to the ultimate overthrow of the regime.

Apparently in the thrall of late 1970s psychoanalytic feminist film theory (and quickly to become enthralling to it), Citron reworks the father's footage so insistently and in such microscopic detail that it is as if she wants to drain it of any and all lingering effects. She replays footage of herself, her sister, and her mother walking on a sidewalk in a leafy suburb of Boston, step-printed in such lilting slow motion that the viewer nearly forgets what standard playback might look like. Her approach is a by now recognizable feminist defamiliarization tactic that attempts to subvert naturalized power relations inscribed in the father's patriarchal gaze. Such a subversion posits the daughter's authorial seizure of control over the images, and hence over the representation, of the family mythology. She effectively replaces the father in his role as family meaning-maker—the woman/child's revenge.[22]

In clear contrast, Berliner allows his home movies to stand, like many family films, as an uncontested record of the past. The film shows a time before his parents' fateful divorce—idyllic in appearance, pre-lapsarian, what Miller calls the "video versions of domestic pastoral"[23] (though the voiceover track tells a different story). It is not the filmed record Berliner wishes to contest, but what happened afterward. Long after the senior Berliner grew tired of his movie camera, outside the parameters of its insistently normalizing frame, his wife was tiring of the marriage and *its* normalizing frame. The son feels implicated in that uncaptured narrative of captivity, but, rather than embracing the liberatory implications, he aims to recapture the mother, his frame a net in the service of nuclear family values, reinstituting the patriarchal position. Where Citron cannot resist the opportunity to displace the family narrative, Berliner sees a chance to put things back in their supposed rightful place. This is precisely where Berliner misses his cue for the oedipal coup. He pointedly refrains from exploiting his role of filmmaker/editor as potential successor, arrogating the authority of the patriarchal gaze. He prefers the version of the family narrative that preserves the illusion of the "domestic pastoral."

Don't misunderstand, the film is not without its oedipal tensions. Berliner, the son, is as mesmerized by the mother's beauty as was the man behind the 8 mm camera. There are countless glam-shots of the mother, some verging vertiginously on cheesecake. The son eyeing and manipulating these shots does raise the incestual specter. Oedipus is never truly out of frame. But it is this son's greatest wish to re-pose the father at his mother's side, not to depose him and take up in his stead. In one scene, where we hear the father's resigned commentary about his doomed mar-

The oedipal gaze in *Nobody's Business* (1996).

riage ("the single bar to that marriage was the age difference," the father feebly claims), we watch footage of the mother on the beach in a comely suit as she stands at an outdoor bar with a come-hither look, and we are shown the father's ill-fated seduction, as well as the mother's complicity, almost entirely from the father's point of view.

Berliner is less the committed successor than the eager apprentice to his father's cinematic practice. His manipulation of the father's archival footage is almost an assist. He makes several attempts to splice his fractured family back together, something we sense the elder Berliner would have also wanted, as if the film family could succeed where the living family had failed. Children may at times catalyze change in families, but they are also often terrified to stand out, to be different, to be exceptional, and this can make them surprisingly conservative in their advocacy. This child of divorced parents in the 1950s is still wrestling with a sense of the injustice of such an imposed difference, and the struggle continues in the hands of the adult filmmaker. The difference is exacerbated by the cultural contrast between the Ashkenazi father and the Sephardic mother, which no doubt had its effects on the family as well. Far from offering a deconstructive critique of the nuclear family such as we see in *Daughter Rite*,

Berliner stands as a staunch proponent of the status quo, an unwilling participant in an untraditional family experiment; in short, he plays the role of the conformist child. That is, this film attempts to reconstruct and repair the nuclear family, ruptured by the destructive force of an independent, protofeminist, and highly atypical Jewish mother.

The divorce was of course a childhood trauma, described in the film as the most traumatic event of both the male Berliners' lives. Where the young child Berliner was powerless to change the course of events, the adult child succeeds, and he does so not only in the past tense of the home movie footage, but in the film's present tense. Berliner is not content to simply recut old footage, masterful though he is at it. For him, as for his father, the divorce is a continual, unresolved source of pain and thus an ongoing event in need of remedy and redress. The child cries out to be heard and, though time has marched mercilessly on and reconciliation is nowhere on the horizon, Berliner takes recourse where he can: in the imaginary world of his film. The clearest example of this filmic "repair," or reconstitution, of the nuclear family is a scene where Berliner has both parents sing one of their favorite songs for his camera: Hoagy Carmichael and Ned Washington's classic, *The Nearness of You*. He then intercuts his parents, bringing them back into relation—that is to say, "near"—through visual juxtaposition and an overlapping sound track. The film wistfully, not to mention wishfully, reintroduces harmony into the discordant family.

Admittedly, Berliner's matchmaking is a childish act, not only because it is totally unrealistic but because he imagines himself at the center of the story, as does the narcissism of any child. The autobiographical family films discussed here are all evidence of a kind of childish hubris, as of children imagining they have powers: to deconstruct, to defy temporality, to reconstruct their childhoods and subsequent events. The filmmaker/child attempts to reconstitute his/her broken family (or broken heart), filmically mending a breach within the family narrative, with an instrumentality that was lacking for the actual child; the medium becomes a device for this repair. These films are also evidence of an acting-out—both in the psychoanalytic sense of a repetition compulsion, returning over and over again to the filmmakers' primal scenes and revealing the filmmakers' ultimate inability to work through the traumas of childhood, and also in the more quotidian sense of an infantile expression of rage against impotence: a proverbial tantrum.

This, however, is not an unmitigated indictment. Done well, these rants enable for all of us precisely what Bachelard claims as the provenance of the poet: they allow us to imagine "a childhood re-animated."[24]

The (Jewish) Mother

Berliner needs to show the world that his parents were once in love, notwithstanding his mother's voice-over protestations to the contrary. That we never see the image from the mother's perspective, that her gaze never dominates the view, is not challenged or even questioned by the son. Her voice-over interpretation of the events leading up to the divorce is, to be fair, given quite a bit of narrative authority. Her analysis of the parents' differences in upbringing, worldview, personality type is obviously more compelling and convincing than the father's insufficiently insightful explanation that centers on the age gap. In fact, the very contrast of their interpretations supports the mother's view. However, the footage tells a different story, a counternarrative that represents the position of the father more articulately than the father can give voice to in words. The son reconstructs the father's testimony: "We were in love, I gave her everything, we could have stuck it out." This story is preferable, for the son, to the alternative narrative, which has the mother marrying only to be free of her overbearing father's clutches and, seventeen years and two children later, abandoning the marriage for a life in the theater. Given the opportunity, the talent, and the requisite footage, any child might have an irrepressible desire to reconstruct a familial story, especially one as classically adaptable as this, into a fairy tale. Here, the father's disingenuous dismay is allowed to absolve him of any wrongdoing. The betrayal rests squarely and solely on the (sexy, seductive) shoulders of the mother, in a unique and unexpected twist revealing the Jewish mother as femme fatale. The fact of the mother's cultural difference (as a Sephardic Jew, raised in part in Egypt, fluent in several languages) slips seamlessly into an implicit trope of exotic uncontainability, as if fueling her irrational, artistic, extravagant, and utterly inexplicable (to the father and son) needs. In truth, she bears little resemblance to the Ashkenazi mothers represented either in the films of this study or in the popular culture, but neither does she resemble a traditional Sephardic mother. She stands as an anomaly.

Ever since Al Jolson crooned to his mammy in 1927, the Jewish mother has been a stock role in the American cinematic and cultural imaginary.[25] Although she appears comparatively infrequently, and is not nearly so familiar to audiences as the black mammy (also, of course, the figure of Jolson's address), she is a well-defined stereotype: matronly, long-suffering, usually stout, always desexualized, and above all, overly devoted to her children, nearly smothering them with care. Over the years, this stereotype has gone through slight transformations: she is still long-suffering and smothering, but she is no longer a product of the old world. In the 1950s and 1960s, she moves to the suburbs and, with newfound wealth, becomes materialistic and status-conscious, pushing her sons to succeed and her daughters to marry well. According to cultural anthropologist Riv-Ellen Prell, representations (often satirical) of the Jewish mother and wife of the 1950s and 1960s show three pronounced attributes: (1) an excess, emotional and material, without bounds; (2) the ability to confer inordinate amounts of guilt; (3) ignorance or stupidity.[26] The Jewish mother is shown as manipulative, overprotective, boastful about her children, ethnocentric, and incompetent about most things.[27] In this remarkably consistent formulation, the Jewish mother never cedes her central role in the life of the child, no matter how old that child grows to be. She does not hesitate to meddle, criticize, or contradict her child (or husband, thus lending credence to the myth of the weak, emasculated Jewish husband). She is a masculinized woman—loud, aggressive, outspoken, domineering—the opposite of the (passive, weak, gentle, soft-spoken) ideal of Western (read: Christian) femininity.

This mother is difficult to find in the films of my present study. The screen mothers in these films are remarkable if only for their near-absolute failure to fit this mold, even when not as culturally alien to it as Berliner's mother.[28] What is also noteworthy is the apparent lack of self-conscious effort on the part of the filmmakers to contest or rewrite that by-now-infamous role. These films are not, by and large, concerned with feminist revisionism that would dictate the accurate or positive portrayals of the Jewish mother; there is no particular political project here to rectify her tarnished image. Surprisingly, there seems little concern about or awareness of the power of the stereotype at all. It seems to warrant neither attention nor deconstruction. It has become simply and inexplicably irrelevant to most of the filmmakers, having uncharacteristically slipped from the scene. Prell argues convincingly that the stereotype emerged with a vengeance at a particular moment in American history when Jews were finding greater access and acceptance than ever before into mainstream American society. According to sociological studies done at the time, the Jewish wife and mother of the 1950s and 1960s was still, by and large, an uneducated housewife whose world was limited to home and synagogue, making her the Jewish gatekeeper at a time when assimilationism was the dominant game.[29] Her world was still provincial and Jewish, while her husband experienced expanded opportunities at work and her children sought to blend in at school. In a word, "the Jewish mother/wife marked difference," at a time when difference spelled stigma—hence the scapegoating of the one member of the family who bore the mark of difference most apparently.[30] Assimilation, or at least economic (class) upward mobility having been successfully effected in the families of most of the filmmakers of this study, the need for the scapegoated mother image appears to have receded. There is in fact a countercurrent in a few of the films discussed, with the filmmakers seeking out and revivifying that which is culturally distinct about their parents or grandparents rather than attempting to belittle or efface it; indeed, when Oxenberg admonishes her mother for never having learned to cook the Jewish foods her grandmother always made, or when Berliner looks to his grandparents' and great-grandparents' generations to find what his parents have not maintained, both filmmakers display classic third generation symptoms.[31]

If the representation (and reputation) of the infamous *Jewish mother* stereotype can be said to be in part an effect of certain assimilatory tensions and tendencies, then it is fair to say that, in this sampling of late-twentieth-century Jewish autobiographical films, there is a different set of challenges being faced than were present in the 1950s and 1960s when the stereotype was popularized (especially in America) in literature, in comedy, and on television. The Jewish mother that Prell describes is nowhere to be seen in these films, or rather, she has softened and grown older and she has become a grandmother.

▶

The Grandmother/*Di Bobe*

If the Jewish mother as a type has evolved beyond recognition in these films, the grandmother has taken her place. There has been a spate of Jewish grandmother films in the last fifteen years, *Thank You and Goodnight* being the best and most elaborated, but there are many shorter autobiographical Jewish films/videos that focus on the relationship between grandchild and grandmother. The grandmother in these representations may surprise, as when she dons a wig and tells of her youthful gender transgression in Sandi DuBowski's *Tomboychik* (1993) or when she accepts her grandson's homosexuality in Andy Abrahams Wilson's *Bubbeh Lee and Me* (1998), but she never plays entirely against type. The grandmothers uniformly conform to the image of the doting, loving, worried, food-obsessed, unsophisticated, unschooled, working-class *balabusta* (good homemaker). In the films I am thinking of—those mentioned above, as well as *Nana, George, and Me* by Joe Balass (1998), which features a Sephardic Jewish grandmother, Chana Pollack's *Revisions* (1994), and Cynthia Madansky's *Past Perfect* (2001)—there are no professional grandmothers, no indifferent grandmothers, no grandmothers who can't cook. The proliferation of what I call the bobe film may in fact be in response

to the absence of traditional Jewish female types (that is, un- or only partially assimilated women) among the contemporary filmmakers' mothers'
generation. When searching for their Jewish roots, the grandchildren
appear to find what they are looking for only when they skip a generation.
This conforms a bit too neatly to what was once called Hansen's Law,
where third-generation proclivities were summed up in the axiom "What
the son wishes to forget the grandson wishes to remember."[32]

There is a strong element of the salvage project in all these works.[33]
Many of the grandmothers are quite old (DuBowski's is eighty-eight during the taping of *Tomboychik*, Madansky's is also approaching ninety) or
infirm (Oxenberg's dies during the filming), and there is the implacable
sense that they are the last bastion of authentic Jewishness. I am sympathetic to this impulse, having experienced the loss of my own long-
suffering, self-sacrificing, old world, Jewish grandmother, who was also
always doting and doling out food. When she died, I too felt the irrevo-
cable loss not just of a beloved grandmother but of the end of an era of
yidishkayt. The desire to document the existence of such a person in one's
life is strong; I have to admit feeling some regret at not having done so.
Yet what is it really that is being documented? What is this sense of seem-
ing authenticity? Almost without exception in these bobe films, this notion of authenticity remains unquestioned in relation to the grandmother.
Yet in reality many of these women's lives represented a rupture with old
traditions, and certainly with the old world. My maternal grandmother,
for instance, no longer kept an actively kosher kitchen, nor was she the
least bit religious, having internalized the optimism of atheistic socialism
in her Warsaw youth. Nonetheless, in these films, the bobes are presented
as the embodiments of *yidishkayt*. Here, the definition of authenticity is
tautological: what the *bobe* does is authentically Jewish because she is
doing it. Her authenticity comes in large part from the Jewish cultural
contexts of her upbringing; regardless of religious observance, these
grandmothers grew up in thriving Jewish worlds. The mother is not accorded the same cultural authority, having been raised in more integrated
(less homogeneous) cultural environments, thus having insufficient indicators of (stereo)typical cultural signifiers. What happens in this tautology,
though, is that Jewishness is reduced to a set of indicators that are so
narrow as to foreclose the possibility of identifying Jewishness outside of
a too-arbitrary limit. There is nothing halakhic, or in traditional Jewish
law, that would preclude the possibility of a scholarly Jewish grandmother,
a professional Jewish grandmother, or even a politically active Jewish
grandmother, yet these (and other) representations do not seem to attract
most Jewish autobiographical filmmaker's attention—and would not reg-

ister in a representational mode as authentic Jewish grandmotherly behavior. Surely there were many women of this prewar immigrant generation who were active in the trade unions and the like, yet few seem to have attracted the focus of the grandchildren's cameras.[34] It is worth noting that, in one of the few first person Jewish films to blatantly defy this typology, the grandmother is neither Eastern European nor working class.

Lisa Lewenz's film *A Letter without Words* is composed of 16 mm footage shot by her wealthy, educated, German Jewish paternal grandmother before World War II. In the film, Lewenz attempts to reconstruct who this grandmother was, on the basis of the people and details she framed. Einstein is one of the luminaries framed by her lens, shown not in an anonymous sighting but within the context of the grandmother's social world, thus associating this amateur cinematographer with the upper echelons of the inter-war Berlin intelligentsia. Lewenz herself was brought up with no knowledge of her Jewish grandmother, her father having converted to Christianity and hidden his cultural heritage from his children. According to most interpretations of Jewish law, this grandmother's origins would not suffice to make Lewenz a Jew. Regardless, Lewenz begins to identify with her as an intergenerational filmmaking partner (she credits her as such) and also as a conduit for her own occluded Jewish identity. This grandmother is unknown to Lewenz personally (having died nine months before Lewenz was born), and she is also unknown, or at least unfamiliar, as a type on our screens. As a wealthy, assimilated, German Jewish woman, she in fact defies type to such an extent that, even in this film, she is only called by her given name, Ella, or *Mutti*, German for mother, never grandmother and certainly not the more *heymish yidishe* bobe.

My paternal grandmother, though not upper class, also did not conform to the bobe image and as a result, I believe, did not stir my salvage impulse. Nor did I feel a great loss of authenticity when she died, even though she certainly represented a legitimate lived experience of a twentieth-century Jewish woman. She was highly literate, fluent in four languages (Russian, Yiddish, Hebrew, and English), a business woman, and an idealistic socialist Zionist. An independent thinker from an early age, she relocated as a single woman, first to New York from Minsk in Belarus, then—twenty-five years later, as a widow—to Israel in the 1950s, fulfilling her lifelong dream to live in *Eretz Yisrael* (the land of Israel). Interestingly, like Lewenz's grandmother she was never called grandma or bobe, insisting that we call her *Ima* (Hebrew for mother). She would likely have been a much more interesting subject for a film than my other grandmother, yet my nascent protodocumentary impulses at the time of these women's approaching deaths was to record my maternal grandmother on audio-tape and not to make any overtures toward my Ima. Apparently I am not alone in this selective recording. The Jewish grandmother in these films is treated as an endangered species, a dying type from the old world, self-sacrificing, family oriented, and performing traditional female roles. Those who do not fit the mold are not seen to warrant our attention. Of course, the mothers are soon to be (or already are) the new Jewish grand-mothers, a fact that will inevitably force a revision of type. But we begin to see the pattern that spurs the salvage impulse: a reliance on preordained categories so that a role only appears worthy of saving when the character closely conforms to type.

▶

The Children/*Di Kinder* Make Good

At the end of *Nobody's Business,* when Oscar Berliner, Alan's father, lists the models he would have preferred Alan to become—an accountant, a lawyer, an engineer, or, in short, any profession but the independent filmmaker he is—Oscar reveals himself finally a more typical Jewish father than the film would have led us to suspect. Since the "children" in these films are the filmmakers, it goes without saying that they have chosen atypical professions, yet each without exception is a professional in some respect—that is, has achieved or maintained the middle-class status to which their parents may have aspired and from which each, nearly without exception, came. The "alternative" nature of the film-makers' chosen profession seems to be articulated as a problem only for the senior Berliner. To his ladies-sportswear-manufacturing sensibility, his son is a *shnorer,* a beggar asking for handouts. In one of Berliner's countless ingenious juxtapositions, and as yet another instance of the child's triumphalism, his father's litany of complaints is heard over a listing of the prestigious "handouts" the younger Berliner received to make this very film (grants from the Corporation for Public Broadcasting, National Endowment for the Arts, Rockefeller Foundation, Guggenheim Foundation, New York State Council on the Arts). In the context of the audience likely to see the film, a group far from the garment district crowd his father knew so well, the younger Berliner has clearly prevailed, getting the last word on his success: a match point in an arduous volley whose elusive trophy is his father's approval. It seems ironic that the man who clearly spent a great deal of time behind a camera is unable to under-stand his son's passion for filmmaking. There is a hidden disavowal here. By deriding his son's choice to validate the film image as worthy of a lifetime's dedication, the father can deny the power of his own passion (to make films, but also for the inspiration of his films: his wife). Had he recognized the son's work as legitimate, he might no longer be able to minimize the importance of his earlier footage, maintaining, as he had all these years, its marginal status as hobby. The son reframes priorities, centering the focus back on the image that the father wants so desperately to ignore. Hence the father's complaint is only partially concerned with traditional expectations and pressures for a son to make good. The complaint is also deeply motivated by the father's need to retain control over the narrative of his own history and to treat it as unremarkable in every respect. Meanwhile, Alan, behind the prestigious awards, grants, fellowships and kudos, reveals himself as the son still in search of his father's approval.

Oscar Berliner's critical view is not reiterated in the other films here. Ravett's parents seem mildly confused about the apparatus involved, and no mention is made of their son's chosen profession, other than generic advice from his father that he should be independent and remain his own boss. The women encounter no disapproval with regard to their filmmaking activities, but neither are these ever compared to a profession, as were Berliner's. When such activity is referred to at all, it is the apparatus involved, not the act, that is privileged. For instance, when Oxenberg's ailing grandmother realizes that Jan's camera caught her during radiation treatment, she has the unexpectedly amused response that the nurses must have thought she was a celebrity. And on her deathbed, she eerily tells Oxenberg that, when she calls on Jan from the "other side," Jan should remember to bring her camera. From the grandmother's perspective, Oxenberg's filmmaking is less a profession than a vocation; it is taken for granted, a fully integrated personality trait that requires a clumsy appendage, but one so naturalized that it is never questioned even during the most painful, intimate moments.

For the women filmmakers, what is questioned by the parental figures is not the filmaker's profession, but rather her marital status or choice of partner; this questioning, too, is not universal. It comes up most notably in *Thank You and Goodnight,* on the part of the grandmother, who would like to see Jan married. The marriage question is brought up twice, both times by the grandmother, and stealthily deflected each time by a bemused Jan. There is no mention, let alone discussion, as to the reasons for Jan's noncommittal attitude toward matrimony. Without the benefit of extratextual knowledge, the ordinary viewer would only have a vague sense of why Oxenberg is so evasive. Her sexuality is never declared, and the clues are not entirely clear even to those in the know. The film is predominantly shot in the 1970s (though finished in 1991), and Oxenberg's presentational style—flannel shirts, big belts, lack of make-up or jewelry—is the very image of the unofficial lesbian feminist uniform of the day. However, these signs can always be misleading; the uninitiated viewer might simply think Jan slightly unkempt or frumpy.[35]

The other children in the family would corroborate that unflattering view. Ricky, the brother closest in age, is an unsavory cross between Woody Allen (physical resemblance) and Leonard Cohen (temperament). He is also an inane pontificator with a morbid streak who fancies himself a latter-day Sartre, a conceit afforded him by his apparent isolation in the the shag-rugged room he still occupies in his mother's house. One imagines he is the product of entirely too much coddling (the family philosopher or genius), mixed with a paralyzing self-doubt that keeps him from testing his mettle in the world. There are other siblings, none so egregiously irritating as Ricky yet all cut from the same cloth. We feel fortunate that the eldest is making this film, as she seems to be the only one in the family to have developed a sense of humor with which to counteract the ponderousness that seems a familial patrimony.

Overall, *der kinder,* the filmmakers, seem to have the unyielding support of their families in these projects; at least, this is what comes across in most of the films (even Berliner's). Without exception, the films demand a tremendous amount of cooperation, time, patience, and forbearance from family members. The extent of the indulgence is thematized in Judith Helfand's *A Healthy Baby Girl,* as she videotapes herself and her family through the crisis of her DES-caused cancer, the ensuing treatment (a radical hysterectomy), and her recovery. At one point, her cameraman can be heard asking Helfand whether her mother's guilt feelings (at having inadvertently exposed her daughter to the toxic DES) are fueling her indulgent cooperation. Helfand, in the film, prefers to see the filming as part of the healing process, but there remains the sense, in this film and others (certainly in Ravett's *Everything's for You* and *The March*), of filmmaking as the habit of an overindulged child getting her or his way. Whether spoiled or otherwise, in these family films the filmmaker is in some sense still and always a child.

▶────────────────────────────────

The Simultaneous Child

With very few exceptions, the family autobiographies in this study are made from the (grown) child's point of view. Family relations are interrogated and contemplated by the child as both an adult and the child she or he once was (Ravett is the only filmmaker considered in any depth here who has children of his own).[36] There is no grand thesis to be deduced from this fact, as there are other Jewish autobiographical films made from the parent's as well as the child's perspective.[37] It is interesting to note that the vast majority of these filmmakers have not had the experience of being parents themselves and their relationship with their parents has not been renegotiated through the potentially transformative experience of parenthood. But the experience is not always or necessarily transformative, and, no matter how many children one may have, one always remains someone's child.

Most domestic ethnographies may be seen as an effort precisely to grow up, to make sense of that which had heretofore been only viscerally perceived and poorly understood. Making an autobiographical film can be said to be motivated by a desire to de-link the mature subject from those embedded, sedimentary narratives of the filmmaker's former, more diminutive, selves. But it is also a method of reconnection, wherein the filmmaker posits herself as intimately related, if not identical to, the child reimaged and reimagined on screen. Filmmaking becomes a mechanism of return, a time travel machine enacting a "temporal dissonance"[38] that creates impossible synchronicities, points where the adult and child exist on the same temporal plane. It is important to emphasize that these filmic renarrativizations of the family remain the child's response: that of the autobiographical filmmaker as perpetual child.

As one of the few philosophers to see childhood as more than a nostalgic remainder, Gaston Bachelard observes that "by certain of its traits, childhood lasts all through life."[39] I want to linger on the ramifications of this statement, in which childhood is no longer conceived of as a phase or a temporally demarcated zone that one crosses at some precise yet unspecified moment, but rather as a state or states that manifest and recede at various points throughout life, never disappearing altogether.

One can imagine that the converse is also true: that if the child inheres in the adult, then the adult may also inhere in the child, or, more soberly put, the adult one becomes is already present in the child. This conclusion may seem overdetermined and counterintuitive, but think of the wizened face of an infant, the uncanny stare of a toddler, the inexplicably acute observation of a preschooler, or even the "grown-up" insights of an adolescent. Bachelard suggests that such a premature adult (he uses the term "premature man"[40]) exists within the child by the time she or he enters into the zone of family, social, and psychological conflicts—that is, at the very beginning of the socialization process.

By suggesting that the adult is already present in the child, the point

I want to stress is that, in looking back to one's childhood via home movies or memories (one's own or borrowed), the filmmaker may well be looking not simply or nostalgically to the innocent or even traumatized child that she or he once was, but for clues, hints, signs of who she or he is today, already present in miniature, in the body of (to borrow from Joyce) "the artist as a young child." I will explore the implications of this complex, multiplanar existence by looking at the externalized child alter ego so exquisitely developed in Oxenberg's *Thank You and Goodnight* (1991).

In this inventive film centered around her dying grandmother, Mae Joffe, Oxenberg externalizes her childhood self in the cardboard cutout figure of the younger, brasher, brattier, alter ego, whom I have taken the liberty of naming Jannie.[41] Jannie is literally the embodiment of the filmmaker's childhood or childish identity. She appears throughout the film to ventriloquize Oxenberg's less than mature feelings or memories, the ones we are meant to grow out of, or at least not express publicly, by the time we reach adulthood, but the ones that the adult Oxenberg clearly still feels the need to express. Jannie is not only meant to represent Oxenberg at a younger age, she is also Oxenberg's child-self who exists simultaneously with the adult. Jannie is depicted crying, looking mischievous, being contemplative, industrious, temperamental, perplexed. This figure comes across as the emotional fulcrum of the adult autobiographical subject: the truer self.

There is a scene in which Jan, as Jannie, attempts to deal with the terminal illness of her grandmother, who is ostensibly the lead character, the "star" of the film. In her inability to accept the scientific evidence, adult Jan might have felt immature or unrealistic, but in the guise of

Doctor Jannie in *Thank You and Goodnight* (1991).

Jannie, she is allowed to voice her irrational, childish thoughts and even to act them out, as if playing make-believe. As we hear Oxenberg's voice intoning naïvely, "I didn't like it that Gramma was sick," we see the two-dimensional Jannie in a doctor's coat, with an expression of firm determination on her caricatured face. We cut to close-up details of what can only be described as a child's imaginary laboratory, complete with bubbling beakers and fanciful gadgets with moving parts. The audio track complements the scene with the requisite mad scientist's laboratory burbling sound effects. We see a sign that optimistically reads "Cure for Cancer," and we can imagine Jannie winning the sixth-grade science prize for her efforts. Oxenberg closes the scene with the unpolished sentiment, "I wished I could make her better." Indeed.

The visual presence of Oxenberg's immature yet precocious alter ego creates an appropriate context for a child's questions to be asked. Existential and pseudometaphysical questions occur frequently through-out the film, questions such as "What is eternity?"; "What's this thing called death?"; "Do you have to keep your same personality?"; "Is it important to face facts, or is that just another illusion?" These questions are spoken in Oxenberg's adult voice, but often in conjunction with an image of Jannie engaged in a comical scene. When asking about the nature of death, Jannie's arms are akimbo, making light of the moment. Jannie creates an environment where such questions and sentiments can be spoken with humor but also with respect. When the grandmother dies and Oxenberg tells us there is more she wanted to say to her grandmother, and that if she could only just say one more thing to her grandmother, she would tell her she loved her, we see Jannie in an astronaut's suit, ready to lift off in a spaceship and find Grandma. The Jan/Jannie character is allowed to dream of making amends with the grandmother; Jan/Jannie, the child and the adult simultaneously, takes stock of all the ways she fell short as a granddaughter, all of the time not spent with her grandmother, the words left unsaid, in a secular version of *kheshbon hanefesh* (the accounting of the soul, traditionally performed during the month before Rosh Hashanah and Yom Kippur).

The externalization of an alter ego is more than a clever device, though it is that, too. It instantiates the multitemporality of the self, raised by home movies and family photographs. Michelle Citron, when ruminat-ing upon her home movies, has asserted that, "my 48-year-old self and my 8-year-old self meet each other's gaze across the gap of decades. I wonder what she will speak."[42] In Oxenberg's work, Citron's "gap of decades" is imaginatively bridged, and we do not have to wonder what the eight-year-old Oxenberg has to say; we are treated to her words.

There is a painful event raised in *Thank You and Goodnight* in addition to the grandmother's death, and that is the unmourned loss of Jan's younger sister, Judy, who was killed by a car at the age of seven. *Thank You and Goodnight* shares the theme of a dead sibling with Jay Rosenblatt's film *Phantom Limb* and several of Abraham Ravett's films *(Everything's for You, Toncia, Half Sister),* though of Ravett's films, only *Everything's for You* is discussed here. Oxenberg's sister died when they were both young, as did Rosenblatt's little brother, and Ravett's died before Ravett was born. All find these deaths unbearably difficult to talk about, yet somehow find their way to language and representation of the missing siblings, and do so almost obsessively. Oxenberg tells us twice that she does not talk about the sister who died. She fools no one with this paralipsis since not only does she "talk about it" by telling us she does not, but she also proceeds to talk quite explicitly about it, and in fact to reenact in considerable detail the events surrounding the sister's death. Her grandmother also talks about it, though she, unlike Jan, seems not to have been bound by the implicit family vow of silence that, in this film, Jan ultimately ruptures repeatedly. The moratorium seems to have been the mother's wish, as she is the only one of the three who is silent on the issue—conspicuously so. Helen, Jan's mother, is never shown in the presence of any discussions of her lost daughter, though as a spectator of the film, she was surely subjected to the words (and the images). The pain caused to the mother is disregarded in order to express the generally unacknowledged loss experienced by the sibling who remains.[43] This is a betrayal of a family law, presumably laid down by the mother, hence another triumphalist moment by the child/filmmaker, yet the betrayal is ultimately in the service of filmically bringing the pieces back together, making the family whole again, a theme to which I will return at the end of this chapter.

Rosenblatt's film, *Phantom Limb*, in its episodic structure and its fragmented, almost schizophrenic images and style, epitomizes the stuttering struggle to utter anything coherent about such a devastating loss. Rosenblatt's brother died as a result of unhygienic medical practices while undergoing surgery for an illness that may (though this remains unclear in the film) have been terminal on its own. We learn very little about the illness except that the treatments caused bloating and the child had trouble walking. What we do know for sure is that, since the brother's death in 1964, the filmmaker's own feelings have hovered anxiously amid shame, guilt, anger, and pain. The brother's illness was an embarrassment to his only slightly older sibling, Jay, primarily because it impeded what appears to have been a latent wish for the perfect American family. The first section of the twelve-part *Phantom Limb* features frequent juxtapositions of home movie footage with black-and-white stock footage. In the home movies, we see the younger brother before his illness, but in order to depict the illness itself Rosenblatt resorts to the generic stock characters of 1950s educational films. As the emotions heighten and the intertitles tell of the family's grief and Rosenblatt's torment, the home movies drop from view, replaced entirely with the stock family in its sanitized, white, middle-class, American "perfection." By highlighting Jewish rituals of mourning in section four of the film, complete with stock footage of kaddish (the prayer for the dead) being read at a gravesite, Rosenblatt implicitly ties the loss of his brother, Eliot, to Jewishness. Up until that point the family movies could be of any white, middle-class family, and the tie to the stock footage of nondescript American families emphasizes this. The focus on Jewish rituals comes as a surprise within the context of the film, and it signals a collapse of categories. In fact the second section of the film is titled "Collapse," but in it we see only the collapse of buildings, structures falling without explanation. The obvious reference is the collapse of the family and the emotional breakdown that ensued after Eliot's death. However, there is more to be read. Eliot's illness calls attention to a difference within the family that perhaps no child would want, since difference is something most children abhor. Yet the generic—perfect, and perfectly non-Jewish—stock family footage situates that difference, that shame, elsewhere. There is a childish conflation playing itself out here—illness equals difference equals Jew—that had weighed uneasily on the unreconstructed childhood memories of a severely traumatized older sibling who was never, until the making of this film in 2005, permitted to mourn this loss.[44] The silences had cut off circulation to Rosenblatt's ability to mourn, leaving him with the acute pain of the memory and loss of his brother and no way to come to terms with it— feelings much like those that amputees report after losing a limb (hence the title). This film is an attempt to work through the adult/child filmmaker's feelings of shame (of the supposed abnormality of his Jewish family, an abnormality signaled by his brother's illness), of guilt (for the shame), and of course of loss, all of which still come across as raw and unresolved as at the time of Eliot's illness and death more than forty years earlier.

Ravett's film, too, is a working through of feelings of loss, but in his case it is the loss of a heretofore unknown, or unrecognized, relationship: a sister on his mother's side and a sister and brother on his father's side, all three of whom perished in the Nazi death camps. He never knew his siblings and never could have known them. In fact, it is not so much a relationship as a rivalry, since had these siblings lived there would almost certainly have been no Abraham. His half-sisters and half-brothers were from his parents' earlier, prewar marriages; the children and spouses had died in the Holocaust, and Ravett's parents had met and married afterward. If the war had not brutally disrupted their lives, presumably his parents would never have met and Abraham would never have been conceived. In the two films dedicated solely to his mother's daughter (*Half Sister* and *Toncia*), and in *Everything's for You,* about his father and his father's first family, this macabre rivalry is never foregrounded or even acknowledged by anyone involved, yet it must weigh heavily on all concerned.

Ravett's children figure into his missing family narrative and, serendipitously for him, he has a son and a daughter, who waft through nonnarrative segments of his films like the revenants of the never-to-be united Abie and Toncia or, alternatively, like mirror images of his father's boy and girl. In their average, typical, sibling tousles, Ravett's children play out a normalized version of Abraham's distorted, disfigured, and war-torn siblinghood, thus burdening the children's interactions with an oppressive history that the child Ravett has unwittingly carried through his whole life. We see the pain transferred symbolically in the iconographic replacement of one generation's mismatched pair with the next.

These films permit the unspoken within the family narratives to be heard. The making of the films provides the permission or excuse to rupture the silences and, in some sense, to revive the dead, at least in name. The films hint at the thanatography that autobiography already resembles, according to Jacques Derrida. Derrida reminds us of Nicolas Abraham and Maria Torok's psychoanalytic theory of mourning, or rather of the failure thereof, where the bereft person retains a space within the living ego, like a crypt within the body. And, according to Derrida's reading, the dead "ventrilocate" through the living from this figurative crypt; it is they who speak our lives, our autobiographies.[45] Thus, for Ravett, the dead prewar half-siblings in effect speak his life.

These films are surely thanatographies, or even Derrida's more awkward "autobiothanatoheterographies," in that they speak the dead who had clearly never been mourned properly, and the dead speak in turn to the heterogeneous and heteroglossic nature of the selves being represented.[46]

▶

Postpain

There are some remarkable parallels between Abraham Ravett and Chantal Akerman. Both are children of survivors, raised with what appears a vast, engulfing, unaccountable, and profoundly disturbing silence about the war and about life before, silence that left the two filmmakers with a lifetime obsession with their parent's past. Both filmmakers' work is autobiographical, though Ravett's more directly so than Akerman's, and both seem to share Akerman's "primal scene" of evacuation (see chapter 1); it courses through their work like a disturbed and wayward muse. They are also both adept in the nonnarrative mode, each with a distinctive lexicon that brands their work as their own. They are obsessive, repetitive filmmakers who often communicate as much through silence as through speech and sound.

But this is where the similarities end. Their films look nothing alike, and someone familiar with the films of both will no doubt be surprised by any comparison between their work. Where Akerman's shots are long, slow, and steady, always allowing an action or gesture to resolve, and often adding a beat or two more for good measure, Ravett's shots tend to be short, at times prematurely truncated without allowing the action to finish. They are often optically altered. Akerman notably eschews archival imagery, whereas Ravett uses it liberally, often slowed down and shot off a monitor, creating horizontal roll bars that interfere with the viewing of the image, or produced in negative where the image is only vaguely decipherable. Although, thematically and formally, Akerman is relentlessly repetitive, she is not known for repeating individual shots in any given film, whereas Ravett often repeats images two and three times, sometimes exactly as they have been seen and other times revealing more of each shot sequentially. Where Akerman works at a remove from her subjects, Ravett tends toward the disorienting extreme close up—a hand, two dangling feet, bubbles in blue water—or partial revelations: a decapitating midriff shot, a decontextualized back of the head. Ravett, perhaps surprisingly (considering his avant-garde training and proclivities), prominently includes interviews, something Akerman has until fairly recently assiduously avoided.[47] Ravett's interview subjects are exclusively his parents; other persons appear in his frame, sometimes in sync-sound footage, but no others are subject to interrogation. Where Akerman refuses to engage the questions of her parents' story directly, even to the extent of avoiding looking at her mother's home town, Ravett cannot stop asking questions. The audio tracks of two early films (*Half Sister*, 1985, and *Toncia*, 1986) exclusively feature an interview with his mother, discussing the circumstances of her evacuation from various ghettos (first Krakow, then Plaszow) and in particular what happened to her young daughter, Abraham's half-sister, Toncia, during that time.

Where Akerman treats personal and family memory as historical,

Ravett treats history as personal.[48] The relevance of the Holocaust in Ravett's films is rendered purely in terms of his parent's broken lives and Ravett's own existence (which is in some sense a direct outcome of those events). For him, his parents are representatives of three distinct pasts: a prewar past, which Ravett can hardly picture and of which there are in fact precious few pictures; the past of the war, with its evacuations, separations, and unfathomable losses, which Ravett can never hear enough about; and his own childhood past, which only becomes decipherable to him once the other two pasts are better imag(in)ed.

The first (prewar) past is a scenario that appears idyllic—indeed, prelapsarian. There are spouses; there are children; there are grandparents, homes, work, friends. The few extant images are of a full and seemingly secure life unaware of its own frailty and approaching demise. It is a history that documents a life before Abraham was born, and it is a history that, had it been allowed to proceed without the radical disruption of the war, would have presumably precluded his birth. If Barthes is right that history is "the time when my mother was alive before me," then in Ravett's case it must also be the time when his mother's and his father's others were alive to the exclusion of "me." Barthes also points out that "history is hysterical: it is constituted only if we consider it, only if we look at it—and in order to look at it, we must be excluded from it." For Barthes, all history entails an exclusion, it happens before we are born. In fact, he adds, "as a living soul, I am the very contrary of History, I am what belies it, destroys it for the sake of my own history."[49] Images of destruction dominate Abraham's past and, in a horrifyingly accurate sense, his parents' prior families had to be destroyed for Ravett's own personal history to unfold. There is clearly a tension between a social, political history and a personal one; however, with Ravett's story, these collapse into each other and terrifyingly it is the "me" for whom the Barthesian destruction, or, in this case, Destruction (*der Kherbn*, the Yiddish expression for the Holocaust), took place. This resonates all too well with the earlier revelation that, had the war not occurred, the histories of his lost half-siblings and his parent's former spouses would have precluded Ravett's coming into being. The child Ravett's very existence is dependent on the cessation and destruction of others' histories, a taxing burden to be sure. Of course, any child might imagine himself or herself as somehow responsible, or at least the guilty beneficiary, of these "pre-historical" tragedies. This is no doubt a narcissistic and highly irrational view, one that entails an inflated sense of omnipotence, yet from such a perspective, the child's very existence could seem to have a dangerous and damaging effect on the historical narrative, on history itself. If we consider that history, as we come to it and as it appears to us, is always in part our own construction, then we can see how Ravett's imagined agency might have devastating and ongoing symbolic implications. The meaning of the child's historical projections wields important interpretive power over a field that persists in its effects. It is no wonder that Ravett pursues his subject single-mindedly, yet as if averting his eyes. The partial frames, the obscured images, the roll bars, the negative images, the clipped cuts all make disturbing sense when we imagine the implications of looking forthrightly at the devastation. Barthes creates an impossible double bind for the child, in this case Ravett. If history is by definition that which happens before you are born, then it must always cease once you appear on the scene; your appearance, in effect, arrests it. However, History is only in fact constituted when we look at it, it does not exist outside our gaze. We create and destroy it simultaneously; we stare into the destruction, which for Ravett is a tremulous ground littered with corpses, and hence the hysteria.

There are ample signs of this hysteria in Ravett's narrative, particularly in the repetitive aspects of the inquiry. No question is posed only once, and many are posed repeatedly, often in at least two languages. The film begins with the question of the name and naming.[50] Over black we see the text "His name was Chaim." It flashes on screen twice. Then just "Chaim," (Hebrew for "life"), again seen twice. Then the name written in Hebrew letters.[51] We find out next, still in white text on black background, that "My mother called him Henyek." Repeated twice, followed by "In New York they called him Herbert." Then "Herbert" is repeated twice. His name, Chaim, through transposition and dislocation, slowly loses meaning. His nickname is Polish, thus effecting the first transformation away from its initial Jewish meaning and resonances. Once the name becomes Herbert there is a further disruption. The de-Judaicization of his father's name is not unique, but, for Ravett, the transatlantic pronominal transformation has important personal implications. It is as if his father was another person entirely when he was Chaim. Chaim had life. By the time he became Herbert he had literally lost life's meaning.

The last sentence to appear before Ravett cuts to an image of his father is "I called him . . ." Like the lines before, it appears twice. The end of the sentence is spoken off camera to a listless and somewhat disinterested older man sitting slightly slumped in what appears to be his apartment. "Pop, what about mishpakha?" he intones in what we soon learn to be the Ravett family's typical multilingual lexicon (a mixture of English, Yiddish, and Hebrew). "What about family?" He is asking his father about the family before the war. "Pop" is impassive. He says little, just that there was a girl who was eleven years old and a boy who was eight, their ages frozen in time as if permanently caught in a snapshot. We never learn for sure, but it would seem that the ages refer to how old the children were at the time of their deaths. We do eventually learn their names, Estush and Sholom David, though it appears as if we, along with Ravett, learn them after the father has already died (from the handwritten text on the back of an old photograph, read aloud in translation by Ravett's ever-obliging mother, Fela). This film is an attempt to reconcile the image of the man Ravett knew as his father with the information learned after the father's death about his former family. In voice-over, Ravett begs, he pleads, he beseeches over and over like a Yom Kippur prayer,[52] "Why didn't you ever tell me you had children? I wanted to know. You never told me anything. Gornisht. Nothing." He has an endless stream of questions for his father, mostly asked posthumously. "What did they do when they sent you from the ghetto? What did the children carry, Pop? How did you eat, the whole day? You never told me anything. Nothing." His tone is plaintive, his need for answers as heartfelt as it is unsatisfied. He repeats his questions sometimes verbatim, sometimes formulated slightly differently, as if, either by sheer repetition or by slight alteration, he might finally get the answers he needs. But as with any hysterical repetition, resolution remains elusive.

Names continue to be of central significance in this film. We learn, about one-third of the way into the film, after having already seen "Pop" and begun to get a sense of the father-son relationship, that "Pop" is dead. We are never told this outright. The information comes in the form of a Jewish clue. We hear Ravett call his son's name, Chaim. In the Ashkenazi tradition one names a child only after a relative who has died, never after a living one. There are no "Juniors" or "Seconds." The boy would only have been named Chaim after the namesake had passed away. In this case, *life* literally goes on. The name Chaim is reclaimed after a lifetime of transformations and dislocations that nearly obliterated all traces of the man who once bore it. The name Chaim appears again toward the end of the film, when it becomes clear that the mother has found a new companion. Ravett tells his deceased father, in Yiddish, "His name is also Chaim. He looks like a good person. I think he's a good man, Pop." In the next frame we see his mother sitting by the window in her apartment, just as her husband Chaim had done when he was alive. Ravett reports to his dead dad in Yiddish, "Now mom sits like you always sat. Every Sunday, every Sunday she sits like that, listening to Shlomo Ben Israel [commenting on the news] like you." Not only does the film become repopulated with Chaims, the mother takes the physical place of Chaim, as he would sit

Everything's for You (1989). Stills courtesy of Abraham Ravett.

listlessly in the living room, ironically showing few signs of life. And this, Ravett would seem to suggest, is paradoxically evidence of revitalization, of the renewal of life, of *chaim*.

It begins to be clear in Ravett's later work, specifically in the inter-actions and communications between his mother and himself, that the mode of communication in the family typically involves such insistent repetition. When the mother speaks in *Toncia* (a film without visual cuts, running slightly longer than the length of one 400-foot 16 mm reel),[53] she often repeats words and reiterates her meaning in different ways. In a sequence about the name of his half sister, Ravett asks his mother, "How did you call her? Toncia?" His mother replies: "She had two names. Tau, Tau, Taybe. Toby, Toby. And Yunta. Yunta was after my grandmother, my father's mother. Toby, they insist [sic], my husband's family, they had a big tragedy in the family. The father from my husband and sister, they died in one year." Again, the naming issue comes to the fore. There is the formal, Yiddish name, Toybe. The nickname, Toncia. And the Americanized name, said presumably for the benefit of Abraham, though no doubt never applied to the actual child, Toby. The mother makes the translation of the name seem necessary, as if speaking the name out of context requires adjustment, and as if the name would seem too distant, too foreign, even to herself. She trips and stutters on her daughter's given name, and seems to settle only once she proffers the Americanized version. Then there is the question of repetition. The names appear two and three times, just as do Ravett's phrases, questions, and names in *Everything's for You*. The convoluted syntax is of course a product of unstudied English, forming unmistakable signs of the speaker's class and age of immigration. But this convolution also signifies a distrust of language, as if the language threat-ens to betray its deafness to her meaning. The words must be repeated to make them obey the speaker's command, as an old dog must be told more than once to sit. In another example, Ravett asks how old Toncia would have been in 1942. The response: "She was, let me think for a second. She was, I think, six years old. She must've been six years old." To which Ravett replies, "Six years old in '42." And his mother confirms, "Yeah, I think so, the school year, I think so, yeah."

Without a doubt, repetition is a mode of communication in the Ravett family. The filmmaker's narrative syntax reproduces the sentence structures of both father and mother, a broken English syntax, a working-class immigrant syntax, a brokenhearted syntax. *Everything's for You,* like many of Ravett's films, has a complex structure akin to the exchange he has with his mother about Toncia's age. He revisits themes over and over again, always using repetition with a difference, each time interjecting a slightly new element, like the mother's belated and inexplicable insertion of the detail about "the school year."[54] Like this interaction, *Everything's for You* is obsessively concerned with the details of the dead, as if the details of the children (name, age, diet, state of mind, circumstances of death) could somehow explain something about Ravett's own traumatic childhood to himself.

Emily Hubley's cell animation scenes unfold dreamlike, as if they flowed directly out of Ravett's memory, in yet another attempt to unravel

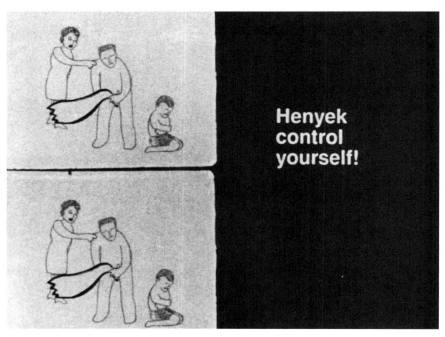

Emily Hubley's cell animation in *Everything's for You*. Still courtesy of Abraham Ravett.

the mysteries of the filmmaker's childhood. The first animated segment is of a man hitting a crouching, helpless boy with something that resembles a towel or a whip. A woman belatedly steps in and touches the father's raised arm. Little of the scene is revealed, at first, but over time we see more of these repeated actions. It takes a while before we understand what we are seeing. The first time the image appears we hear Ravett in voice-over, prompting his mother to say in Yiddish, "Henyek, *derbaremdik*" (Ravett translates this as "Henyek, control yourself"), which she does with rising conviction six times before she stops and declares, "That's enough. What for do you need that?" Ravett needs it to help reenact the scene of his father beating him for something he did accidentally (he broke a lock). These scenes are of course meant to unlock the meaning of a memory. Ravett re-animates these scenes for himself but also, as the film's title suggests, for his father, returning to the painful memories to better understand his father's actions. In the scene about a broken lock, Ravett is in effect looking for the key. The violent excesses of his strange and distant father were inexplicable to the child at the time, yet armed with this new information (about the father's other family, his dead wife and children, his destroyed life), Ravett hopes to understand them and his father better. In this regard, the film can be seen as a catharsis, a working through of the kind resisted in Akerman's obsessive quest. Yet these hysterical repetitions remind us that ultimately these traumas will find no peaceful resolution.

There is so much Ravett did not understand as a child and so little adequate explanation given for his father's behavior that no amount of detail could possibly satisfy his need to understand. Yet Ravett does not conclude, as Susan Korda does in her film *One of Us* (1999), that his father's distorted worldview and radically unforgiving approach might have preceded the devastating events of his life and that the Holocaust merely provided him with the necessary pretext for his abusive and erratic behavior. His is a compassionate reproach toward the father. Abraham comes to Chaim as one father to another, not simply as the child of a difficult man. Ravett's experience as a father seems to allow him an identificatory position vis-à-vis his father, imagining, as we are all forced to do when watching Ravett's two feisty children, what it would mean to lose something so precious. Yet as compassionate and comprehending as Ravett is, he does not ultimately work through his relationship with his father. Most of the questions posed to the father are never answered, they are in fact, unanswerable both because the father has died before Ravett could ask and, more importantly, because none of the answers could ever begin to mitigate either the father's or the son's pain. This pain is intergenerational, with effects that can be felt even when the source is unknown.

This is a case where the memory was evidently not passed on to the next generation. Ravett is not the recipient of "postmemory" that we saw in Akerman's film. As a child, he apparently knew nothing of his parent's past lives, but he is nonetheless haunted by the pain that clings so tenaciously to the father that he would be unrecognizable without it. What Ravett has inherited is not the memories per se, but the unbearable pain—call it *postpain*.

It is difficult to convey the devastating melancholia of this film. It is not sentimental nor is it excruciatingly difficult to watch. It is prosaic in its deathly confrontations, and stoic in its refusal to indulge in self-pity. This is no afternoon special on child abuse, no straightforward documentary on children of survivors. It is a love letter to a father in the form of an experimental, nonnarrative film, which speaks in a language of fathers, mostly in the father's native tongue. Ravett revives his father periodically in the film; after we ruminate with Ravett on his inability to ask his deceased father one more question, he proceeds to ask his father one more question. The film was shot in two separate periods, the first from 1974 to 1977, the second from 1984 to 1989, yet the footage is intercut in such way that time appears to reverse and eventually to realign, making it suddenly possible for Ravett's father to have actually known Ravett's two young children. When Ravett informs his dead father in voice-over that "I have two children now, just like you had," it thus seems yet another redundancy of the film. It becomes unfathomable that the father could *not* know. Ravett's film twists time to the extent that his father and his children can coexist on a plane that life denies them. He attempts to do the same with his two half-siblings, but the stillness of the photographs and the incompatibility of the presentational styles inhibits this reunion, emphasizing rather than minimizing the distance between them. The mute siblings refuse to testify to their family relations, as is only right. Were they still able to speak, Ravett himself would be rendered mute.

The contemplation of the three old photographs, apparently found after the elder Chaim's death, engages Ravett in a process of recontextualizing these family images so as to reconceive his family mythology. They represent the missing pieces to a puzzle Ravett had not previously realized was incomplete. The silences and occlusions of his childhood suddenly make sense as absences, not mere incoherencies. The father's violence is linked to a substantial source, the pain of the unfathomable loss of those glimpsed through the foreign and unfamiliar faces in these fading photographs. Ravett passes these images before our eyes, moves them around the screen, fades them in and out, duplicates them, blows them up, pixelates, and otherwise dissects them. I imagine he is looking for familiar and familial signs.

Can he recognize in this younger, dapper man, dressed fashionably in the costume of another time and place, the eyes, the nose, the forehead, the demeanor or expression of his scowling father? Can he see this as the same man? Can he detect any family resemblance between the two children—his missing siblings—and himself? There is something threatening and ultimately destabilizing in what Marianne Hirsch calls the "perpetual present of photography," in these pictures.[55] The man in the photographs must be younger than Ravett was when making this film. His older siblings are perpetual children, not much older in the photographs than Ravett's own children are in the film.[56] Yet, in the case of the missing siblings, there is no "after" to compare to this "before." By virtue of their frozen childhood, his older siblings become his younger siblings or, more eerily still, his own children. The solitary childhood of Ravett's memory suddenly becomes crowded with more strains and tugs, more needs and desires, more cries of despair than he could ever have dreamed. His adult family, the modern, American, alternative-lifestyle family he has made with his non-Jewish wife and their two unsuspecting kids, is suddenly (re)populated with this belatedly discovered mirror family that parallels their every move from the remove of insurmountable distance. These English-speaking, country-living, thoroughly assimilated kids could never have suspected what forces have ransacked their lives, just as their father was ignorant of these forces before. Yet the weight of the lost lives, of these relations whose destruction meant the possibility of new life (Ravett's and his children's), lingers like a debt to be repaid. Ravett offers his film's "everything for you" as a form of recompense, his gratitude and art as payment for his life and that of his children. One wonders however, if such a debt is ever fully compensated or if it remains unpaid and unpayable in perpetuity, permanently spellbound by, and beholden to, the stare of those perpetual children.

Ravett's camera and editing create alliances and a web of *looks* that bind family members together who never knew of one another's existence. He creates a version of a family *eruv*,[57] a line drawn loosely around family members, corralling them into a network of *looking* relations that binds them to one another. These looks are not mutual; the dead siblings cannot look back at Ravett or his children, but the hope that there is some reciprocity is present in Ravett's gaze. Like Barthes describing looking at the picture of his mother in the winter-garden, as Hirsch notes, "His desire is . . . not only to recognize but to be recognized."[58] In this way, Ravett attempts to create, rather than instantiate, what Hirsch calls a "familial look," whereby there is a mutuality within the gaze, so that one is "both self and other(ed), both speaking and looking subject and spoken and looked at object: I am subjected and objectified."[59] Ravett's film brings

Abraham Ravett's prewar siblings. Still courtesy of Abraham Ravett.

his dead siblings and his more recently deceased father into a relational realm where glances are exchanged (that is to say, traded-in) for a new version of the family narrative. These filmic narrativizations of the family construct another dimension, a filmic plane, in which the disparate and indeed disjointed elements of the family narrative can be reunited. Hamlet's famous phrase, "The time is out of joint" is exemplified here through the construction of impossible unities along a filmic plane, long-dead siblings brought into a set of transhistorical "looking relations." The new relations developed through this filmic operation alter the conceptualization of the autobiographical self; through his filmmaking, Ravett creates a new and more complex family and thus a new understanding of himself within it.

▶
_____

Jewish Moments

In *Thank You and Goodnight,* Oxenberg wonders aloud about things like the perpetuity of death. As mentioned earlier, she too lost a sibling, though unlike Ravett's, Oxenberg's was known to the filmmaker. Another key difference from Ravett's film is that, in Oxenberg's case, the Jewish historical component of the loss is missing. Where Ravett's story implicitly resonates within a larger Jewish history of catastrophic loss, Oxenberg's loss of a younger sister hit by a car is random and individual. There is no attendant persecution, no mass destruction of a people, in which to contextualize it. Oxenberg's grandmother's death, however, as suggested earlier, does have significant Jewish resonances; the loss of the grandmother implies the loss of what appears the last generational link to cultural Jewishness, or *yidishkayt*. Without ever saying so explicitly, the drama of the whole film turns on the bitterness of the irremediable loss of that link.

Here, as with Ravett's film, we have a work about a relative who has died (both the sister and the grandmother have died, but the bulk of the film focuses on the grandmother), and about the filmmaker's attempt to reconcile her relationship with the dead relative through a series of meditations. Both Ravett's and Oxenberg's films were shot in two distinct periods, before and after the family member's death. In *Thank You and Goodnight,* we are not spared a moment's agony as we watch the steady and relentless decline in the grandmother's health. Oxenberg's camera shies away from nothing as the grandmother lies skeletal and moaning in her bed. We are told by Jan in voice-over, "Members of my family have a tendency to hold onto the last drop of misery in any experience, even life itself. It wouldn't be our style to drop dead of a heart attack or die peacefully in the night." It also, as it turns out, would not be their style to turn the camera off and leave some of the misery to the imagination.

In contradistinction to Ravett's depiction, in Oxenberg's film the Jewish family is constituted in and through this film as a tragicomic spectacle. The suburban seventies motif would not have drawn much comment in its day, but the film, though shot in the late 1970s, was released in 1990, and the dated style (the garish flowered yellow-and-brown wallpaper, the shag rugs, the green eye shadow) all seem slightly excessive and embarrassing, as seen from a perspective of the 1990s and beyond. The family members are not always intentionally funny; they can be self-involved, manipulative, even dull. It is Oxenberg's droll sensibility that allows the humor to emerge. A particularly clever scene shows Oxenberg and her mother dividing up the recently deceased grandmother's possessions. Each item that Oxenberg mentions, her mother wants as well—and works a not so subtle guilt trip on her daughter, who appears to relent. The scene is played deadpan and the mother in particular does not seem to recognize the humor in her performance. Oxenberg only once, toward the end of the scene, glances toward the camera after one of the more egregious moments of manipulation; with only the faintest hint of a raised eyebrow, she clues us in to the absurdity. In a "where they are now" epilogue, Oxenberg revisits those characters in the film still living, to see how things have ended up. She tells us that she has a new apartment, and in it, of course, are all the items she had coveted of her grandmother's. As the master manipulator of everyone's image, and apparently of her mother as well, the filmmaker daughter triumphantly gets the last laugh.

There is a stealthy power play in and around this scene that acts out a mother-daughter battle for ascendancy. What they are vying for is their claim to the grandmother's affections, her memory, and ultimately her Jewish legacy. Oxenberg wins on all counts. The mother seems to have disqualified herself innumerable times by not being more attentive to her mother, by not appreciating her, by not learning how to cook from her, by leaving the children to be cared for by her, by being unable to relate to her. But as the daughter of the dying woman, she shows a remorse and desire for a better relationship that could not be more apparent—yet the grandmother and granddaughter have conspired not to see it.

This scene is particularly poignant in displaying the dynamic between the filmmaker daughter and her mother. The two women sit on a couch, not quite close enough to touch, yet not pinned in separate corners. They face each other in profile, cheating slightly to camera so that there is the impression of a three-quarter view of each face. The women are neither intimate nor alienated, not warm yet not estranged. They are familiar in a familial way, they resemble one another slightly but are by no means carbon copies. The conversation plays out more like a set-up for a punch line than an honest, heartfelt interaction. The question of whether the scene is indeed set up for the film remains unanswered, though the unselfconscious performance, especially by the mother, indicates that it was at the very least not pre-scripted. The mother asks Jan if she wants the TV from grandma's apartment; Jan demurs at first but then says yes. The mother half-seriously says "I'll choose you," referring to a child's game similar to tossing a coin, where fingers are used to determine the outcome. Jan looks at her mother disbelievingly and laughs. Then her mother launches into one of the better renditions of Jewish guilt captured in a documentary:

> MOTHER: You can have it if you want it. Just because mine is broken and can't be fixed [camera zooms in on Jan's face smiling uncomfortably as her mother continues to talk] and doesn't play, you know. That's no reason for me to take it. [Pan over to mom] No, you can have it, Jan. She would've wanted you to have it.
>
> JAN: Well, it's all right, Ma, you can have it.
>
> MOTHER: [too quickly] O.K. [both laugh]
>
> JAN: [after a beat of realization] Wait a minute . . .

This scene continues in the same vein as Jan names one item, then another, that the mother does not want to part with but cannot forthrightly deny to her daughter. This is merely one of the ways cultural Jewishness is subtly inscribed in this text. Guilt, as an unofficial Jewish mode of communication and emotional connection, is skillfully portrayed here at its operational level. We see Oxenberg's mother performing (convincingly) an aspect of the classic "Jewish mother" so rarely seen in the bulk of these films. Other indicators of Jewishness in the scene are difficult to place. Jewishness is not locatable in the objects being fought over, or in any direct statement made. Can there be said to be specific Jewish mannerisms, speech cadences, modes of interaction? Certainly such a claim used to be said of Eastern European Jews in Western Europe; think of *Mauscheln*, the supposedly Jewish speech that was said to reveal the boorishness of the Eastern European Jew as she or he tried to pass as Western and modern.[60] And in Europe, more generally, Jews were sometimes said to speak in singsong, nasal voices, with full command of no language but their own secret one (Yiddish). But here are two American-born, middle-class, secular Jewish women with full command of English, no hint of Yiddish, and scarcely any other detectable Jewish cultural indicators. To ask a basically rhetorical question (since there can be no conclusive answer), what makes this guilt so classically Jewish?

Similarly, the Jewish family in *Thank You and Goodnight* is a subtly recognizable entity, yet it is difficult to say exactly how. One has to be a detective of Ashkenazi Jewish American ephemera to pick up the overtly Jewish signs, like the black ribbon with the slash cut in it on Jannie's lapel after the grandmother's funeral. The children of the deceased are supposed to rend a garment when a parent dies; the bourgeois version of this ritual has Jewish mourners pinning this ribbon onto the lapel so as not to damage presumably expensive clothing. There is a quick cutaway shot of a *yizkor* (memorial) candle at Jan's mother's house after her grandmother's funeral; one sees a candle burning in a large glass with an embossed Jewish star, next to pictures of her grandmother. Whether or not one knows what such a candle is called, it is not hard to figure out its meaning or to detect its Jewish symbolism, but it is held in a brief shot in which the depth of field directs the eye toward the photographs.

There is also the funeral service, which the rabbi leads in Hebrew. And then there is the film's most overt reference to Jewish culture by Jan, when she tells us that after the funeral the family came home to her mother's house to sit shiva. She says, "During the next week, the week of sitting shiva, we mourned." Hers is not exactly a detailed ethnographic explanation, or even an attempt to render the ritual intelligible to the uninitiated.[61] But she does state the Hebrew name of the delineated period of mourning, and it is, for those who know, a clearly Jewish reference.[62]

I appreciate Oxenberg's lack of concern about the legibility of the Jewish context of this film. She is not trying to translate the terms or references for those unfamiliar with Jewish rituals or traditions. Yet I wonder if this apparent lack of concern over translation and transparency belies a lack of consciousness on her part about the Jewish specificity of her family and her film. Here, I want to offer a series of Oxenberg-esque questions. Is it important that this family be seen and recognized as Jewish? Or is Jewishness entirely incidental and arbitrary here? Could it have been any culture that Jan was raised in, and just happenstance that it is Jewish? Is Jan attempting to create a universal story about death and loss, and (thus) efface the Jewish specificity of this family's experience? Is there a Jewish specificity to this family's experience? (A case could be made defining the absence of visual cultural indicators as one aspect of contemporary Jewish American culture, a kind of "distinction without difference.")[63]

What is left of the family's Jewishness, once the grandmother dies? Aside from an ephemeral and barely traceable sensibility that seems impossible to pin down, there is left to them basically their memory of her. The recognition that a memory is not a viable replacement for the last bastion of *yidishkayt* makes it all the more difficult for the granddaughter and her surrogate, Jannie, to accept the grandmother's death. In a comical scene, set in a mock-therapist's office, Jannie lies two-dimensionally on a red couch as a "therapist" (played in voice-over by Oxenberg's editor, Lucy Weiner) tells her that she has to learn to let go: "Imagine you're looking at a photo album. Now close the album. You haven't lost your loved one. You have made them into memories. You can look at them again and again and they will enrich your life. If you don't close the door, you can't open the door. We have to stop."

It is no wonder Oxenberg has such trouble mourning. The loss is compounded. She lost not only a deeply loved, though severely under-appreciated, grandmother, but also the embodiment of a tradition and a point of ethnic identification. This is quite similar to the fear expressed by Alain Finkielkraut when contemplating the passing of his parents,[64] and is reiterated in the Baal Shem Tov parable of the Jew who goes to pray at the tree in the forest and eventually his descendents forget the place and even the prayer and are left only with the story to tell. Yet as the parable ends, "and God heard him," there is the suggestion that memory itself is sustaining, and that it is enough to remember the existence of such *yidishkayt* in one's family to be recognizable as a Jew.

Oxenberg, in her resistance to mourning, may not have accounted for the fact that all was not lost. In fact, her family represents a new tradition that has sprung up in place of the old. The Oxenberg family is a fairly typical late-twentieth-century, secular, assimilated, Ashkenazi Jewish American family. It is not uncommon for such Jewish families to have a tenuous connection to the religious practices of their culture. Nor is it uncommon for Yiddish to fade out of practice, or for Jewish iconography to cede its place on the walls to modern art.[65] The cultural signs may be more difficult to read, perhaps intentionally so, but this does not render them nonexistent. It is difficult to articulate what remains of Jewish culture, once the religious, the historical, and the traditional elements drop out, but there are signs that point to its existence. Jewish culture in its secular and assimilated American forms is readable as a series of behaviors, a type of humor, an overt emotionalism, a love of food, a way of interacting, even certain high-cultural aspirations. This Jewish culture may not be an exclusive or rigidly defined set of attributes, but it has become an identifiable set nonetheless—which is precisely what Kirshenblatt-Gimblett means by her phrase "distinction without difference." The film itself, with its particular brand of sardonic humor and cynical nostalgia, is both a symptom of this phenomenon and a contribution to its effectiveness and legibility. Oxenberg unwittingly produces a piece of contemporary Jewish culture just as she is produced as an effect of it.

Further, in Oxenberg's film there are many of what Jon Stratton would call "Jewish moments," such as the mother's guilt-tripping session. A Jewish moment (a concept Stratton has adapted from Alex Doty's "queer moments") is a "variable textual attribute" that is available to be read, though not, in Doty's words "an essential, waiting-to-be-discovered property" of the text.[66] A Jewish moment can be interpreted variably, and is by no means a fixed or permanent aspect of the text; rather, it is essentially a product of reception.[67] In Stratton's usage, a Jewish moment can be read into a text that has no Jewish content or intent whatsoever, and it can be read by non-Jewish as well as Jewish spectators, depending as it does not on heritage or genealogy but rather on "degrees of knowledge of Jewish/Yiddish religion and culture."[68] In this regard, there are countless Jewish moments in *Thank You and Goodnight*. For instance, during the scene depicting the week of shiva, Oxenberg tells us what the family and visitors did: "We talked and we ate. We cried and we ate. We pondered the meaning of life and death, and we ate." The cadence and structure of the sentences are meant to convey the humor of the situation, and, I believe, its Jewishness. Litany, repetition, and irony here stand in for—indeed, create—Jewish affect. The emphasis on eating during highly emotional times has also become viewed as a Jewish cultural attribute. The discussion the family has about death and suffering, with the parsing of the terms and the arguing of ethical limits (Jan chides her philosophizing brother, "Who gets to say if it's enough? If you stub your toe, are you suffering too much? Or if you have cancer, are you suffering too much? Or if you're in a concentration camp?"), is a form of domestic *pilpul* (the traditional term for the penetrating and hair-splitting detail with which scholars debate the precepts of the Talmud).[69] Also, the scenes immediately following this dialogue, where we watch the family argue about the meaning of death, exemplify Jewish moments in the extended family's verbalization of thoughts and beliefs not usually articulated in so-called polite company.

Stratton elaborates this concept of the Jewish moment by suggesting that Jewish culture in Western society has long signified a (potential) rupture in civility. That which is "simply not done" in civil or "polite" society, may be done with alacrity among Jews. Stratton suggests that Jews, according to Western standards, are "improper," "impolite," and ultimately "uncivilized.[70] Although this may at first seem a potentially offensive overstatement, it does reflect popularly held beliefs about the Jew from the nineteenth and twentieth centuries and before. This stereotype has translated, in contemporary cultural terms, as the ability of Jewishness to counter the stoicism and asceticism of Christian culture. Jews of Eastern European descent effuse, emote, argue, eat, and complain volubly. This has been lovingly hyperbolized in scenes of films like *Annie Hall* (1977), where Woody Allen's character, Alvy Singer, sits at his girlfriend's WASP parents' table unable to join the polite dinner conversation, and is distracted by his flashbacks to his own family dinner scenes, the apartment quaking under the Coney Island Cyclone, with family members yelling and interrupting and reaching over one another to get to the food. Woody Allen's is an exaggerated version of the cultural contrast, played for comic effect, but it does signal the disruptive threat represented by Jewishness in the midst of WASP supposed civility. *Thank You and Goodnight,* with its emphasis on pain and suffering and death and food, its obsessive and unrelenting questioning, its exposure of less than flattering family dynamics, and, perhaps most important, its humor in the face of deadly serious issues can be read as a sequence of Jewish moments challenging the limits of (gentile) standards of "decency" and "good taste." This is not to say that *Thank You and Goodnight* is indecent or in bad taste, clearly, but that it refuses to tread lightly on issues deemed by dominant culture to be "delicate," and thus raises the specter of *uncontainability* that Jewishness has represented in Western culture at least since the Enlightenment. In this respect, *Thank You and Goodnight* could not be more Jewish.

In *Nobody's Business,* Alan Berliner is determined not to lose what
Oxenberg fears she has already lost: history, heritage, filial and ancestral connections. He too is from a secular, assimilated family and he too
seems to feel on the precipice of some irremediable loss. Berliner is willing
to put up a fight, waged in this case with his father, to produce a historically accurate family narrative. He is obsessively concerned with his past
and that of his family, an obsession fueled by his father's maddening indifference. Berliner is a genealogist as much as a filmmaker. And, though
he played the eager young apprentice to his father in reconstructing their
nuclear family narrative, he also plays the determined opponent against
his antagonistic and uncooperative father in the effort to save the extended
family narrative for posterity. The battle must be won, even if only as a
technical knockout, as the boxing footage in the film attests. Although
it remains to be seen whether he does win, and if so, what he wins in the
end, one of the key areas of contestation in *Nobody's Business* is between
official history and personal memory. For Berliner, the nuclear bomb-
proof vault that he visits in Utah that contains a gold mine of genealogical
data kept under very strict Mormon control is, ironically, more accessible,
and yields more information in Berliner's search for family history, than
he can extract from his own living relatives. Slowly and surreptitiously
(as the father duly notes), Alan does elicit cooperation from his resistant
father, and he does manage to pry some information in the form of memories from his father's still agile mind, but the insistence upon the relevance
of family ties and genealogy remains the son's obsession, in direct opposition to his father.

Any connection to a past not experienced firsthand (but instead
abstract, ancestral, unfamiliar) is categorically refused by the father.
For Oscar Berliner, family is constituted strictly through direct contact.
Family must be familiar for it to be kin. Kinship is more likely to be
created for him with army buddies or workers in his factory than with
ancestors whom he has never met. When Alan presents his father with a
photograph of his father's paternal grandfather, Oscar defiantly declares,
"He's just another Jew in a yarmulke." There is a categorical rejection
of any meaningful connection to past generations as family relations. As
a Jew, Oscar Berliner retains a modicum of concern for, perhaps even an
allegiance with, other Jews, but no more binding than his allegiances to
other collectivities of which he considers himself a part (New Yorkers,
Americans, World War II GIs). Berliner claims in an interview that his

father "likes to hide in these large rhetorical crowds."[71] For Oscar there are three states of affiliation: the known quantity, which can imply family regardless of blood ties; the generic collective, such as national, religious, geographic, or ethnic, with which he may identify abstractly but bears no deep personal connection; and the stranger, who may even be a blood relation but, being unknown personally to Oscar, inspires no feelings of closeness, let alone kinship. There is no crossover between the intimate circle and the broad generality: he may be an American, but that does not make all Americans his family; he may be a Jew, but that does not make all Jews his kin; he may be a Berliner, but only those he knows or knew personally inspire any family fealty in him.

Given his father's radical resistance to the naturalized discourses of kinship, Berliner is forced to explore more broadly the meaning of family relations. He desperately attempts to (re)create the ties that bind his immediate family to a broader kinship network of relatives and ancestors and ultimately to the "family of man." His bonds with his father are strong, but he feels the need to claim ancestry to connect him not only to a particular history and geography (Jewish, Eastern European, on his father's side) but to a universal history. He seems to derive tremendous pleasure and affirmation in the knowledge that "according to some genealogists . . . no human being on earth can be any further related than fiftieth cousin and that most of us are a lot closer than that." Considering the zealousness with which he pursues his genealogical interests, one can surmise that his passion for the subject is partially in reaction to his father's refusal of all but the most immediate ties. One also suspects that, for the younger Berliner, there is a moral imperative to this work. His underlying conviction, albeit naïve, is that the key to world peace and harmony lies buried in this genealogical connectivity. His idealism is dashed when confronted with his father's absolute obstinacy in the face of the evidence presented. Oscar barks, "If you're trying to convince me that the whole world is cousins, I don't believe it."

From the raw data of photographs, letters, birth and death certificates, marriage and divorce decrees, and interviews with father, sister, mother, and cousins, Berliner attempts to construct his family tree. He desperately wants to engage his father in this painstaking pursuit, but his father, predictably by now, resists. He complains, "You have one flaw, Alan. You think just because you're interested in something, everybody else should be. Well, I'm not." Oscar Berliner may not be interested and may never have been interested in his son's genealogical passions, but part of the family drama that plays itself out in this film is the son corralling the interest and sympathy of the audience (the rest of the world) to prove his father wrong. Both the fact of the impressive funders' list and the highly engaging nature of the film itself attest to a broad audience for it. It was broadcast on American national television, won an Emmy Award, and was invited to be screened at the Clinton White House. Apparently, someone besides Alan was interested.

But the father's resistance to his son's insistence has another function, too. In forcing the son to sidestep his immediately preceding relative in order to fabricate a bond to his ancestors, the film unwittingly calls attention to family relations precisely as an imaginary bond. For all of Berliner's pseudoscientific pretensions, he is no doubt well aware of the constructed nature of these family narratives, adept as he is in (re)constructing his own (as we have seen with his efforts to rejoin and reharmonize his parents within his frame). The father's resistance to genealogical explanations of family exposes the bare fact that there is nothing "natural" about familial affinity, even though by and large it tends to be naturalized. The father introduces the possibility of the irrelevance of phylogeny to identity or self-knowledge, something that the filmmaker son adamantly wants to reject but that nonetheless the film has to contend with.

There is a very different conception of family lineage and genealogy at work in Jeremy Benstock's short, quirky, film *Orders of Love* (2004), whose tagline reads "Some family trees get more twisted with every branch." In this playful jig of a film, Benstock uses the occasion of his son's birth to explore a family that seems heretofore to have eluded his attention. Suddenly it occurs to him that there is a lineage he is passing down to his son. His concern is not simply genealogical for the sake of it. He takes a genealogical approach to psychological inheritances. With a neurotically tinged sense of humor, unkempt red hair, oversized glasses, and a genealogical psychotherapist doling out well-meaning platitudes, Benstock plays up his resemblance to Woody Allen, albeit with a Scottish brogue. He may not expect, in the manner of Berliner, his genealogical quest to contribute in its small way to world peace and global understanding, but he does seem to believe that a more detailed knowledge of one's lineage may contribute to one's peace of mind and to peace in the family. He takes this literally, admitting to all that in every generation of his family there has been mental illness and suicide, and declaring, in line with featured family-constellation expert Bert Hellinger, that facing the unspoken in one's lineage is the key to breaking the cycle of dysfunction. Hellinger believes that a family's traumatic experiences and figures are often enshrined in silence, and that those silences haunt a family's unconscious, passing from one generation to the next, causing untold psychological disturbances. This philosophy is in line with Marianne

Hirsch's theory of postmemory, where spoken or unspoken traumatic experiences are transmitted from parent to children and the child experiences the memory and trauma as his or her own. The difference, in Benstock's film, is that the filmmaker indulges in the overly hopeful notion that simply recognizing what has been repressed within the family memory (in this instance, the memory of his uncle Malcolm, who, after a battle with mental illness and unsuccessful shock therapy treatments, committed suicide and was rarely if ever alluded to again) will cause the pall of generational transmission to be magically lifted. The mixing of genetics and pop-psychological analysis makes for an awkward and fairly unconvincing denouement, yet the process of discovery in the film is so lighthearted and entertaining that one wants to share Benstock's enthusiasm.

Memory—accessing it, cajoling it, buoying it with official facts and figures—plays a key role in both Benstock's short and Berliner's better-known feature. Indeed, both filmmakers build not only their case but their own sense of belonging upon memory. But what happens to identity and communality in the complete absence of family recollection? What if the sole remaining witness to a family history is no longer capable of remembering?

▶

Identity Blank

In *Complaints of a Dutiful Daughter,* we encounter a different type of resistance to genealogical excavation: involuntary resistance. We are forced to contemplate the consequences on identity and family history of a memory gone blank. Hoffmann's mother's Alzheimer's leaves her with only vague, jumbled, random memories that have no narrative cohesion and no significant impact on the mother's identity. She is no longer greater than or even equal to the sum of her memorized parts. She is constituted anew at every moment, living exclusively in the present (pure presence), and as such is nearly unrecognizable to her (remembering) daughter. In the absence of memory, one is forced to realize its critical importance in creating and sustaining family and identity. One can even say that family is constituted through memory, and that identity is constructed, in large part, in relation to family memory. If the mother loses her memory, and her memory is partially constitutive of the daughter's identity, then who does the daughter become when the mother cannot remember? This is a painfully disorienting prospect, faced bravely and forthrightly by a (hardly complaining) daughter who for a long time does not seem fully able to grasp what she is up against.

Marianne Hirsch argues that the familial gaze within and toward family photographs is in part responsible for the sense of relation among family members. What makes people *family* is in fact the discourses built around these interactive "looks." As Hirsch says, "The 'family' is an affiliative group, and the affiliations that create it are constructed through various relational, cultural, and institutional processes—such as 'looking' and photography, for example. 'Families' are shaped by individual responsiveness to the ideological pressures deployed by the familial gaze."[72] Oscar Berliner may be the exception that proves the rule. And if it is true that family is enacted through looking relations, then one's self-identity must in part be a product of such a performance. Our recognitions of one another within the family create and sustain our mythic narratives of the self. We have multiple, competing narratives that are not all centered around the family, yet family mythology, reinforced through shared memory and recognitions, is central to our self-conceptualization. Hirsch usefully defines *familial mythology* as "an image to live up to, an image shaping the desire of the individual living in a social group. This myth or image—whatever its content may be for a specific group—dominates lived reality, even though it can exist in conflict with it and can be ruled by different interests. It survives by means of its narrative and imaginary power."[73] And this power, we learn from Oscar Berliner, can be partially resisted but is one to which most of us nonetheless succumb. What happens, though, when a family member is unintentionally unresponsive to the pressures of the familial gaze, when she no longer shares the memories that contribute to the recognition of family as such? We see with Hoffmann that complete breakdown of self-identity does not necessarily ensue. But elements of an identity crisis do unavoidably emerge.

It is not just that Hoffmann's mother no longer recognizes her daughter. This would be traumatic enough. But the mother's loss of memory makes her, in turn, unrecognizable to Hoffmann. The loss creates a mutual nonrecognition. A mother who cannot differentiate between her daughter and her college sorority-mate, or, alternatively, is equally embracing of her daughter and her daughter's girlfriend, toward whom she had previously been quite hostile, creates a cognitive dissonance: she is no longer the mother Hoffmann thought she knew. The Alzheimer's affects not only the mother's identity but the daughter's as well; both find themselves, as a result of the mother's illness, unmoored from the past and thus from prior definitions of self. Hoffmann's mother becomes unrecognizable to her in all but the most elementary ways. The mother Hoffmann has known most of her life is gone, yet the body, the voice, the affect, the touch, the smell, all live on. Hoffman can no longer see herself reliably reflected in her mother's responsiveness, which brings up the troubling question of whether she (or any of us) ever reliably could.

Relatedly, Hoffmann's tenuous tie to her Jewish identity seems to teeter on the brink of extinction, with the loss of her mother's memory. There are only the most discreet Jewish references in this film, and they can barely carry the burden of cultural representation. Jewishness has been invoked explicitly in this film (as we see in chapter 4) only as an afterthought, and in an effort to expand Hoffmann's distribution outlets, rather than as an integral concern. Yet, in an unpublished article about the film, Faye Ginsburg asserts that the mother-daughter relationship is one of the core elements that make the film undeniably Jewish. Ginsburg acknowledges that there are elements to this narrative (specifically the fact of the mother's misrecognition of the daughter and the mother's loss of memory) that "upend two of the most fundamental elements of American Jewish identity whether religious, assimilated, or ethnic: first, the proverbial overwhelming attachment of Jewish mothers to their children; second, the inseparability of Jews from historical, collective, and kin-based memory."[74] Of course, we have seen with Oscar Berliner that not all Jews maintain such an inseparability, yet the efforts of the younger Berliner, as well as those of Benstock, Ravett, and Oxenberg, attest to a strong affinity with Ginsberg's second assertion. Ginsburg goes on, nonetheless, to cite several formal as well as substantive devices that may be seen to ground *Complaints* as a Jewish text. The one to which I will attend concerns *khidush* (Hebrew, from the word *khadash,* or "new").

Toward the end of her essay, Ginsburg assesses the treatment of the mother-daughter relationship in *Complaints of a Dutiful Daughter* as rising to the level of Talmudic hermeneutics. She argues that what ultimately makes the film Jewish, more than its admittedly paltry overt signs of Jewishness, is its formal strategy that she likens to the Jewish scholarly practice known as *khidush.* She defines *khidush* as "renewal of Jewish knowledge through interpretation." *Khidush* traditionally refers to any new interpretation of or insight into a Jewish text (Talmud, Torah, etc.), but here it is extrapolated to mean a new interpretation or insight concerning not a sacred text but a sacred relationship, that of the mother and daughter.

Again, for something to be *khidush,* it must revisit or rework a traditional Jewish text or concept. I am thus not certain that Hoffmann's reworking of the mother-daughter relationship constitutes *khidush.* For one thing, although it does achieve some new insights, in terms of the possibility of identity without memory, these are not insights that contribute greatly to an understanding of Jewish identity per se. In addition, I have

to wonder if the relationship between mother and child, or, even more unlikely, mother and daughter, is distinctly sacred for Jews. Is the reconsideration of the nature of this relationship on the basis of a mother's illness
a specifically Jewish impulse? Surely this transcends Jewish specificity.
This reinterpretation of the relationship (as "play," as free of the past, as
"in the moment") may in fact contribute little insight into Jewish culture
or tradition. Yet, although I am not convinced that this reevaluation of
the "sacred relationship" is a clear example of *khidush*, I understand the
desire to read the presence of Jewish attributes in structural terms. If
Complaints is to be seen as a Jewish film that negotiates its Jewishness
through the mother-daughter relationship, then it is necessary to search
for clues at the formal level, since almost none exist in the diegesis. And,
though I am skeptical that Hoffmann's effort to, in Ginsburg's words,
"manage a disorderly narrative and give it meaning"[75] is any more Jewish
than any other narrativizing attempt, I recognize that it is the absence of
substantive cultural references that motivates Ginsburg's reading (not unlike my reading of Oxenberg's film).[76] However, what I find striking here
is the absence rather than the presence of Jewishness. The parent-child
(here, mother-daughter) relationship, often constitutive of an individual's
Jewish identity, is transformed in *Complaints* into a deracinated expression of universal loss, with nothing specifically or especially Jewish about
it. With the loss of memory—suffered by the mother, accepted (grudgingly)
by the daughter—comes the loss of specificity, rendering the daughter's
complaints generic.

▶

Filmic Repair

If khidush does not present a convincing "Jewish distinction" for *Complaints,* then perhaps there is another distinction to be made, one this film
shares with the other films considered in this chapter. These family autobiographies, each in its way, go beyond the problem of displacement and
loss, attempting to filmically mend a breach within the family created by
time, historical events, lack of communication, generation gaps, differences
of belief, or the vicissitudes of memory. The medium becomes a device
for this repair, bringing fathers and mothers together again in harmony,
as when Berliner intercuts his parents as they sing "It's Just the Nearness
of You"; impossibly reuniting family members who never could have coexisted yet meet on the same filmic plane, as in Ravett's film; reconstructing memories obliterated by war (Ravett), disease (Hoffmann), disinterest
(Berliner, Benstock), or death (Oxenberg, Rosenblatt); reengaging the

dead in a dialogue with the living (Oxenberg, Ravett, Rosenblatt). All of these reconstitutive gestures are constructed filmically through visual and aural juxtaposition, rhythmic intercutting, use of archival or home movie footage and family photos, and of course the creative use of family interviews. By making these links and staging these cinematic reunions, the films provide an unusually effective platform to perform an important Jewish activity or duty, *tikkun,* or "repair." *Tikkun* can also mean emendation or improvement, concepts applicable to the way these films seek to rewrite family narratives to correct or improve the errors, omissions, or grave injustices of the past. When seen in this light, with family as an extension of the self, and its interrelationships constitutive of self-identity, the films may also be seen as constituting a *tikkun,* or repair, of the self.[77]

A Treyf Autocritique of Autobiography

*Why should I not speak of "myself" since this "my" is no
longer "the self"?*
:: Roland Barthes, *Roland Barthes by Roland Barthes*

In 1998 I finished an autobiographical film with my then-partner, Cynthia
Madansky, titled *Treyf* ("unkosher" or "impure" in Yiddish).[1] The film
explored Jewish lesbian secular identity and politics from our two first
person perspectives. The work made the usual festival rounds, especially
Jewish and gay/lesbian film festivals, and was broadcast on the Sundance
Channel. Women Make Movies picked it up for distribution. Shortly after
completing the film, we were invited as filmmakers to participate in a
symposium at the University of Southern California; the symposium, "Eye
and Thou," focused specifically on Jewish autobiographical film. Although
I had been aware of a handful of other Jewish autobiographical films, I
had not until then thought of this field as encompassing a large or interesting enough body of work to warrant an entire weekend's consideration.
As it turns out, it warranted two. In March 2001, just as I was finishing
my dissertation on this subject, New York University held "Eye and Thou
II," in which I also participated, this time as a moderator. Beginning in
1998, I put my mind to the study of what, until then, I had not imagined
worth studying, even as I strove to enact and represent it: the construction
of contemporary Jewish subjectivity in recent first person documentary
film. In the making of *Treyf,* I had passed through and around an entire
range of representational issues that, given the style of the film we were
making and the general specifications of film as a medium, I had to conjure
visually and/or present within the narrative structure we had imposed.
Many issues were glossed, some resolved economically, others rendered
with a richness that theoretical writing rarely attains, but none were

explored in the depth that critical writing allows. It became clear to me subsequently that the two endeavors, making a film and writing critically about it, could be mutually informative, allowing for the exploration and elaboration of differing aspects of the issues raised.

As mentioned, I was invited to the first "Eye and Thou" as a filmmaker. The sessions consisted of a filmmaker (in our case, two filmmakers) paired with a Jewish scholar of repute (not necessarily a film scholar). The scholar then either presented a formal paper or engaged in a dialogue or interview with the filmmaker(s) in front of the audience. As an impertinent graduate student, I proposed to Michael Renov, one of the organizers, that perhaps Madansky and I could do without a scholar and could instead perform an autocritique of our autobiographical film. Wisely, perhaps, Renov politely refused. What follows is an elaborated version of what I had in mind.

Here I approach *Treyf* as a vehicle for looking at autobiographical concerns raised in recent Jewish documentary from a self-critical perspective, while simultaneously considering the vicissitudes of autocritique. As I struggle to define the paradoxical space from which to position myself to speak as both critic and filmmaker, I prey on the notion of being both insider and outsider, an intriguing contradiction that, as becomes clear, is directly linked to the idea of treyf in the film. That is, I endeavor to produce a treyf autocritique of my film *Treyf*. As I am an autobiographical filmmaker with scholarly training, to broach the subject of autobiography without performing an autocritique would be to miss an irresistible opportunity.[2] In the case of autobiographical film specifically, to consider criticism the exclusive domain of the theorists and critics would maintain a division of labor that the act of autobiographizing seems to strive to overcome. On the other hand, the work itself can be seen as an invitation to the world to look, comment, and critique. Derrida has written that the autobiographical work is not constituted as such until received by another.[3] As much as autobiography demands an audience (by asking for an "ear," to use Derrida's word), its logic invites autocritique as an extension of the motivation behind autobiography, the desire to represent oneself.

To be clear, not all autobiographical filmmakers would choose to write about their own work in a theoretical or critical vein, nor would this necessarily be desirable. In some cases, autocritique may be an integral part of the filmmaking project itself, rendering a written supplement superfluous. Further, autocritique should not be misconstrued, as a result of my advocacy here, as the only valid form of theoretical engagement for autobiography. In fact, I have reservations (contrary to possible interpretations of this autocritical intervention) about the value of a filmmaker's own estimation of his or her work. Often our commentary about our own work is less interesting and incisive than others', yet our words may nonetheless be overvalued in the consideration of that work, taking precedence over other possible readings. Statements of intentionality, which comprise the majority of authorial commentary, have some limited historical interest, but they have little theoretical value and may even inhibit valid and imaginative hermeneutical engagement with the work.

Presumably the reader will keep this in mind as I proceed to elaborate aspects of my intentions in making my film. I am emphatically not arguing for autocritique to replace other forms of criticism; rather, I am proposing, to extend the logic of autobiography, to speak critically and theoretically about my work in the first person, keeping in mind that the autocritic's voice should merely be considered one among others.

▶

On the Impossibility of Lifting Oneself Up by One's Hair

Treyf is a film by Cynthia Madansky and myself that uses our autobiographical narratives to explore our contemporary queer Jewish secular identities and the ways we are products of, yet outsiders to, mainstream American Jewish culture.[4] We, the filmmakers of *Treyf,* invented our characters, Cynthia and Alisa, based, like many compelling representations, on true stories. I have always loved the phrase "true stories" since in it "truth" is revealed to be modified by the narrative imperative, of which the transformative effects should never be underestimated. Truth demands a story, for it cannot be told otherwise, and in the telling it is always altered—truth being, then, alter to itself. So, too, Alisa and Cynthia, the onscreen characters, are other to ourselves, no more or less true than any other story we tell about ourselves.[5] In our effort to make a film about the conflicts and contradictions inherent in contemporary queer Jewish secular identity, we put ourselves squarely at the center of the narrative. The characters are us; we shopped in those West Jerusalem markets, we traversed the West Bank, we wandered the streets of New York's Lower East Side—but we did so for the camera. These characters are alter egos, that is, constructed for the purposes of this one film. *Treyf* is not a video diary, nor an impromptu "have camera, will shoot" proposition. It makes no pretense of being an unmediated window on our world. Shooting on 16 mm film on a limited budget with a largely volunteer crew, we could ill afford to leave much to chance. Of course, chance did occur, interfering with our plans at nearly every turn, but we had to maintain at least the illusion of control, for our own sake, if not for our funders. The element we wanted least to leave to chance was the development of the lead characters. Yet I must not speak dispassionately about them/us. I am not a disinterested party. My performance onscreen, considering that I am not a professional actor, is by default a slightly self-conscious rendition of my everyday self, already a performance of sorts. My autocritiquing character writing these words is no less crafted (with her academic pedigree in hand), though perhaps less artful. With all of these constructions and performances of various selves, a careful consideration of self-representation is in order. Hence, before delving into an in-depth discussion of the film, I intend to tease out the imbricated rhetorical selves about which "I" speak here.

Both the notion of representing one's self (autobiography) and the self-critique (autocritique) of that representation may seem to assume an uncritical belief in the viable and coherent self, and in the availability of a perspective outside of this self from which to critique. Yet, from its Enlightenment conception, autobiography has posed simultaneously an awkward and an unresolvable challenge to these notions of integration. Even Rousseau, the Enlightenment philosopher and, by all Western accounts, the father of the modern autobiography, managed to sow the seeds of the dissolution of the unified self in his *Confessions*. As much as he claimed to know himself and to be the willful and conscious master of his own fate (a claim he did make), he also frequently gave reason to doubt such certainties, as he insisted on his double identity as man and child, recognized his conflicting states of mind, and highlighted the aesthetic construction of his narrative as he repeatedly called attention to both style and story.[6] Preeminent autobiographical literary critic James Olney argues that it was Rousseau "who fragmented the I and dispersed it among various hes. . . . He cut the self loose, leaving it without ties, anchor, or direction, and to modern descendants he left as a starting-point what for him was the end-point: a free-floating self, uncentered except in itself, and quite unreal."[7] Remembering Nietzsche's famous assertion that "the subject is not something given, it is something added and invented and projected behind what there is,"[8] we see clearly that the trouble with the self and subjectivity is neither new nor finally resolvable. The very fact of representation (in words, in images, or in both) brings with it the inevitable realization of constructedness and alterity. The dissolution of the unitary self has always been ineradicably bound up with the project of representing it.

In the last half century, the foundational concepts of truth, objectivity, autonomy, and free will have been radically reevaluated in light of the historicization of power relations and in light of insights into the discursive nature of identity (Barthes, Foucault, Derrida, Butler, and, before them,

Wittgenstein), theories of fragmented subjectivity (Lacan and the post-Lacanians), and narrativity (de Man, White). To posit, at this point in time, that autobiography, let alone autocritique, involves an unambiguous assertion of autonomous will and an objective critical perspective in relation to one's self would be in flagrant disregard of much critical thinking that has emerged in particularly the latter half of the twentieth century (and, as we have seen, well before).

So, how does one make a documentary about a self that somehow evanesces as we attempt to represent it? Who or what is being represented? If autobiography can never simply be considered the direct articulation of an individual's own story—that is, if the self being represented is already fragmentary and divided and the story told is a narrative invention that constructs, indeed subtends, this illusory and fictively unified self—then who is it who intends to write the autocritique of this fiction? No doubt another (or the same) imaginary projection of the coherent, simultaneous self. At the risk of sounding like a postmodern drone, I am compelled to ask: how can "I" claim a more privileged relation to the "real me" than my image claims on screen? Under what discursive regime can "I" hope to transcend the boundaries of the self I have represented as myself? In other words, who is the "I" who critiques and how does she differ from the "I" who performs or represents herself on screen? Finding herself in a somewhat similar predicament, Judith Butler has boldly claimed her right and intent to use the first person even as she problematizes the unity or coherence of that "I." In fact, she insists that there is no doing without the "I," even as we wish to displace it. She says, "You will note that in the making of [my] formulation, I bracket this 'I' in quotation marks, but I am still here."[9] Thus the first person "I" takes hold regardless of whether, or how tightly, I hold onto it. It is not something I can do without, write without, even as its credibility is subject to debate. It is also not something I can thoroughly interrogate, as there will always be an unanalyzable remainder, something the "I" can never see.[10] But this does not mean "I" cannot write, or "I" cannot represent myself in film or otherwise. This crisis of subjectivity is not an impediment to the representation of the self; it is the very condition of its possibility.

Self-representation as much as autocritique is always a crisis: of temporality, of credibility, of authorship. The temporal disjuncture has been claimed to be uniquely bound to filmic autobiography, where editing, in particular, demands temporal distance from the events portrayed, yet clearly the disjuncture is inherent in all self-representation, whatever the medium.[11] The experiencing self is never simultaneous to its telling; whether we highlight the disjuncture and discontinuity or strive to deny and efface it, the disjuncture is always there.[12] So I will persist in the operating fiction that I am simultaneously and paradoxically one and the same as the image of myself onscreen, and rhetorically distinct from it, yet I will desist in the attempt to exhaustively enumerate and calculate the "I"'s myriad effects.[13]

As both theorist and filmmaker, the "I" who speaks from the position of my identity (the "I" who speaks as "me") draws from my own experience. This experience is by no means irrefutable, nor does it pretend to be exhaustively represented. Rather, it is a composite of memories of places, ideas, people, images, and things, and of cultural, social, and family mythology as remembered through sensations, dreams, pictures, and stories about pictures, navigated through the choppy seas of contradictory tellings, mixed liberally with a large dose of wishful thinking, and political and philosophical beliefs that motivate the selection of, or emphasis on, certain details to the exclusion of others. This statement would pertain as much to the onscreen representation of myself as to my critique of that process. In other words, the experiential narrative is not meant to be taken as a seamless presentational given. Rather, it should be seen as a constructed, partial, complex, and even contradictory mobilization of so-called experience—no less in my critical writing than in my filmmaking, autobiographical or otherwise. Here I am trying to avoid the invocation of the notion of experience as occupying a fixed, incontestable, position, or of experience as a naturalized, honest, transparent discourse of sincerity.[14]

It should be noted however, that the "I" who writes occupies a distinct rhetorical position from the "I" onscreen. For example, the writing "I" critiques many of the discursive and rhetorical conventions that the "I" onscreen engages.[15] The autobiographical "I" onscreen speaks about herself, the autocritical "I" speaks about herself speaking (and representing). Additionally, in the case of *Treyf*, there is more than one onscreen self-representation; indeed, there are two autobiographical subjects playing different yet related roles in the unfolding tale, which is not then reducible to biography, but is instead an ungainly, two-headed subjectivity. Like any other kind of freakish anomaly, this dual autobiography is a rarity, not something we can take for granted.[16] The implications of the bifocal autobiography will be explored further, but for now I call attention to the fact that the multiple "I"s in this narrative are not reducible to a repeating mirror effect. The "I"s occupy distinct rhetorical positions and also emanate from multiple perspectives, some of these interpersonal. The relational aspect of autobiography in *Treyf* is not only in terms of other's biographies (as discussed in the Introduction) but actively performs a parallax view of subjectivity.

More than the distinct voices or positions articulated within the film, which at times are admittedly neither very distinct nor particularly varied, it is the collaboration of two very different approaches, styles, and perspectives that creates the amalgam of aesthetics, politics, memory, and history giving the film its multilayered texture. But the perspectives that Madansky and I brought are at least partially self-aware, designed to create a narrative that would ideally have certain cultural and political effects. What this design is meant to indicate is that the choice to represent in the first person is not inevitably or exclusively naïve. Though there are many who pick up cameras to make their autobiographical documentary with little or no consideration of the elements (pretenses, myths, defenses, fabrications, normative proscriptions, and generic prescriptions) that subtend this act, the choice of autobiography is in many instances, and in our case certainly, a strategic decision.[17] I hope to make the reasons Madansky and I chose this particular representational strategy clear.

With such multiple articulations of subjectivity resonating within and around autobiography, and within *Treyf* in particular, autocritique posits yet another position vis-à-vis an autobiographical text and the life to which it refers. Autocritique delineates and elaborates, in effect, a borderline, suggestively disturbing the implicit relations between oneself and one's (autobiographical) work, and raises the question: when analyzing that work, can one ever be inside and outside oneself and the work at once? For a film that thematizes the insider/outsider conundrum, the treyf answer would have to be a qualified yes. Trinh T. Minh-ha has developed the figure of the Inappropriate Other to describe this condition, wherein the "I" is both "a deceptive insider and a deceptive outsider." It is the very idea of outsiderness that is the deception; rather, the attempt to be outside is always also inscribed internally.[18] Simone de Beauvoir phrased it thus: "To put oneself 'outside' is still a way of living the inescapable fact that one is inside."[19]

▶

Treyf: Insider/Outsider Simultaneously

Treyf is predicated on a formulation of queer, secular, politically progressive Jews as being outsiders in the Jewish world yet still having antecedents in modern Jewish history. Jews, particularly in the context of European history, are of course also the perennial outsiders nonetheless suspected of being the ultimate insiders (we should not forget the *Protocols of the Elders of Zion*). To be treyf in the context of this film is to maintain a delicate balance between being integrated into one's identities and being radically alienated from them. As my character says, in direct address, early in the film, "'Treyf' is an insider/outsider term: you have to be insider enough to know what it means, yet to be treyf is to be an outsider." As I continue to discuss my film here, consider the awkward straddle of this treyf position, being inside and outside the text simultaneously.

Treyf (the title and the film) trades in the currency of belonging and outsiderness: negotiating the boundaries of Jewish identity (who is and is not treyf); challenging the borders of national(ist) sovereignty (Zionism and Israel's occupied territories); stretching the margins of accepted sexualities within our Jewish families; formally abutting the borders of fiction from a documentary position; testing the permeability of assimilation by reversing its flow (e.g., when Alisa goes in female drag to a Hassidic synagogue to watch the Purim service from the women's section); even testing the bounds of propriety, treading a fine line between what can and should be said publicly and what by rights, laws of discretion, tradition, or good sense, might better remain unsaid.

Obviously, I, as one of the autobiographical subjects of *Treyf,* am inside, or insider to, this film. Clearly, I was integral to the process of writing, performing, and editing the piece. My physical aspect is on the celluloid. I am framed, I have framed myself in a portrait that I recognize simultaneously and contradictorily as a strategic deployment of self for the purposes of this film, and as a "true" or "authentic" projection of my experience of myself. Yet, stubbornly, I maintain that the character on screen, Alisa, is a strategic construction. As much as one can claim to have control over one's representation (not an ultimately finalizable claim), Madansky and I made a series of decisions as to how to draw and build the character, what elements to include in her biography, what role to give her. We constructed *Treyf* based on the not atypical narrative arc of a journey, beginning with the establishment of the two characters as guides, and then charting one of their transformations through a fraught political landscape, with the other character as the more anchored interlocutor. After much deliberation, for instance, we decided that the character known as Alisa would go through a political transformation and that the character Cynthia, though conflicted at times, would anchor the journey with her more rooted analysis and experience, particularly with regard to her relationship to Israel/Palestine.[20] Did this narrative arc approximate our actual experiences and political transformations in relation to our subject? To a certain extent, yes. Yet this strategic deployment of our autobiographical characters was as politically as dramatically motivated. Its effects rest on the verisimilitude of my performance of myself and Cynthia's of herself.

Let me state upfront that we made *Treyf* with the intent to persuade. Perhaps all too grandiosely, we hoped to catalyze a shift within the American

Alisa on the West Bank in *Treyf* (1998).

Jewish public debate around the question of the occupation of Palestine. We felt an imperative to speak out, and to do so from an avowedly Jewish position. Thus we posited both the Israeli occupation of Palestine and the Jewish silence in the face of the occupation as untenable breaches of the Jewish values in which we were raised. To my knowledge, until *Treyf*, no film made by a Jewish filmmaker outside Israel had taken a critical stance on this issue, certainly not from a Jewish perspective. Although there were already several books written by Jewish Israelis, in Hebrew, on post-Zionism and anti-Zionism, very few could be found in English and even fewer by American Jews.[21] The Jewish group that most closely approximated our political views, the New York-based Jews for Racial and Economic Justice,[22] was avowedly local in its remit—precisely, it seems, to not have to contend with the divisive issue of Israel (the group has since officially changed its bylaws and taken a public stance against the Occupation, but not until 2002). It would be a full three years after *Treyf* came out before Jews against the Occupation[23] appeared on the political scene, and five years before the publication of Alisa Solomon and Tony Kushner's groundbreaking edited volume *Wrestling with Zion*.[24] With the notable exceptions of N'tureh Karta, Noam Chomsky, and a handful of other Jewish artists and intellectuals, there was hardly a whisper from the contemporary Jewish Left in America. The American pro-Israel lobby, with the American Israel Public Affairs Committee (AIPAC) at its center, was working overtime to create the impression of a unanimous pro-Israel American Jewish block. I felt very much that we were going out on a limb, and at times (I'm ashamed to admit) my conviction wavered, terrified as I was to be so public with my unpopular (among Jews, or so it seemed at the time) but principled position. "Maybe," I anxiously wondered aloud as we drafted and redrafted the script, "we should just focus on the lesbian piece and leave Israel out of it." After all, who authorized us to speak about anything other than identity politics? In question-and-answer sessions after screenings of *Treyf,* we were frequently confronted with a distressed audience member questioning our judgment, not to mention our authority, in steering what they expected to be a film about Jewish lesbians into the deep and unwelcoming waters of geopolitics. We had clearly taken unexpected liberties by insisting on our right to enter into political debates beyond (though not entirely unrelated to) the scope of questions of ethnicity and sexuality. Many seem to have come expecting to have their liberal views on homosexuality affirmed, and instead found themselves confronted by the limits of liberalism and its appalling inadequacy in the face of brutal repression and occupation.

Despite, or because of, this anticipated response, we went to great lengths to establish our credibility to our audience, calculating that our critique would fall on deaf ears if we did not take pains to situate ourselves as authentic members of this community. Yet the discourses of *authenticity* is not without its detractors, myself among them. What constitutes authenticity and how is it achieved? The oppressions and exclusions that have been practiced in the name of authenticity are not to be underestimated or ignored, and certainly not to be validated. As postcolonialist critic Asha Vadarajan has said, "Authenticity is bought at the price of the decimation of others."[25] The so-called authentic subject is a tautological construct who exists only as a justification of a conservative impulse, not as a true or autochthonous entity who can verify an authoritative version of a given cultural identity. There is no sustainable authenticity, no true essence to be verified, yet, however vacuous the concept and unsustainable its claims, the appearance of authenticity is still lamentably necessary to achieve certain political ends.

Familiarity with the theoretical arguments against an authoritative model of authenticity does little to augment a filmmaker's credibility for most audiences. It can be said that the desire for political effectivity led us to suspend our disbelief in authenticity. It would be too easy for our Jewish audiences to dismiss our critique, largely directed toward the American Jewish community, if we were perceived to be completely outside that frame of reference. Although self-critical Jewish humor is widely embraced within Jewish circles, Jewish political autocritique is not. It is, in fact, singularly unwelcome, as seen by the relentless attacks by Jews against Jewish critics of Israel or Zionism. Hannah Arendt writes of being nearly skewered for her critique of the Eichmann Trial by what appeared to her then the monolith of the Jewish community.[26] Things have hardly improved since.

To reiterate, the credibility we felt we must establish was that of the insider: the knowledgeable Jew, raised in demonstrably Jewish environments, integrally involved in the issues and debates that most concern American Jews. Interestingly, very few of the other films in this study went to such lengths; to the contrary, they more often would tend to erase specifically Jewish markers, a fact that points to the varied aims of these diverse films. Madansky's and my primary aim was political, and our primary audience was American Jews. Our credentials included being raised, respectively, orthodox and Zionist (it barely matters which of us was raised orthodox, which Zionist); being familiar with the foibles of the community, aware of the silences, the oversights, the prejudices, the often justifiable (and as often unjustifiable) paranoias; and, perhaps most important, being adept at the humor with which Jews have laughed both at ourselves and at the outside world for generations. It seemed important to establish our insider status in these ways, to make an effective insiders' critique.

To dissent credibly from within the Jewish community, we felt the need to do two things in particular: (1) to establish our Jewish credentials (a task raising a range of troublesome authenticating practices already briefly delineated here); and (2) to construct sympathetic characters with whom viewers (primarily but not necessarily Jewish) could easily identify, recognizing that identification is film's primary mode of cathexis for viewers. Although admittedly our performances were not as thoroughly convincing as we had hoped, nonetheless naturalism in performance was the key for us, knowing that the film would not be successful in its cultural, political, or aesthetic aims if either my performance or Cynthia's appeared too unnatural by the realist conventions of the day.[27]

▶

Interchangeable Selves, or the Double Life of Autobiography

The characters Alisa and Cynthia are based on two actual lives, our own two lives, yet they are also a performance of those lives constructed so as to appear natural when we (our characters) sit on the floor clipping newspaper articles about Jews or tour the West Jerusalem neighborhoods in which Cynthia had lived. Our performances are not so far from our everyday offscreen personas that we would be unrecognizable to the people who know us. In fact, the distinction between my onscreen character and who I take myself to be in actuality often seems artificial even to me, aware as I am of the considerations that went into the construction of my filmic character's performance. I often identify that character onscreen as me, even knowing that a shot may have been one of many takes, that I had to memorize my lines, that the production circumstances may have had a determinative effect on the outcome of a scene, and how the use or placement of the shot or scene may have changed from its originally intended slot, thus changing its meaning or effect. I suspend my extra-textual knowledge, however, and simply (or not so simply) identify with the image onscreen (in a more fully embodied spectatorial projection than Christian Metz ever imagined).[28] In fact, I often experience the image as an actual projection of my self, not merely a fantasy of my ideal or constructed self on the screen. It would take tremendous discipline and the complete dismantling of a set of psychological associations with my own image to fully resist such a patently logical identification. I seem unable to fully deconstruct these associations of and with myself. Instead, as I look on, a moment of proliferating selves is effected, a kind of spectatorial mitosis, and I am both inside and outside of this film at once.

In terms of voice, I also, not surprisingly, recognize myself in the film, though it can be said that I sound *like* the self I have become accustomed to hear as myself. We are all familiar with the jarring sense of alienation experienced when we first hear our voices played back through a recording device. I have come to accept the sound of my recorded voice as the sound of my actual voice, though there is a trace resistance to this identification that does at times usefully hamper an unfettered relation to my reflected image.[29]

In *Treyf,* with Madansky's and my voices often commingling in voice-over narration, and given the similarities in the accent and timbre of our voices, we made little attempt, for the most part, to distinguish or even identify who is speaking. This creates an experience for the viewer where the voices are of indeterminate origin, often creating a slight confusion as to who is speaking of whose experience at any given time. The point was not that our voices were or should be regarded as interchangeable, that as a couple we had become indistinguishable from each other, or that our stories were virtually the same, but rather that it made little difference to which of us the film experiences were ascribed. Our filmic bodies were not bound at all times to our filmic voices, and our onscreen autobiographies could not be attributed verbatim or by voice to either of us individually. When we see, for instance, Alisa driving in an affluent New York suburb, we hear Cynthia's voice telling of the insular Jewish world in which she grew up. It was of little consequence to us that the footage was mostly shot in New Rochelle, where, in fact, I grew up, or that we mixed details of my biography (such as the reference to the working-class cousins who remained in the Bronx while my parents marched us up the socioeconomic ladder to Westchester) with hers. Cynthia's biographical details may have been slightly different, with her academic father and the family's

Los Angeles–Long Island–Chicago trajectory. But, in this instance, the stories of the upwardly mobile midcentury Jewish American families, regardless of the minor biographical differences, were fairly interchangeable. The stories were told with intent and purpose: to construct an impression of an historical moment, to characterize a certain stratum of American Jewish culture, to build a foundation of Jewish cultural experience and knowledge from which to launch a credible cultural critique, and not as expected, from a purely autobiographical endeavor, to elevate or emphasize our personal autobiographical details.

To a certain degree, we undermined audience identification by refusing to ground the voice at all times to an identifiable subject. Yet this occurred in an effort to reduce the relevance of our individual characters in favor of the effect of creating a common cultural context from which to speak. What we sought to avoid was the literal assignation of narration with story, of voice with authenticity. Our voices were just voices; the stories were stories told by disembodied voices whose origin was or could be open to debate. These stories were ours and not ours. They could easily have been told by another. They simply had to resonate emotionally with the viewer.

Here we begin to see the ways that the double-autobiography in *Treyf* actually adds up to more than two voices. The doubling brings with it an ambiguity or ambivalence (*ambi* equals *both*) that further undoes that which is already fragmentary in autobiography. There are others beyond the "each other" of the text. The illusion of multiple others within a given text is not an unknown documentary practice, though it is generally created by intercutting a chorus of interviewees chiming in on the same point.[30] I had begun to suspect the documentary convention of finding others to ventriloquize the filmmaker's position; the dynamic of turning the camera on others only to edit them to speak, essentially, the filmmaker's own words amounts to pulling strings behind a curtain, and in this case seemed patently unnecessary. To construct a film in such a way that the autobiographical subjects' stories resonate with larger concerns is to send one's voice(s) rippling outward like an echo with multiple reverberations, rather than like a puppet-master controlling marionettes.

Treyf is billed as a semiautobiographical film in its promotional materials. What the "semi" is intended to signify is a degree of interpretation and creative license that went into the construction of the onscreen characters' narration. Without specifying the elements that were enhanced, embellished, or outright fabricated, this "semi" attempts to call attention to the fictionalization that inevitably accompanies the process of narrativizing one's own history. With this definition of autobiography, the "semi" is admittedly superfluous, but it calls attention to the process of narrativization that may not be understood or assumed by most viewers. Whether or not an individual account refers to an actual historical event that happened to either of us, or only points to a generalized phenomenon common among American Jews of our generation, was immaterial to us. By speaking ourselves, we were also speaking others, again attempting to exploit the reverberant potential of the medium.

Minor Autobiography

These are, in fact, some of the reasons for choosing the autobiographical register in the first place. In addition to these ideological and aesthetic considerations, we quickly realized that autobiography has been an effective vehicle for cultural memory and critique for some time. The facts that we were not famous and that we could not expect our characters to have star appeal did not deter us. Autobiography has a venerable history of minor characters. The history of first person film consists of a continuous stream of nobodies, some of whom may have become recognizable through their films but were generally unknown before.[31] Even literary autobiography has a long and split history—a strain by "great men of history" and an equally valid and thriving strain by the ordinary person, the unknown writer. Women, minorities, the underrepresented, and the disenfranchised have taken up autobiography (written and filmic) as a mechanism to give voice to their condition, to their humanity, to their struggles. This strain might be described, following Deleuze and Guattari, as "minor autobiography," in which the individual biography is secondary to the way it reflects and resonates with broader cultural themes. Presumably there was something noteworthy about some aspect of the author's life that warranted the telling, usually something sociological or political as narrated through the personal. An example of a minor autobiography would be Mary Antin's *The Promised Land* (1912), which remains the writer's only enduring work. Its success lay in its representative quality, the author speaking as a member of the young immigrant class and documenting the process of becoming an American. Antin's was a model American melting-pot tale, its interest not strictly in her as an individual. That is, the trope of the melting pot narrated her story as much as did Antin, the individual. In hindsight, it will perhaps be as easy to identify the tropes that have narrated ours.[32]

It is fair to say that most first person filmmakers do not consider their personal biographies interesting or engaging in and of themselves. Even within the small sampling of films in this study, very few of the filmmakers approach their story for its own sake. Deborah Hoffmann uses her experience as caretaker of her Alzheimer's-afflicted mother to speak to others in such a situation. Alan Berliner engages the father–son dynamic as a vehicle to explore generational memory and genealogy. Gregg Bordowitz deploys his HIV-positive condition and AIDS-activist status to address a range of political, ethical, and representational concerns. Similarly, Madansky and I recognized autobiography as an extremely effective medium for engaging sensitive subject matter. Autobiography does not rely on fact-based analysis; rather it privileges an experiential narrative (one, I again emphasize, strategically deployed), evoking a different dimension of truth, subject only to emotional verification. Autobiography allows, to use an invasion metaphor, maximum penetration with minimum resistance. In short, it is an excellent tool for propaganda.[33]

To reiterate, the stories we tell about ourselves in the film are true, but this is an interpretive, politicized truth. And here, this is yet another treyf intervention into the meaning of truth. It is not the accuracy or inaccuracy of the account that matters, but the effective projection of a valid account. Whether an event happened to me or to Cynthia or to one of our friends is less important than whether it can stand as a representative event in the lives of American Jews of our generation and class, and whether it effectively promotes a particular point of view. To a large extent, the credibility factor is essential in these stories, for we must be believed for our narratives to have their intended political effect. Yet whether one's stories are believable depends on the telling, not on the facts; any good storyteller can tell you that.

Here, as elsewhere, truth is an effect, not a cause, of credibility. If the film resonates with individual viewers' experiences, and if it catalyzes questions, challenges assumptions, and motivates dialogue, then it is true—or, perhaps I should say, has generated truth effects (to mobilize a Foucauldian concept). The spectator, in his or her engagement with the film, imbues it with a truth value to the degree that it affirms, corroborates, engages his or her own perception of what seems true.[34]

▶

Treyf Aesthetics

Our task, as we conceived of it, was to imagine what a politically engaged, queer, secular, progressive, Jewish text would look like in all of its contradictions and ambivalences. We had to decide how best to construct characters that embodied these at times conflicting sensibilities. We realized quite quickly that the most obvious, visible, Jewish signifiers were either religious or anti-Semitic, and we were forced to mine the depths of our memories and cultural ephemera to develop a visual language that signified Jewishness as we lived it.[35] In this, we attempted to develop an aesthetic to parallel our complex identity construction, drawing from Jewish iconography, imagery, music, ritual, and pedagogy, yet always working to decontextualize these referents to the point where they teeter on the edge of recognizability, verging on, and at times crossing into, treyf territory. The music was one key factor in constructing this ambience of treyf Jewishness. Working with composer Zeena Parkins, who was Jewish but not known for making classically or typically Jewish music, we asked her to find (lesser-known) Jewish musical themes and strains and defamiliarize them. So, for example, she found traditional tunes, *niggunim,* which she then rewrote or recorded with nontraditional instruments and arrangements.

Another example of the treyf Jewishness that we worked hard to develop occurs in the visual register: the two interstitial scenes where we parade Jewish mementos, or *tshatshkes,* across the screen against a white background. These form a momentary break in the onslaught of voice-over, a reflective interlude in an otherwise high-paced, tightly packed film. The trinkets are the kind that might have been found in many American Jewish households: gaudy metal medallions that say *Jerusalem* and *Shalom,* tie clips with engraved Jewish stars poking fun at the stereotype of the "rich Jew," colorful plastic lamps shaped like a Jewish star, etc. Yet in the context of the film, these mundane objects are transformed from high kitsch memorabilia into daunting talismans. After our tour of the illegal settlements on the West Bank, our visit with the irritatingly cheerful American settler, self-satisfied in her role as colonizer taming the Wild West Bank, the glimpse into the relentless humiliation of the checkpoints, it becomes difficult to see these as the breezy souvenirs they were once thought to be. By the time the image of the birthday cupcake sporting miniature Israeli flag toothpicks and the camel-and-palm-tree ashtray with "Israel" in Hebrew roll by, the mood has changed. Alisa and Cynthia have walked through the labyrinth of the Valley of Communities in Israel's Holocaust Memorial, Yad V'Shem, and meditated on the ways in which the dream of Israel as a safe haven for Jews has turned into a nightmare of militarization and occupation. The exterior valley of death, a graveyard of bones, the endless and increasingly senseless battle over stones, leaves an empty satisfaction of having secured neither safety nor a sense of righteousness. The images are infected with the dark tones of the sound track, signaling a more complicated narrative of complicity, and turning the onus onto the viewer as delight in the familiarity of the mementoes fades into a moral morass.

The Mythical Embrace of Community

To return to questions of voice, credibility, and authority, we are not the only voices heard in the film. One distinct and recurrent voice is that of an unidentified Jewish male who speaks informatively and authoritatively on several aspects of Jewish tradition (halakha), though he does so in a manner patently out of place in the context of this film. The filmstrips are meant to revive collective memory, since they were a pervasive pedagogical tool in U.S. Hebrew schools in the 1970s, and this male's accompanying voice lays down the law as we learned it. His is a thoroughly disembodied voice. His authority is undercut very early in the film when, in a stereotypically Jewish-accented voice, he introduces a kitsch educational filmstrip, "Koshering Meat and Chicken," over filmstrip imagery of pork and shellfish (food decidedly *not* kosher).[36] His words are entirely out of sync with the imagery; he is clearly not in command of the image.

Upon thus undermining the traditional Jewish voice of authority, we immediately replace it with our own, considerably less identifiably Jewish-accented, voices. The unintended consequence of this supercession, however, is that in the process of stripping this man of his perceived patriarchal Jewish authority over us, we avail ourselves of the accent of a equally pernicious authority, the accent of dominant American culture (white, Christian-inflected, nondenominational "newscasterese") that has historically been ready to repress signs of Jewish specificity. Our power is derived in part from our ability to speak in the voice of assimilated Jewry; our voices, our accents, our intonations are not coded Jewish in the way that this heavily accented male's are. We unwittingly participate in an erasure of overt Jewishness right at the moment of our ostensibly empowering coup. Our authority, seemingly uncontested in the context of our film, thus comes at a price. The game of supercession yields its usual reward, one blunt instrument of authority replaced by another. The dynamic forces of cultural capital at work on an unconscious level reveal themselves in these moments.

Of course, the authority we wield is circumspect and illusory. We present ourselves as authorities (but only partially) over our own narrative, created for the film, not over facts and figures, laws and traditions. The film only veers into the territory of historical facts when in its most contentious territory, critiquing the Israeli occupation of the West Bank and Gaza. And we all know that these facts have been in dispute for years. Even at *Treyf*'s most polemical, the verifiable data are kept to a minimum and a visceral, personal, and emotional relationship to the politics is emphasized. This was, as I have indicated, a strategic decision.

At the point of strategizing, one cannot help but notice the constricting logic of denominators. A filmmaker is always encouraged to target an audience. Grant applications require it, producers expect it, distributors make a science of it. Yet once you begin to set your sights on an audience you have no choice but to reduce these people to a set of assumptions, already underestimating their diversity even if not their intelligence. There is no Jewish community per se, nor were we raised "within it" as such. Such a proposition resides in our minds, imagined—though through material indicators and effects, as Benedict Anderson has so convincingly argued. Yet, the power of the myriad Jewish film festivals to concentrate an audience into a supposed community should not be underestimated. And our aim was to play to that aggregation of Jews, who range the gamut of political affiliations, though for many Zionism remains an unquestioned allegiance. Of course, we intended for our film to be seen by more than Jews (and queers) and we made an effort, in fact, to be accessible and decipherable on some level by those with no exposure whatsoever to Jewish or queer culture. But central to our project was sending a message back to the Jewish community, constituted as a festival-going audience—back to ourselves, if you will, in yet another level of autocritique.

As I have said, we felt the most effective method of critique would be from an insider's perspective, yet there would have been no need to establish our insider's credentials had they not already been in question. Even though halakhically Jewish and unimpeachably culturally credentialed (Hebrew day schools, observant upbringings, Israeli Day parades, relatives in Israel, etc.), we render ourselves immediately suspect once we declare ourselves treyf.[37] The title of the film immediately signals the ways we differ from the mainstream Jewish community, however broadly or narrowly that community is conceived. Our status as lesbians alone would be enough to indicate a rupture with convention that would make us outsiders in many persons' eyes.

By insisting on calling ourselves treyf, we obviously wanted to resist full integration or any uncomplicated relation to insiderness. In fact, many gay and lesbian Jews who struggle (often successfully) in their daily lives to gain access to and legitimacy from existing Jewish institutions, refuse to embrace the term treyf as a valid or desirable description of their lives, insisting that it is important that the Jewish community consider them kosher—i.e., legitimate, full-fledged members of the mainstream Jewish community.[38] There are those who have voiced their disappointment that we would want to appropriate what they perceived a negative appellation.

There are others still, Jewish conservatives of all stripes, who have been all too eager to embrace the term "treyf" to describe us and anyone else they deem undesirable. Both positions refuse to register or accept the reappropriative implications of our title.

Although our aspirations to achieve an exclusive (and elusive) membership have always been ambivalent at best, and we have tried adamantly to problematize the terms of acceptance, we did nonetheless make concessions to the beliefs and value systems that have historically perpetuated the very exclusions we would contest. By attempting to establish ourselves as, at the least, knowledgeable, engaged Jews, steeped in the (Americanized) traditions of our culture, we have tacitly affirmed some key elements of inclusion and authenticity even while we purport to challenge their legitimacy.[39]

All this has been in an effort to establish a modicum of credibility, which would likely still be denied us by those disinclined to hear our message in the first place. This result leads me to question our choice to mobilize what is tantamount to a conservative, even reactionary, strategy in the service of what we believed was a politically progressive agenda. It is entirely possible that these messages effectively cancel each other out by working at cross-purposes. Certainly the film failed to directly catalyze the political debates and dialogues we had envisioned. I have to concede that what appeared the most efficacious plan was ultimately a move toward reinscribing the exclusionary and impermeable border we had intended to transgress, without yielding the outcomes for which we so willingly compromised. The delicate and often permeable *eruv* that separates the insider from the outsider within the Jewish community became a fixed border with its own set of enforced exclusions, legitimated by our tacit endorsement.

▶ ──

Dialogism and Community Unity

Legitimacy and authenticity are bound together in a set of mutually affirming criteria, all working toward a troublesome unity and unanimity of the subjects in question. The desire to establish the credentials of our authenticity undercuts the double-voiced, treyf, countercurrents of this film. The more we insisted on our authenticity, the more we capitulated to the monadic force, the unitary, univocal, monologic of traditional autobiography. We implicitly proclaimed: we are one of you, and (perhaps more disturbingly in the context of this essay) we (the two of us) are one. To the extent that we speak through the film in a unified voice, we have reduced the potential to rupture the narrow confines of monologic autobiography.

It is not only a question of speaking in unison with one another on the diegetic level, however. Returning to yet another aspect of the problem of split subjectivity and doubled, insider/outsider, autobiographical articulations, it is important to ask, What is the relation between the onscreen voice and the voice of the film in an autobiographical film? Can these different registers be read separately in autobiographical film, the way Bill Nichols suggests they must be read in other documentary films? Never an easy separation to make, this proves even more difficult with autobiographical film than with other kinds of documentary. Autobiographical films can have a strong tendency to appear univocal, where the enunciation within the film seems at one with the *enoncé* of the film. The indexical affinity between the image and the pro-filmic real that documentary traditionally exploits would appear further corroborated in autobiographical documentary when the film functions as an extension, not merely of the filmmaker's vision, but also of what looks, acts, and sounds like the filmmaker's very self. The stubborn conflation between filmmaker and character(s) is all but inevitable. Even when, as in our film, there are two autobiographical voices, there exists the temptation to collapse the represented positions into one unified textual voice, a voice that directly and immediately speaks in unison with its subjects. The illusion of an unmediated experience of the filmmaker(s) as subject(s) makes these documentaries seem considerably less polyphonous than they may actually be. Nonetheless, the registers are, and must be understood to be, as distinct as Bill Nichols argues they are in other types of documentary.[40] I hope to convey an impression of *Treyf* where we as authors are neither entirely in unison with the enoncé of the film nor entirely distinct from it. Even an autobiographical film attributed to only one author need not be monologic. All discourse is relational and potentially dialogic.[41] Given the fact of two main voices in *Treyf*, it is doubly imperative that the film maintain a complex dialogic dynamic.

Thus, with regard to the diegetic, the film's bi-vocality leads us to expect that at the least it would rupture any monologism. But it may well be that the slippage of our voices only serves to reaffirm such monologism, too often making our two voices one.[42] My (perhaps unrealistic) hope for *Treyf* was that the film would somehow transcend the perennial problem of naïve autobiography by knowingly deploying the autobiographical register without fully subscribing to its conceit. We wanted to portray a complex contradictory subjectivity, one that questions, that wonders aloud, that shifts over time, and that slips in and out of character. But autobiographical generic imperatives may have all too effectively deployed us. Formulated in an effort to authenticate our characters and thus authorize our message, our method may have undermined our purpose, thus endorsing the very image of the subject we wished to avoid: a monolithic, monologic, unitary, speaking subject. This result is partially, of course, a necessary consequence of the film's political aspirations. The project is characterized by a tension between the yearning for an alternative representation of selfhood and the desire to locate the self in a sociopolitical environment from which to speak. These tensions at times risked undoing the project entirely, but I would not say our failure was complete. Even if I concede (grudgingly) that the slippage of the two voices can be seen as a tacit reaffirmation of the unitary subject, and thus as contributing to the monologism of the piece, literal voice is not the only register to consider. The visual and the aural registers often resist a one-to-one correlation in the film, creating competing strata of meaning that necessarily complicate each character's words. At the film's best and most complex, there are multiple levels of dialogism at work, vying for attention and adding dimension to the narrative.

One scene in particular comes to mind as an instance where the attempt to create a multilayered dialogic is realized. This is the final scene in the film, with Cynthia and Alisa filmed walking the streets of New York's Lower East Side, in an inelegant late-twentieth-century version of flaneurie. Amidst the Jewish shops and bakeries that we walk in and out of are the signs of cultural syncretism: the synagogue turned Seventh Day Adventist church; the leftover sign from the long-closed kosher Chinese restaurant (Shmulke Bernstein's on Essex) in what has since become an

Alisa and Cynthia on the streets of New York's Lower East Side in *Treyf*.

actual Chinese neighborhood; the occasional observant Jew glimpsed among the neighborhood's predominantly Chinese and Hispanic residents. These images epitomize our palimpsestic relationship to geography and history, culturally rooting us to this place while displacing us simultaneously. In voice-over, I speak first, reading an imagined letter addressed only to an alphabet letter. It begins "Dear C," immediately identifying (if elliptically) the addressee and distinguishing her from the addresser (hence not an instance of the previously mentioned indeterminate-origins effect). The letter is poetic if predictable, imagining a life not lived or at least not recorded: a lesbian love story in the heart of the early-twentieth-century Jewish Lower East Side. The nostalgia of this letter is laced with an obliquely heretical tinge. Mixed with the reverential awe for the struggles and creativity of our immigrant progenitors is the iconoclasm of insinuating lesbian desire and a lesbian presence into what has become a sacred cow of Jewish American history. The letter is a love letter, but it is also a reinvention, a nostalgia released, to some extent, from the reactionary longing for traditions of days gone by, instead reconfiguring an image of the past to conform to the articulated desires of the present.

Nevertheless, the image of the past, however reconstituted, is still overly romanticized in this letter, and in need of a counterpoint. Cynthia's response, in her letter to a letter ("Dear A"), provides an arresting intervention. She disrupts "A"'s reverie to remind us of the harsh conditions, the scarce resources, the inhospitable environment of America for Jews, and of the Lower East Side for lesbians, in the early part of the twentieth century. Yet there is a double movement here, a prevarication. As Cynthia decimates the pleasures of one nostalgia, she replaces them with another, one less guiltily sanctioned by a class-conscious, politically engaged contemporary audience. To mitigate the unchecked political correctness of this revised nostalgia, our characters are seen browsing in the streets of today's Lower East Side, shoe-shopping as Cynthia proclaims her dream to have marched in the streets with labor activists and other radicals of that bygone era. Consumerism invades idealism, and the two coexist uncomfortably in the chronotope of the narrative, sound and image subtly mocking each other. The passionate engagement of the characters with each other, with the audience, and with Jewish history is not diminished by this use of irony; the irony simply strips the film of a facile romanticism that would deprive the subjects of the paradoxes and contradictions that texture their lives.

In *Treyf,* we vacillate between nostalgia for a life never lived and a skepticism, verging on agnosticism, of the redemptive potential of nostalgia. We struggle to establish an insider's status even while we undermine the validity and value of membership. We insist, in contrarian fashion, on being treyf, and then proclaim treyf to be a quintessentially Jewish value. We speak in two voices that intersect and divide, just as the film's voice bifurcates from its speakers. The intersections of history, geography, culture, memory, identity, sexuality, and politics motivate the film, and our two characters enact the interplay among these forces, grounding them in the delicate plexus that has constituted our lived lives. That these lives are fabricated for the purposes of the film is a regulative necessity of the field. Any claim to the unmediated reality of an autobiographical character only adds dimension to the illusion. It does not succeed in making that character, or that film, any more real or true.

In the interest of fulfilling any unsatisfied expectations raised by the term *critique* in this autocritique, I want to focus on the final moments of the film, on what I have come to see as a filmic surrender, where I believe we lose the power of the momentum we have gathered, precisely when it should have been harnessed and actualized. After taking the viewer through a highly selective tour of Manhattan's Lower East Side, and attempting to mitigate the Jewish American nostalgia for those immigrant days, we simply abandon the dialectical critique—or rather we artificially synthesize it into a false/forced retrospective optimism. Walking past the Streit's matzo factory, "C"'s character proclaims in voice-over that, though we may be treyf, we are not alone, and history has eventually, with some coaxing, revealed that our politics, our secularism, and even our sexuality have antecedents in the modern Jewish world, as if to say: we come from somewhere, there have been others like us, we are not alone. This feels like a desperate turn, both to affirm to ourselves that we are not anathema to Jewish history (not actually treyf!) and to send a warning, at the very least, to those who would further marginalize us. The film then cuts to the final filmstrip; this one (much like the first seen after the opening title) is purely constructed from images we have chosen—in this instance, still photographs of women who participated in the "Jewish lesbian party" scene held in the ex-synagogue on Norfolk Street (a few blocks from the Streit's factory). We gathered nearly one hundred Jewish lesbians together for that scene, having no idea ahead of time how it would turn out. Luckily, the event really did turn into a party, with the dancing happening spontaneously, and mostly without the cameras rolling (we had to cobble the dancing scene together from what footage we managed to film; there was a desperate flurry to catch the moment since, when the dancing erupted, the camera was not loaded with film, the camera assistant was nowhere in sight, and the rest of the crew was busy breaking down the set). Although some of the women had known each other before the shoot and participants were invited through word of mouth, signifying some semblance of informal community, it would be an exaggeration to call this particular gathering a *community*: the group had never gathered before and has not gathered since, and the uniting factors of Jewishness and lesbianism proved much thornier than expected.

The answering-machine messages heard immediately prior to the synagogue scene (while Cynthia and I prepare a technicolor *kiddush*) give some indication of the obstacles and impediments to constituting this secular, politically progressive, multiethnic, mixed-class, Jewish lesbian community. As each woman responds to her invitation, a differing aspect of identity is at issue. The phone messages, recorded for the purposes of the film, were based on actual messages we received on our home answering machine several times a day during the lead-up to the shoot. We were amazed, amused, and bemused by the way the compound identity "Jewish lesbian" threw some people into fear and self-doubt ("while I'm Jewish and a lesbian, I've never really seen myself as a Jewish lesbian"), while others gaily embraced its paradoxes. This scene economically reveals, even as it undermines, the fantasy of such a unified community. As one caller proleptically laments while sending her regrets, "[a gathering like this] never ever happens in my lifetime."

This community is clearly a filmic fiction. Why the necessity, then, at the very end, to take haven in its mythical embrace? What purpose does this rhetorical crowd serve? What might a more treyf ending have looked like? If we had had the answers to these questions, the ending of the film would have looked very different. But even in retrospect I am left with no better idea of how to conclude either the film or this chapter, how to ultimately embody treyf individually or communally, how to fully deploy treyf in the first person register. I humbly and dialogically open the floor to suggestions.

[4] *Ambivalence and Ambiguity in Queer Jewish Subjectivity*

> *To attain his truth, man must not attempt to dispel the ambiguity of his being but, on the contrary, accept the task of realizing it.*
> :: Simone de Beauvoir, *The Ethics of Ambiguity*

When I informally interviewed British filmmaker Ruth Novaczek, she told me that her way of dealing with the dual identities of lesbianism and Jewishness in her films is to "just stick them in the same room and make them get on."[1] To her credit, she does at times attempt to force the issue in her films, though it is not always certain that these identities do get on. However, what concerns me here is that the issue needs to be forced at all. It is not only Novaczek's Jewish queer self-representation that struggles with the integration of these identities. Other first person filmmakers, as becomes plain in this chapter, have difficulty even negotiating these two identities in the same frame, developing, rather, a puzzling circumspection with regard to queerness, Jewishness, or both. For instance, Jan Oxenberg, an out lesbian feminist since the early days of the second-wave women's movement, never once mentions her sexuality in *Thank You and Goodnight* (1991), a film about her maternal grandmother. Akerman typically leaves any direct references to her girlfriend of decades, Sonia Wieder-Atherton, out of nearly all of her autobiographical representations, though the sounds of Sonia's cello are almost always somewhere on the sound track. This omission takes place even while both Oxenberg and Akerman concern themselves on some level, however elliptically, with their Jewishness. Only three of the films treated here— *Treyf* (1998), *Tarnation* (2004), and *Complaints of a Dutiful Daughter* (1994)—represent sexuality in relation to a sexual partner (lover, crush, trick), and even these are noticeably timid and restrained in the depiction of these relationships.[2] The most that *Treyf* manages is a kiss and an occasional caress. *Complaints* does not even go that far. It is almost as if any explicit sexuality would confirm the stereotype of the hypersexual Jew, a stereotype that not only coexisted paradoxically with the stereotype of the impotent (male) Jew but was one of the few stereotypes applied equally to Jewish men and Jewish women. There are five films in this selection that loudly proclaim their queerness—*Treyf, Fast Trip, Long Drop* (1993), *Rootless Cosmopolitans* (1990), *Cheap Philosophy* (1992), and *Tarnation*—but of those, *Treyf* prefers to dwell on issues of the protagonists' Jewishness and Bordowitz's proud proclamation of his gay identity turns out to be more political strategy than exclusive sexual preference. *Rootless* and *Cheap Philosophy* have trouble integrating their queer and their Jewish elements, and *Tarnation* takes this problem to an extreme, with Jewishness twice flashing by as an anomalous, almost hallucinatory, glitch whereas the filmmaker's gay relationship is the main stabilizing element throughout.

Of the films in this grouping (aside from *Treyf*), Novaczek's films make the most concerted effort to integrate queerness and Jewishness in the same frame, though each emerges more as a symptom of an all-pervasive neurosis than as a coherent identity. In *Cheap Philosophy,* Novaczek plays a bevy of bewigged beauties, running the gamut from lovesick lesbian sociopath to spaced-out kabbalist. Of Novaczek's many personae in the film, it is that of the belligerent butch in the baseball cap, repeatedly blurting out "Don't you call me neurotic," that best brings together Jewish and lesbian, and here she comes out as a defensive, hostile, paranoid figure. Amusing as this characterization is (and it is), if this is "getting on," I shudder to think what love might look like.

The films I discuss in this chapter include Ruth Novaczek's *Cheap Philosophy* and *Rootless Cosmopolitans*; *Tarnation,* by Jonathan Caouette; Chantal Akerman's *Chantal Akerman by Chantal Akerman* (1996); Jan Oxenberg's *Thank You and Goodnight*; Deborah Hoffmann's *Complaints of a Dutiful Daughter*; *Treyf* (1998), by Alisa Lebow and Cynthia Madansky; and Gregg Bordowitz's *Fast Trip, Long Drop*. Although these represent only a select sample of queer Jewish autobiographical documentaries, they do represent a range of practice spanning a decade when queer visibility politics, as well as a Jewish cultural revivalism, were well underway in the United States and Europe (though Jewish revivalism, perhaps, to a lesser extent in Europe). In this context of relative openness and unprecedented exhibition opportunities in both gay/lesbian and Jewish film festivals, what prompts these films' multiple and often simultaneous evasions?

In queer Jewish autobiographical films, the two identities coexist uneasily, at best, and, at worst, ambivalently conflict with or negate each other. Ambivalence is a running subtext of many of the films discussed here, and it is, I argue, a result of mutual, if at times competing, historical survival strategies. Further, in addition to this symptomatic ambivalence, there is a disquieting ambiguity of expression. Considering that all the films were made in an era and in geopolitical contexts where visibility and forthright identification were generally (though not unproblematically or universally) considered signs of pride and self-acceptance,[3] it is ironic that the films at times still straddle a zone of unintelligibility that would seem a remnant of an earlier age.

In this chapter, I examine, through the analysis of a handful of contemporary films, the complications that attend a coherent and forthright expression of these two multivalent and interpenetrating identities. In the process, I attempt to anatomize the surprising parallels and paradoxes of these two identities, not the least being that they emerged as modern political identities at roughly the same historical moment. I will argue that the difficulties in articulating this hyphenated identity (which is at all times co-implicated with other key identificatory positionalities such as gender, class, and nationality) are the curious effect of a pernicious historical conflation of the homosexual and the Jew, rather than resulting from inadequacies of the filmmakers' personal or political evolution.

This is not a case where the filmmakers have not yet come to a point of openness and full acceptance of their identities. Progressive historicism inadequately describes the syncretic conditions of queer Jewish identity formations in the late-twentieth-century Euro-American context. These films can be seen in part as a response to the competing demands of two complex and conflicting identities, both historically suffused in tropes of ambivalence and ambiguity. The syncretic coexistence of these two mutually implicated yet distinct identities has led to a queer Jewish aesthetic of ambivalence that manifests itself in different ways (sometimes by not being manifest, or apparent at all) in each film considered in this chapter.

Writing specifically about lesbian Jewish identity, though in a way that may be relevant to Jewish gay men as well, literary critic Bonnie Zimmerman proclaims Jewish lesbian identity to be inherently, though fruitfully, contradictory."[4] Since it is impossible to determine which identity is meant to be the subject and which is meant to be the modifier, she questions whether the issue is not more a matter of both functioning "as subjects held together in uneasy union."[5] She refuses simplistic, mollifying gestures that would either ignore or artificially overcome what she sees as inherent and irreconcilable differences. She insists, perhaps too forcefully, "that certain influences and traditions cannot be harmonized smoothly, that being lesbian [or gay] is a decisive break with [Jewish] tradition that cannot be repaired easily, and that contradiction is a fruitful, if difficult, state in which to live."[6]

This emphasis on contradiction, however, obscures the ineradicable fact of the common histories of these identities during the last two centuries, at least in Europe and America (histories of, e.g., phrenological and criminological associations, Nazi persecutions), as well as related if distinct survival strategies. Indeed, there are compelling places of sympathy between these two identity positions that Zimmerman, in line with other theorists, does not fail to point out.[7] In fact, Zimmerman calls the parallels between Judaism and homosexuality "obvious and compelling."[8] For instance, there are analogous racial, geographical, national, and economic diversities; correspondent civil rights struggles; immanent and actual persecutions by shared oppressors; the comparable complexity and perplexity of assimilation, passing, and coming out—all questions of visibility that have weighed heavily on the experience and performance of each identity. These questions of visibility, in particular, can be meaningfully traced back to the late nineteenth century, when, as Hannah Arendt points out, the rise of the historical category *homosexual* is simultaneous and often entwined with the rise of political (that is to say, modern) anti-Semitism.

I propose that the parallel historical circumstances of these two distinct but by now filmically flourishing identities has unwittingly shaped the filmic self-representation of contemporary lesbian and gay Jews. How else to explain the persistent presence of themes and tropes that seem to resurface from an earlier age? With or without an awareness of the anti-Semitic, homophobic tropes of the past, some filmmakers of the late twentieth century have revisited the terrain plotted out in that previous era with decidedly distinct implications.[9] When Gregg Bordowitz seemingly forges new territory in his first person documentary about life as an HIV-positive, Jewish, AIDS activist, he is, as we shall see, updating and recasting the notorious triadic interpenetrations among homosexuality, Jewishness, and disease. When Ruth Novaczek plays twelve different versions of herself, she reinvokes images of the Jew as chameleon as well as the association between psychopathology (not to mention psychoanalysis) and Jewishness. When Sandi DuBowski, in *Tomboychik* (a short video I do not analyze in any depth here but that fits nonetheless within this rubric), coaxes and goads his elderly grandmother to confess her adolescent gender transgressions, one is moved, beyond the initial (not unpleasant) surprise, to remember the accusations of gender inappropriateness of both male and female Jews at the turn of the last century. When Chantal

Akerman, Jan Oxenberg, and Michelle Citron bury explicit references to their lesbianism in their films, one is prompted to consider comparisons between the assimilatory strategies historically ascribed to Jewishness and to homosexuality. I read these films in part for their autobiographical revelations and generic innovations, but also in light of their intersections and interarticulations with a panoply of tropes from the past that refuse to disappear, even as they are remade anew.

The declarative and affirmative statement of identification, *coming out,* is central to both gay and Jewish visibility in ways that many other identificatory regimes navigate only marginally. Like other border identities that entail a crossing of a boundary (racial, national, linguistic, sexual, gendered, economic, etc.), whether explicit or assumed, queers and diasporic Jews have to negotiate the terms of their visibility.[10] Wherever the question of passing exists, so too the problem of the closet. Yet the paths toward or away from visibility of various Jewish communities are historically distinct from those taken by gays and lesbians, at least in the last quarter of the twentieth century in the West. There are competing strategies at work in these films, and the result is a contradictory ambivalence, evidenced in an ambiguity of representation of one or other of these identificatory positionalities. As we shall see, especially with regard to Hoffmann's and Oxenberg's films (but also with Michelle Citron's and Chantal Akerman's), Jewishness or queerness is often only discernible in the subtext. Surely, as chapter 1 on *D'Est* attests, this subtext can be an enormously rich and interconnected set of allusions, associations, insinuations, and inclinations, yet the ambiguity persists.

I wish to make a brief aside about my apparently interchangeable usage of the terms *ambiguity* and *ambivalence.* Many times I detect an ambiguous representational strategy, one that raises more questions than it answers about a given identity or cultural configuration. In this chapter, I generally read these ambiguities as evidence of a constitutive ambivalence. This ambivalence may be internal and personal, reflecting the individual blind spots or discomforts of the filmmaker toward a forthright identification with her or his sexuality or culture. Ambivalence is more fraught with contradiction than is ambiguity, and is the aspect of conflict and contradiction that, I believe, overtakes the self-representations in these films; hence my emphasis on ambivalence. In this chapter, I use Zygmunt Bauman's theories of the Jew as modernity's ambivalent excess to explore the idea that such ambivalence is motivated by, though not necessarily intrinsic to, the particular cultural configuration portrayed. In short, I am investigating a structural ambivalence created by the confluence of these particular identity positions in representational terms. Ambiguity is read here as a symptom of ambivalence.

Ambiguous representation of queerness and Jewishness creates an unavoidable challenge for me, since I have to resist the desire to name or categorize (a counterambiguous operation) or to try to ascertain ways that what appears to be ambiguous can actually be clarified and revealed to be more transparent than originally perceived. Any of these invasive strategies would refuse the logic of ambiguity, when the films often ask to be read on their own (ambiguous) terms. Ambiguity here is neither a virtue nor a curse, neither inevitable nor unlikely, but the fact that it is a prominent, if unsignaled, self-representational strategy in several of the queer Jewish autobiographical films suggests that its presence is more than coincidental, given the particular identity configuration involved.

From the perspective of identity politics, there would seem little justification for such elusiveness. As suggested earlier, given the emphasis on visibility (and its corollary, pride) as a liberatory strategy prevalent in identity discourses, it is not self-evident why so many of these films decline (or neglect) to articulate a clear queer/Jewish positionality. However, identity politics may not be the ideal frame to contextualize this phenomenon. The ambiguity of these films is not necessarily in direct response to, or strictly readable as a repudiation of, the demands of identity politics. Rather it evinces a more overarching ambivalence that may be seen as quite an apt expression of a queer Jewish positionality, given the categorical crisis that both the queer and the Jew pose for modernity, as the following discussion indicates.

British sociologist Zygmunt Bauman has identified Jewishness as categorically ambivalent within modernity, contending first and foremost that Jews are "indefinable by definition."[11] Bauman explains that, in Christian religious terms, the Jew is long obsolete yet (unfathomably) not extinct. In social terms of the Christian West, the Jew is the perennial stranger, never fully belonging anywhere yet present everywhere. In the categorical terms of (secular Christian) modernism, "Jews mean the impossibility of order."[12] Given what Bauman considers modernity's "obsessive preoccupation with ordering," the Jew stands out as a painful and unwelcome reminder of the impossibility of the ordering conceit.[13] The Jew does not fit easily into established categories (already, if cursorily, rehearsed in this chapter) of nation, race, class, and, at least in the Western cultural imaginary of the late nineteenth century, gender and sexuality.

Although Bauman never writes about homosexuality (or sexuality at all), I shall extrapolate his insights to render a relevant rejoinder to his assertion that "Jews are unlike all others."[14] Without considering the condition of homosexuality within modern Western paradigms, Bauman can find it easy to declare the Jews unlike all others. Yet, if the ambivalence represented and inspired by the position occupied by the Jews in Western culture has to do with national, cultural, racial (and gendered and sexual) indeterminacy, as he claims, then in fact there is one other like the Jews. Queers too cross national, racial, cultural, gendered, and of course sexual boundaries and incite similar ambivalence and, to understate the case considerably, indignation within the dominant culture.

The question (to which I return repeatedly in this chapter) begs to be asked: even if this parallel is so, why do contemporary queer Jews tend to self-represent in ambiguous terms? It is one thing to be identified by others or within a cultural context as ambivalent; it is quite another to self-identify, and perform a representation of oneself, in a manner rife with ambiguity. To do so can too readily be seen as evidence of (queer) Jewish self-hatred, of the type that Sander Gilman writes about. But the ambivalence can also be read as an unconscious symptom of a cultural positionality or indeed the performance of a prescribed role. It is fair to say, especially in light of the theme of ambiguity, that such self-identificatory schemes are generally unintentional (that is to say, unclear or ambiguous even to the filmmaker). Ambiguity of cultural as well as sexual indicators is, appropriately enough, never overtly thematized in the films discussed here. Nonetheless, when writing about queer Jewish self-representational strategies in these films, it becomes unavoidably apparent that Jewishness and/or queerness are very nearly elided in some cases, avoided in others, minimally addressed in still others, and in uneasy collusion in the remainder. If one identity (queer, for instance) is loudly proclaimed, it may at times follow that the other is just as "loudly" suppressed. If both are proclaimed loudly, as in *Cheap Philosophy*, the result is very nearly a shouting match. Thus ambiguity and ambivalence emerge as unavoidable themes in the discussion of the films in this chapter.

If ambiguity marks the expression of Jewish and queer identity in these texts, ambivalence marks my response. I find myself struggling to identify what (if anything) makes many of these films queer or Jewish. I am interested in, but frustrated by, the almost agnostic identity politics displayed in some of the films; not my patience but my attempt at interpretation often finds itself strained. Each film considered here (even the most explicit like *Treyf* or *Fast Trip*) can be said to be defined by a degree of indefinability or indeterminateness in queer/Jewish terms, thus approximating Bauman's definition of Jewishness, and mine of homosexuality, in filmic form. I consider issues of tradition, religion, Jewish continuity, visibility politics, and assimilation in terms of the complex and generally elusive ambiguous and ambivalent approaches of the filmmakers; toward the end of the chapter, in an extended consideration of Gregg Bordowitz's

Fast Trip, Long Drop, I explore the ways that the ambivalent trope of the pathological Jew has been appropriated and rearranged to create new sets of ambivalences and ambiguities, this time from an insider perspective.

A particularly vexing example of cultural indeterminateness can be found in the otherwise extraordinary autobiographical tour de force that is Jonathan Caouette's *Tarnation.* This film is as explicitly queer as they come, with the autobiographical protagonist performing flawless drag at the age of twelve and seamlessly integrating his long-term boyfriend as the one stable element into an otherwise vertiginously nonnormative narrative. Queerness is the grounding on which the narrative and formal excesses of the text alight after their dizzying forays into the wilderness of family dysfunction. In a film that matches the instability *in* the text with the instability *of* the text, a film where almost nothing is too outrageous or excessive to mention or depict, a film that leaves no personal boundaries uncrossed, there seems only one element of the filmmaker's identity that, although hinted at, remains almost entirely un(re)marked. Viewers may forgive themselves for overlooking a brief, one-second shot of a family photo of Caouette's grandparents' wedding, where we see the groom wearing a Yarmulke. The photo flashes by so quickly that one almost wonders whether it was imagined. A full three-quarters of the way into the film, in one of Caouette's mother's many seemingly interminable, incoherent rants, soon after she has suffered irreversible brain damage from an accidental lithium overdose, she is filmed singing the first stanza of the Sabbath morning prayer, Ein Keloheinu, in Hebrew. This Jewish moment flashes by almost as quickly as the first and, for those unacquainted with the Sabbath service, might not seem extraordinary. The moment could be simply another arbitrary and disconnected memory shard from a shattered mind, a fragment picked up along the tortured and twisted road of life too full of strange and disturbing details to notice. Or, if one thought further, one might decide that here was a song taught her by a fellow mental-health patient while she was institutionalized, or perhaps a legacy from a Jewish ex-boyfriend. More likely, considering the range of random outbursts emanating from this highly unstable character, one might think nothing of the song at all. Yet, for those viewers who recognize the prayer, it is nothing short of astounding to hear it come out of the mother's mouth, as it is a prayer that one would only know if one was raised going to synagogue regularly—a not entirely minor detail otherwise elided in the film. Nothing else, not even the fleeting yarmulke, prepares us for this Jewish moment, one that indicates considerable immersion in and identification with Judaism (not just with the culture but with the religion). This Texas family is so well integrated into lower-middle-class

Christian-American culture that news of its Jewishness comes as a jolt more stupefying than all the years of the mother's shock therapy. How to reconcile this moment with the opening shot of the mother, wearing a cross and singing a hymn to Jesus? How to account for what clearly must have been a Jewish upbringing, when no other signs of cultural immersion are available? This late and latent surprise in the film may prick a memory of the earlier skullcap in the wedding photo, yet both shots are so thoroughly out of context that they only add up to two errant blips on the cultural meter, easier to forget than to make sense of. Caouette offers no explanation. No mention is made of either Jewish moment, or indeed of Caouette's own Jewishness, in interviews with the filmmaker or on his Web site—or in any but three (as of this writing) of the many reviews of this, his only film to date. In this film that thematizes excess, there is still an unassimilable remainder, an excess to exceed all excess, an ambivalence that cannot be explained—Jewishness.

Novaczek's films force the issue of visibility, though, as already suggested, this does not necessarily lead to any kind of thorough (or even partial) integration of identities. *Cheap Philosophy*, like *Tarnation*, is an unstable text, and, with the filmmaker playing at least twelve different but interrelated characters, it is a film driven by the illogic of a multiply split personality. Each of the personae (all named Esther Kahn) is a familiar if idiosyncratic type that fills the viewer with a mixture of amusement and trepidation, as Novaczek treads deliriously close to the bygone dreaded figures of the imaginary queer and the Jewish sociopath. The characters,

Ruth Novaczek as alter ego Esther Kahn, playing her character, the Tragic Opera Singer, in *Cheap Philosophy*.

who often speak as if giving an account of hostile lovers' exchanges, include: the suffering opera singer ("She said, 'What are your hobbies?' I said, 'Suffering, opera singing. Suffering, opera singing. Smoking'"); the seventeenth-century kabbalist ("I said, 'You cannot possibly accompany me on this journey'"); the psychopathic (American) analysand ("I wish you were dead. I wish I were dead. I wish my parents were dead. I told this to the therapist. She didn't think it was funny"); the not much saner French/Israeli Mai '68 analyst ("It's more complex than that, and you know it"); the "I'm OK, You're OK" revolutionary ("Change, Progress, Revolution"); the baseball-hat-wearing lesbian ("Don't you call me neurotic"), the tragic Tennessee Williams character ("I have a bad case of Stanley Kowalski and Blanche Dubois"); the Yeshiva boy/girl ("Everything is governed by laws"); and more. Some of the characters are more identifiably Jewish than others, some more identifiably lesbian; all ride the edge of social acceptability. Esther Kahn, Novaczek told me, "has a multiple personality disorder and likes dressing up." And, of course, Esther Kahn is Novaczek, sitting in her apartment alone with a camera, some wigs, and four blank walls.

Novaczek's play with lesbian types mixes a well-worn feminine romanticism ("Of course I believe in that true love shit") with an uncomfortable and unwelcome violence that lurks just under the surface and erupts at sudden moments ("My mother's a bitch, so is my lover"; "Yes, it's Armani, secondhand. My girlfriend tore the top button off when she was trying to strangle me"). Her Jewish types verge on internalized anti-Semitism ("She said, 'You're a living anachronism. You know, like all the rest of you. You didn't accept Christ, why should you accept the contemporary approach to existence?'"), of which Novaczek says some uncomprehending critics have accused her. In the end of the film she deliberates between identifying as "just another disillusioned Jewish lesbian alcoholic" and identifying simply as a neurotic. The choice is a dubious one, yet this is her precarious visibility strategy. When asked directly about her dangerous flirtation with stereotypes and her ambivalent representational strategies, she says she embraces the stereotype "because I really think that that's how people see us," but she then returns with another question, saying, "But also, how else do you make us visible? What do we do with visibility?" Visibility here is necessarily a reduction, a shorthand, an unavoidable oversimplification that is nonetheless meant to bring with it an embrace of difference. How this will happen is left an open question.

The play of types, the embrace of difference, the multiple personalities: it is all a monologue, addressed as much to the filmmaker as to her imaginary audience. Like Sadie Benning's early Pixelvision work, made around the same time, this low-tech video was shot in a room with no witnesses, no crew, no community. It is an internal performance for an audience of one, the camera lens playing the eye of the filmmaker's I. This is an autoplay, staged for the self, exploring the contradictions of an identity that switches and swaps but never resolves into a coherent whole. If this is visibility, what precisely is seen? A highly conflicted and contradictory (i.e., ambivalent) character, an amalgam of types, a chameleon; a lesbian whose neuroses keep her from love and intimacy; a tragic Jewess out of sync with the times. There is no redemption and no relief in these ambivalent characters, no way to smooth their edges or make them more socially adept. They occupy an indeterminate space (an ambivalence, if you will), falling through the cracks of a positive identity politics.

It should be reiterated that not every film discussed in this chapter is equally elusive or ambivalent on the subject of its queer and/or Jewish identifications. As noted earlier, Bordowitz's *Fast Trip* is, on the contrary, quite forthright about its identifications; nevertheless, Bordowitz's particular self-representational strategies reveal further complication, wherein the representation of the queer Jewish male begs to be read in terms set out by nineteenth- and early-twentieth-century anti-Semitic discourses. As with *Cheap Philosophy,* this film reveals another type of ambivalence, another remainder that exceeds the terms of rational discourse and instead relies on the highly charged connotative discourse of stereotype and innuendo. The late-nineteenth- and early-twentieth-centuries' linkages between Jewishness and a venerable host of disorders ranging from vices and diseases to overt criminality have been duly documented in the genealogical work of several prominent scholars, among them Sander Gilman, Daniel Boyarin, Jay Geller, Ann Pellegrini, and Daniel Itzkovitz.[15]

Before turning to the nineteenth-century resonances in Bordowitz's film, however, I attend to the more apparent contradiction in the clash between religion and sexual identity, as I trace the way Jewish tradition presses uncomfortably on some of these works.

▶

Traditional Tensions

One might expect that at least some of the queer Jewish first person films made in the past fifteen years would make some reference to Judaism, the religion. With the exception of *Treyf,* none of the films in this chapter, nor any others that I know of to date, chooses to explore a queer Jewish religious identity or even to consider ways in which Judaism (Jewish law and custom) impacts on queer Jewish lives, or vice versa.[16] Of course there have been several nonautobiographical films to do so, most prominently Sandi DuBowski's *Trembling Before G-d* (2001) and the Israeli production *Keep Not Silent* (2004), by Ilil Alexander. In *Treyf,* Cynthia Madansky and I come close to articulating a position on religion, only to eventually offer a secular definition of our Jewishness that does not require us to integrate Jewish religious teachings and practices into our decidedly nontraditional lives. Rather than twisting ourselves into halakhic knots to fit an image of a pious, though still queer, Jew, we choose to twist the boundaries of Jewishness around to allude to its porous limits.[17] Thus, when Alisa sits in Katz's, the "kosher style" delicatessen in the formerly Jewish Lower East Side, with an unkosher though Jewishly identifiable corned beef sandwich on rye placed tantalizingly before me, I ask defiantly, "Who gets to say what's treyf? Who's treyf? We're all treyf." "Treyf," the word that signifies that which is not halakhically kosher (and that has often been informally extrapolated, as in this case, to refer to a broader categorical repudiation of all that lies outside the bounds of Jewish "taste"), becomes instead the signifier of a Jewish brand of resistance ("kosher style"). The concept of treyf (discussed in chapter 3) is invoked here as a type of border identity, an ambivalence, where one both is and is not fully identified with the communal identity *Jewish.* Or, as Simone de Beauvoir phrased it, "To put oneself 'outside' is still a way of living the inescapable fact that one is inside."[18]

Even if religion per se is scarcely thematized in the films considered here, tradition remains a forcefield to be navigated through or steered around. In many films by self-defined gays and lesbian secular Jews, tradition often finds its embodied signifier in the figure of the grandmother; the bobe film can almost be considered a subgenre of Jewish gay and lesbian autobiographical film.[19] As discussed in chapter 2, Jan Oxenberg's *Thank You and Goodnight* clings to the memory of the grandmother as if for dear life because, at least in part, she represents what appears the last remnant of Jewish tradition in the family. Oxenberg insists on extricating the grandmother's culinary secrets, a gustatory synecdoche for traditional Jewish life. She persists even as her grandmother fades in and out of consciousness, desperate to eke out one more Jewish recipe before her grandmother's final fade to black. The remarkable thing is that, even semiconscious and crippled with pain as the grandmother is, she does remember her recipes, signifying that she is indeed the proverbial conduit of tradition, requiring neither sound mind nor sound body to reproduce and transmit it. Oxenberg's salvage impulse, trying to ensure that some symbolic traditions are passed on even as their human embodiment passes away; is not entirely successful.[20]

The grandmother ultimately succumbs to her pain and is unable to continue her cooking lesson, signifying a rupture in Jewish cultural continuity. One wonders why Oxenberg even pursues these cooking lessons—why, in fact, she is so nostalgic about her grandmother's cooking. In a scene where she, or rather her alter ego, Jannie, remembers and somehow (mysteriously) reproduces her grandmother's delicacies (*cholent, tsimes,* chicken soup), the memory is always marred by one unpleasant and unavoidable detail: the ubiquitous carrot. In nearly every dish her grandmother made, carrots were a prominent ingredient, to the apparent dismay of her granddaughter. Even in the mist of rhapsodic reminiscence, the carrot protrudes (literally, sticking out in each of the re-created dishes) as a red (or orange) flag of ambivalence. The memory that the filmmaker holds so dear and the tradition that she longs to resuscitate are rife with reminders that in fact this tradition does not entirely suit her taste. But, as a gesture toward continuity, the life-giving implications of cooking replace the more common link to Jewish continuity, procreation, which is notably absent from this filmmaker's set of concerns.

The pursuit of tradition in this film seems to require the virtual erasure of any reference to the filmmaker protagonist's sexuality. It is as if the grandma (as embodied tradition) and *lesbian* (as embodied rupture of tradition) must never explicitly coexist in the frame. If Jan can be in the frame, she can do so only if she remains in the closet. Her silence on the issue of sexuality in this film indicates that the grandma may never have known that Oxenberg was a lesbian. She repeatedly asks about Jan's marital status, wanting to know when (if ever) Jan will get married and give her grandmother a measure of (traditionally codified) pleasure.[21] If the film is attenuated in its representation of Jewish cultural signifiers (as described in chapter 2), sexuality is almost totally occluded. The embrace of tradition in the limited arena of food seems to allow no room for exploration, or even explanation or articulation, of untraditional sexuality; the cooking lessons operate as a surrogate (though abortive) offering of continuity—and here we may see the ambivalence toward the protruding carrot cast in a slightly different light: its unwelcome and inflamed tumescence may signal another undesired signifier. Suffice it to say that sometimes a carrot is not just a carrot.

Akerman's self-portrait, *Chantal Akerman by Chantal Akerman,* is, like Oxenberg's film, more explicitly engaged with her relationship to tradition than with representing her sexuality. Sexuality in Akerman's films is addressed through the inclusion of a few scenes where Akerman's protagonists seem to long for other women, as in the protracted dance scene from *Portrait of a Young Girl at the End of the 1960s in Brussels*

(1993), where the lead character is clearly and touchingly infatuated with her best friend, but other scenes are included in this compilation self-portrait in which Akerman's alter egos have sex with men, creating an uncertainty about her sexual identification. Akerman is well-known for her unwillingness to be seen as a "lesbian filmmaker," routinely denying gay and lesbian film festivals the opportunity to screen her films (with the notable exception of *Portrait of a Young Girl*) and refusing to discuss her sexuality in interviews. Her reasons, though unstated, are presumably less about personal ambiguity than about the professional placement of her work. Yet in the context of other queer Jewish work, her evasiveness seems to fit.

Tradition, too, is represented somewhat ambivalently in *Chantal Akerman by Chantal Akerman,* but it does emerge as a surprisingly frequent subtext. The film is composed of two parts. The first is an onscreen monologue, delivered by Akerman directly to the camera, that gives the barest biographical details while revealing a tremendous amount about her idiosyncratic way of thinking and her minimalist (sometimes even anti-) aesthetic.[22] The second part comprises a reassembly of scenes from the films of her oeuvre, creating (as indicated in chapter 1) a portrait of the artist *as* her work. In this formally nontraditional "compilation autobiography," a concern with tradition emerges, in four distinct ways. The first is, as with Oxenberg's film, through the figure of the grandmother, who apparently was a traditional woman in every respect except one: she was a large-format portraitist of women's faces, a portraitist whose legacy, Akerman implies, lives on in her granddaughter's films. The second manifestation of a concern with tradition is Akerman's revisiting of the introduction to her film *American Stories,* wherein Akerman's voice-over laments the loss of traditional engagement in her own life by invoking a Jewish parable that nonetheless allows that even without the substance of tradition, connection to the spiritual core of that tradition remains strong.[23] The third manifestation is the recurrence in Akerman's work of the Second Commandment, the commandment that most closely ties the Jewish people to their God, and to which (see chapter 1) Akerman adheres in spirit but not in letter.[24] The fourth manifestation is in fact more enactment than concern: the reappearance and the affectionate rendering of the Jewish joke also quoted from *American Stories.* Jewish humor becomes a touchstone for a beloved and beleaguered sensibility, a shtetl gestalt. In truth, *Chantal Akerman by Chantal Akerman* does not feature the best of the Jewish jokes from *American Stories;* however, it is noteworthy that Akerman chooses to represent the less amusing, less endearing anecdotes in this reedited version. The traditional Jewish state of being represented in this self-portrait is, after all, that of memory and displacement. As demonstrated (at some length) in chapter 1, memory and displacement are central tropes in Akerman's own contemporary sense of her Jewishness. For those of us familiar with the original film, the funnier jokes are never far from memory; this mnemonic function transforms Akerman's work into a signifier of tradition, whereby we refer back to the earlier, more complete, and "authentic" work for the necessary resonances, just as, in the parable of the forest and the tree, the descendants of the rabbi had to recall the story of the prayer to retain their increasingly diluted connection to tradition.

At the end of this Jewish parable, Akerman adds an autobiographical note, still in voice-over, telling that not only does she no longer know the words of the prayer, or even the woods to pray in, but she does not have a child to pass the story on to. Thus she ruefully acknowledges that her life, as a nonprocreative Jew, represents a break with even the adulterated tradition that she has inherited. Although her (unstated) sexuality is not determinative of her childlessness (lesbians obviously retain the biological capacity to procreate, and indeed, increasingly, many are choosing to), her tone of regret and resignation inclines us to read a measure of remorse. With her interest in the past, the laws, the traditions and cultural mannerisms of her people, she paradoxically represents both a link to and a rupture with Judaism—an ambivalent gesture, to be sure. The continuity that she (along with Oxenberg and the rest of the filmmakers discussed in this chapter) offers, implicitly and by example, is through creativity rather than procreativity. All these representations of a lost *yidishkayt* turn out to be as much these filmmakers' progeny as their patrimony. The filmmakers revive and revivify a discourse, give it life, and, in this gesture, offer their offspring, in the form of the films themselves, back to the community. But the anxiety over the potential rupture that homosexuality (signaled through childlessness) poses to the continuity of Jewish traditions is particularly evident here.

These films do not represent a traditional way of life, nor do the filmmakers harbor some nostalgic longing for the religious life of their youth (if they had it) or that of their ancestors. Neither Oxenberg nor Akerman, for instance, leads us to believe that the answer to their spiritual and cultural quandary is to return to traditional Judaism.[25] To reiterate the recurring question, in altered terms: why is it that these particular filmmakers seem unable to explore their questions regarding tradition in a way that is integrated or at least coeval with their identities and experiences as lesbians?

One likely answer is that the ability to integrate a lesbian or gay identity into daily life often entails a turn away from traditional Judaism. Yet consider too the proposition that there is an incompatibility among historical survival strategies that vie awkwardly for ascendancy in each of these films. In other words, these silences specifically relate to how each group has dealt with the necessity to negotiate visibility at different points in history. The question becomes which closet door, Jewish or queer, tends to remain shut, when, and why.[26]

Degrees of Visibility

For Jews, visibility, like continuity, is a concern that throughout the nineteenth and twentieth centuries and into the twenty-first has required, and may continue to require, vigilant monitoring and highly adaptable strategies. In *Treyf*, there is a scene where Cynthia Madansky and I are shown sitting on the floor, clipping a variety of newspaper articles having to do with Jews and Jewish culture. The voice-over is a kind of call-and-response between Madansky and myself, in which we articulate our inherited obsession with tracking and monitoring the treatment of the Jews in the mainstream press. We declare this an obsession, itself ambivalent, for we are never certain whether we approve of public acknowledgment of Jewish achievements and failures or whether the exposure is ultimately too menacing for comfort. Foucault's famous warning from *Discipline and Punish* comes to mind here, "Visibility is a trap."[27] The scene attempts to delineate the double bind of Jewish visibility with which most Jews in the Diaspora are all too familiar. I am not certain that, at

Clipping
Jewish-
themed
headlines
in *Treyf*.

least in Western Europe and the United States, gays and lesbians carry the same degree of Pavlovian paranoia (or pride, for that matter) when faced with the mention of their "own" in public. In part, this has to do with the senses of belonging distinct to each community. Gays and lesbians do not constitute a *people* in the way that Jews have historically understood themselves (and been understood) to be, and are only beginning, relatively speaking, to develop cultural inheritances that are being passed along to younger generations (in myriad ways—writing, film, cultural, social and political institutions, community organizations, Internet sites, etc.).

Yet surely the closet has historically required very sophisticated and elaborate mechanisms of partial and selective visibility for homosexuals. Even today, visibility means radically different things to different queers. A transsexual may aspire to undetectability of passing, either as a queer survival strategy or as an ideal success story, while radical anarchist queers may choose a visibility that brings them in line with a global anticapitalist movement in which sexual and gender politics are only one aspect of a broad political agenda. There are some important parallels to be drawn between many middle-class, mainstream gays and lesbians and some middle-class, mainstream Jews, both of whom hope to achieve "distinction without difference" (discussed in chapter 2), which would grant them the same rights, privileges, and access as their straight or non-Jewish counterparts.

Despite such examples, the main thrust of Western gay rights movements has been essentially to advance a queer visibility imperative. Visibility has been the major hue and cry of the U.S. and Western European gay and lesbian liberation movements since at least the 1980s, and coming out of the closet has signified the one imperative act in the struggle toward greater acceptance and empowerment. It has been widely and unquestioningly assumed that the making visible of the homosexual (whether in all or only in some of his or her permutations and variations) will indeed accomplish such acceptance and empowerment. Peggy Phelan was at the forefront of the politically engaged theorists who challenged this assumption, arguing that hegemonic power at its most consolidated and effective operates from an unmarked or invisible position, not in the full exposure of visibility.[28]

Looking from a Jewish historical perspective, one also approaches the question of visibility more gingerly, not so as to consolidate some (invisible) power, as the anti-Semites would have it, but rather from an awareness of the dangers and pitfalls of visibility, as reflected upon in *Treyf.* The matter has historically been cast less as a matter of personal moral integrity than as one of diasporic survival. Survival strategies have depended, at certain moments in history, on the ability to pass undetected.[29] This is

not necessarily an argument in favor of invisibility or unmarked assimilation strategies; think only of the fate of the most successfully assimilated
Jewish community in nineteenth- and twentieth-century Europe, the
German Jews. Yet it would seem that the lessons of Jewish ambivalence
about visibility, not to mention the ambivalence of Jewishness within the
context of Western culture, have had a determinative effect on the queer
Jewish films in this study. How else do we account for the extreme discretion of so many of the queer Jewish representations, flying in the face of
the "loud and proud" proclamations of the gay and lesbian movements?
There are three basic ways in which these queer Jewish first person films
resist, or only reluctantly conform to, the demands of visibility politics: one
identity is expressed at the expense of the other, as is the case in *Rootless
Cosmopolitans* and *Tarnation*; both identities are equally repressed, as in
the case of *Complaints of a Dutiful Daughter* (as discussed in the following pages); or, indeed, Jewishness or queerness constitutes an ambivalence
in and of itself, as in *Rootless Cosmopolitans* and *Fast Trip, Long Drop*.

I devote the rest of this chapter to discussing three of these films:
Deborah Hoffmann's *Complaints of a Dutiful Daughter,* Ruth Novaczek's
Rootless Cosmopolitans, and Gregg Bordowitz's *Fast Trip, Long Drop.*
First I address the ways in which Hoffmann's *Complaints* performs a
delicate and not always successful balancing act between Jewish and queer
visibility. Then, *Rootless Cosmopolitans* further complicates notions
of visibility by (re)introducing into the equation the notion of race—an
element long repressed in the popular Jewish imaginary yet still inherent
in coded allusions to Jewish difference. At this point, my discussion of
visibility opens up more fully to the repercussions of nineteenth-century
racializing and "perverse" categorizations of the Jew. *Rootless* then leads
into an extended consideration of a film that best exemplifies the multiple
intersections of nineteenth-century pathologizing discourses and contemporary queer Jewish self-representation, Gregg Bordowitz's *Fast Trip.*

Add Jewish and Stir

Hoffmann's film, about a daughter's struggle with her mother's advancing
Alzheimer's, was geared toward an audience concerned with Alzheimer's,
an audience imagined to be too general to sustain explicit reference to
either Jewish or lesbian identity. In an unpublished paper, Faye Ginsburg
recounts that Hoffmann only added what few explicit Jewish indicators
are present out of concern that her film would be excluded from the San
Francisco Jewish Film Festival. Apparently Janis Plotkin, the found-

ing director of this festival, had seen the rough cut and had reservations about including the film in the festival since it lacked explicit Jewish content.[30] An excerpt from an e-mail from Hoffmann to Ginsburg explains Hoffmann's thinking: "I had only two things left to do—reshoot the suitcase opening and closing and have the music composed. So I stuck the book [Abba Eban's] *The Story of the Jews* in the suitcase and I asked Mary Watkins—the African American very un-Jewish composer—if she could make the music a little Jewish. She did and I marched back to [Janis] with my Jewish movie and she took it."[31]

Hoffmann's strategy of "add Jewish and stir," to borrow and amend Gerda Lerner's famous phrase, is surprisingly effective. As Ginsburg notes, "These hints are subtle and so well placed that I thought that this must have been a well thought out strategy from the beginning."[32] In fact, Jewishness, we learn, is something of an afterthought in this film. For Hoffmann (and also perhaps for Jewish film festivals) it is possible to make a music score "a little Jewish" (whatever that might be) and have this carry the full weight of Jewish representation in the film: Jewishness as flavoring, atmosphere, spice.[33] An alternate interpretation is that, for Hoffmann, Jewishness is internal and in no need of visible representation except under duress (threat of exclusion from a film festival, for instance), in which case it can be hinted at subtly yet effectively. Pressure was needed for Hoffmann to Judaicize her film. And, as a German Jewish descendant in the Mendelsohnian tradition,[34] Hoffmann's response was to be extraordinarily discreet. One wonders what, if not Jewish, the film appeared to be before its modifications.[35]

In general, this film is not easily identifiable in Jewish terms yet could not ultimately be other than Jewish. Neither accent nor affect, content nor context, makes this film recognizably Jewish. The ambiguity of Jewish specificity in the film could perhaps itself be said to be a Jewish indicator, since assimilation has ensured that Jews occupy a cultural space that is frustratingly indeterminate, neither fully integrated nor wholly other. This ambiguity more than anything else may in fact qualify *Complaints* as a Jewish film. Bauman declares the central defining characteristics of both modern and postmodern Jewishness to be precisely its indefinability. Hoffmann's film instantiates this claim.

There are no Jewish accents, no Jewish expressions, no Jewish tshatshkes or trinkets, no Jewish neighbors, nothing reliably indicating the film's Jewishness, with the exception of the two aforementioned markers: the Judaicized sound track and one unambiguous visual—Eban's *My People: The Story of the Jews,* stuffed in a suitcase half-hidden under a pile of bananas. The metaphor deserves to be unpacked, as it were.

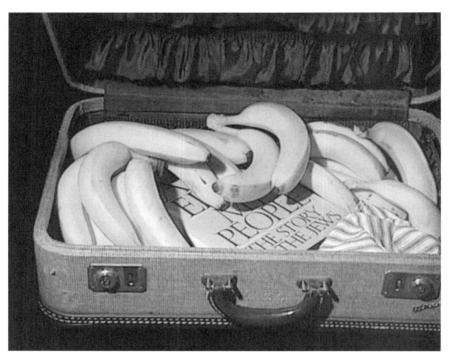

Unpacking Jewishness in *Complaints of a Dutiful Daughter.*

This suitcase segment of the film is the one period in her mother's illness that Hoffmann chooses to read symbolically. The other periods, all marked by excessive repetition of some activity or behavior (such as "the banana period," where Doris Hoffmann is said to have consumed untold numbers of bananas, having forgotten that she had just eaten one, or "the podiatrist period," where Doris repeatedly shows up for a podiatrist appointment she does not have) seem simply to indicate the mother's mental decay, whereas the suitcase period constitutes for Deborah a signal from her mother that she wants to move out of her apartment. In the scene, Hoffmann splices shots of the same suitcase magically opening and closing, each time to reveal new and unexpected contents. The cuts are supposed to be seamless and the contents are meant to reflect the arbitrariness of the mother's frenzied activity. In a feat of low-budget movie magic, the suitcase opens to reveal a box of Lorna Doone cookies nearly covered with wire clothes hangers, then closes, and then opens to reveal an eclectic assortment of household items: a phone, a boot, three forks, one lightbulb, a teacup. The third opening reveals one banana, a small bowl, a black-and-white photograph of Einstein, and a white carnation. Although Einstein can be read as an oblique moment of affinity with another German Jew (one whom, in fact, Hoffmann's mathematician father is said to have worked with and subsequently become biographer for), the symbolism in the next opening is more overt. With this fourth opening, we see the film's single most unambiguous Jewish referent, the Eban book. The book's title is barely decipherable, as it is virtually smothered in bananas. The prior mess of wire hangers is, in a visual rhyme, here echoed with bananas while the suitcase duplicates a portable closet in which to hide, yet coyly reveal, Jewishness. Bananas are not only a period in the filmmaker's mother's mental decline, but also a symbol of insanity ("She's gone bananas!")—as if to say, just beneath this madness there lies a hidden Jewishness. If only the madness could be lifted off, removed, then Hoffmann's mother's Jewishness (along with the rest of her lost identity) could emerge. This detail is telling, considering the lack of explicit Jewish reference in the film. Clearly this "Jewish moment" does not quite amount to Jewish visibility politics; rather, the visibility politics of the gesture are muted, at best.

Hoffmann is less obscure when it comes to outing herself in the film as a lesbian, though apparently she was considerably more reluctant. In reference to the moment in the film that actually names Hoffmann as a lesbian (in the scene that immediately precedes the magic suitcase), we learn, from an article that Hoffmann had to be coaxed and cajoled into retaining the scene. Without it, the film would have simply appeared a thoughtful if quirky personal account of a daughter dealing with a parent who has Alzheimer's. Including this scene meant challenging an implicit heteronormativity and the assumption that sexuality has no place in a film about Alzheimer's. It meant confronting those interested in Alzheimer's, asking them to consider and sympathize with another, seemingly unrelated, concern: homophobia. Presumably it would have been easy to make the film without reference to lesbianism, but, Hoffmann tells us, neither her mother nor her editor would allow this. Hoffmann says: "So here I am, making a film that would appeal to people who don't usually see films I work on. And yet, my mother kept looking at Frances [Reid, Deborah's lover and cinematographer] and saying Frances' name. She insisted Frances be in the film, basically. So I had to decide: am I going to throw this monkey wrench into this nice, middle-American subject of Alzheimer's? Suddenly, it's a gay film."[36]

Apparently, Jennifer Chimlund, Hoffmann's heterosexual editor, had to hold the closet door open while Hoffmann debated how to proceed: "Jennifer was the one who really insisted when I would get cold feet. 'No, you really have to put this in,' she'd say. And she's right."[37]

Given these accounts, it would seem that Hoffmann, left to her own devices, might have tried to represent herself as a de-ethnicized and desexualized subject, one not entirely unlike her post-Alzheimer's mother, who lives her life without reference to, or encumbrance by, the compromising contingencies created by identificatory regimes. The difference, of course, is that for Deborah Hoffmann identity is sustained by memory, something on which her mother can no longer rely. Here, it emerges that identification is based on a self-conception that requires memory to be meaningful; as discussed in chapter 2, conscious subjectivity relies on memory for its constitution. Hoffmann's mother is beyond subjectivity, having no reliable reference for her own self-conception, and requiring none for those around her. Hoffmann reads her mother's newly found, post-Alzheimer's, acceptance of Frances and consequently of Deborah's lesbianism as revealing the baselessness of homophobia;[38] I tend to disagree with Hoffmann's assessment here. Rather, Alzheimer's reveals that prejudice as well as identification requires, at base, the capacity to remember (who one is and what one believes). When prompted, Hoffmann does consistently choose to remember to identify (as Jewish and lesbian), albeit somewhat reluctantly. It is to her credit, I believe, that she ultimately realizes the value of "throw[ing] a monkey wrench into this nice middle-America[n world]," but it seems that this projected image of her middle-American audience has contributed greatly to the ambiguities and repressions of identification in her film.

▶
_____

Fin-de-Siècle Queer Jews

If Hoffmann's strategies in *Complaints* reveal ambivalences in her identifications, then *Rootless Cosmopolitans* and *Fast Trip, Long Drop* reveal more profoundly ambivalent representational strategies. These two films awaken, like few others I have seen, disturbing nineteenth-century associations between the Jew and the homosexual, two bogeys of the Western European imaginary that began to appear at the same historical juncture. Writing about the rise of political anti-Semitism in late-nineteenth-century Europe, Hannah Arendt perspicaciously makes the connection between the precarious social position of the newly emancipated Jew and that of the homosexual. Apparently, for a brief time in the salons of Faubourg Saint-Germain, it was considered fashionable to be Jewish and/or an "invert." Arendt finds these linkages in the singular figure of Proust. Proust, she believes, "was a true exponent of this society, for he was involved in both of its most fashionable 'vices': the 'vice' of Jewishness and the 'vice' of homosexuality, and which in their reflection and individual reconsideration became very much alike indeed."[39] Since both were conceived of as vices, and vices were generally seen as "an inherent, psychological quality which man [sic] cannot choose or reject but which is imposed upon him from without, and which rules him as compulsively as the drug rules the addict," the immutable conditions of both Jewishness and homosexuality were nonetheless subject to the rapidly changing winds of prevailing social mores. Tolerance or embrace were merely the flip sides of repression and persecution, as they each depended on the current cultural attitude toward "vice." In short order, the image of the "invert" could (and often did) convert from social butterfly to social reprobate, and that of the Jew from welcome guest to inveterate traitor—or as Arendt would have it, from pariah to parvenu, or vice versa. Neither Jews nor homosexuals had any recourse through which to defend themselves or hold their ground. Arendt suggests that this condition of partial or qualified acceptance led to:

> a complicated game of exposure and concealment, of half-confessions and lying distortions, of exaggerated humility and exaggerated arrogance, all of which were consequences of the fact that only one's Jewishness (or homo-sexuality) had opened the doors of the exclusive salons, while at the same time they made one's position extremely insecure. In this equivocal situation, Jewishness was for the individual Jew at once a physical stain and a mysteri-ous personal privilege, both inherent in a "racial predestination."[40]

It is the vexed question of Jewish and queer visibility and racialization raised by Arendt that Ruth Novaczek engages as a key theme in her experimental film *Rootless Cosmopolitans. Rootless Cosmopolitans,* like the previously discussed *Cheap Philosophy,* is a peripatetic film with a short attention span, jumping distractedly from one character type to the next, though in this film none of the parts are played by Novaczek herself. The loose nar-rative (if there can be said to be one) is of two Jewish women, one loud and unapologetic about her Jewishness and her lesbianism (Lilly Klein), the other more repressed and awkward (Estelle Levine), who meet and become close.[41] They fall in love, much to the surprise of the latter, who expects to be em-barrassed by Lilly's overt Jewishness but is instead comforted by it. We learn all this from a choppy voice-over that, along with scraps of images and some imagination on the part of the viewer, fills out the tale. The editing style, as in all of Novaczek's work, has a cyclical, fragmentary pacing, returning to recurring themes while consistently disrupting any fluid identification with characters or ideas. Her films are made up of many bits and shards, broken up and put back together with a sense of timing that Novaczek calls "Mosaic," clearly punning on the proper and common meanings of the noun. This Jewish mosaic wants nothing more than to bring all of the bro-ken, disenfranchised, alienated people back in frame, in a kabbalistic version of tikkun, though the film seems to accept that fragmentation and gaps will remain and *wholeness* will continue to elude.[42]

Even the title of the film harkens back to a late-nineteenth-century and early-twentieth-century euphemism for Jews that references their displacement and their difference, their "not quite belonging." Jon Stratton quotes Timothy Brennan as saying, "'Any student of the late nineteenth and early twentieth centuries is aware that 'cosmopolitan' was a code word in Eastern Europe for the Jew, where rootlessness was a condemnation and a proof of non-belonging.'"[43] Long left to lie fallow, the claim of Jewish national and racial difference is raised in Novaczek's work with a critical and knowing difference, in that she embraces it with pride. Breaking the unspoken pact of silence among British Jews, Novaczek in effect wants to proclaim and reclaim Jewish alterity, specifically in the form of racialized difference, not as a stigma but as a link to other nonwhite identities and a way to disidentify from the hegemonic whiteness with which Jews had eagerly, and, to her mind, problematically, come to be thoroughly identified.[44] Recognizing racialized Jewish difference—i.e., recognizing Jews as nonwhite—is seen by Novaczek as a way to forge ties with other nonhegemonic identity formations. Jewish identification with whiteness and dominant cultural values in England is explicitly challenged in her work. Her defiance helps to bring the contours of British Jewish assimilatory strategies (elocution classes, emphasis on decorum, etc.) into relief, whether or not it may bridge cultural differences or create alliances.[45]

In a key scene in *Rootless Cosmopolitans* where Jewish alterity is played out through discourses of race, a little girl in a frilly party dress dances daintily and playfully for the camera. We first see her immediately following a scene where a classically Jewish-looking Lilly Klein (played by nonactress, and friend of the filmmaker, Vicki Klein) has a non-sync-sound (the entire film is non-sync), somewhat pedantic discussion with her black friend Inez (played by filmmaker Inge Blackman, also a friend of Novaczek's) precisely about Jewishness, race, and Jewish alliances/identifications with nonwhites, a subject to which Novaczek is always attentive. Lilly notes that she has never felt white and has never been accepted as white. Inez affirms a connection with Jews, but admits that there is a sense of betrayal when Jews can and do accede to white privilege. The lack of synchronization between sound and image contributes to a sense of the incongruity of the two characters' words and experiences. Something does not jibe, and it would seem to be the incommensurability of the two women's experiences as nonwhite. The parallels are compelling but not convincing. Lilly's lament is a familiar theme in Novaczek's work, and it is a position with which Novaczek is thoroughly identified.[46]

Novaczek is not satisfied with this fitful and unresolved discussion, and the incommensurability seems to leave her (typically) restless. She attempts to resolve it in the following scene, as she abruptly cuts to a little, nameless, mixed-race girl prancing out of what appears to be a kosher butcher shop, holding a woman's hand that we presume to be her (white) mother's. We hear a young girl's voice on the sound track. She tells us how much she loves being Jewish. The girl's appearance is racially indistinct, perhaps black and Jewish, her figure tying the discourses of Jewish racial difference and indifference to a concrete point. Suddenly too, broader racial discourses of the nineteenth and twentieth centuries begin to resonate, with this body standing in for the Jew as feminine and not (quite) white, a status always suspected (if not stated outright) by anti-Semites all along but rarely instantiated in Jewish self-representation.[47] For Novaczek, Jewish identity is inevitably and implicitly racialized, having more in common with the colonized and the oppressed than with the privileges of whiteness. The girl is a poignant repository for these weighty histories because she carries little else. Her speaking role (in voice-over) is perfunctory and deceptively uncomplicated. She functions here more as a visual symbol, a Rorschach test upon which we may project the full force of identity claims and their attendant anxieties. The signs of her body are not yet even remotely within her performative control. For Novaczek, she is innocence incarnate, yet what we see of her is our own *vorschrift* (pretext), written, without the girl's consent, on her body. She stands in as the filmmaker's preferred rendition of the Jewish self—relieved of its power and white-skinned privilege. With this and the previous scene, *Rootless Cosmopolitans* indulges the belief that Jewish victimization and ambiguous racial attribution mitigate any privileges experienced (through passing) as whites, a fact qualifying Jews to unreservedly and unapologetically (re)join the ranks of the oppressed. The little girl here signifies, in short, the desire to project an idealized, subaltern image upon an unsullied tabula rasa.

In the collapse of black and Jew, Jewish visibility is highlighted as the problematic and ultimately unstable signifier that it is. Of course, in the Manichean order of today's postcolonial Britain, this little girl can be black, the film wants to say, but can she be Jewish? What does a Jew look like? Like her and not like her. The ambivalence of Jewish looks is foregrounded in this casting choice that flows both with and against type. Late-nineteenth-century writings ascribe "Negroid" features and dark skin to the Jew, while late-twentieth-century Western assumptions about the Jew are equally suspect and erroneous, in coding the Jew simply and unproblematically as white.[48] This returns us to Bauman's point, made earlier, about the disorderly Jew, perennially resistant to categorization

Lily as tabula rasa in *Rootless Cosmopolitans*. Photograph copyright © 1989 by Chris Jordan.

and epitomizing ambivalence. As Jon Stratton has said, "For the Jews, whiteness itself is the ambiguous category."[49] Differently put, Jewish racial indeterminacy unhinges simplistic racial binaries and throws the entire taxonomic project of race into question.

Novaczek plays with the desire and impossibility of exposing or revealing a quintessentially Jewish physiognomy. As discussed earlier, she often works in stereotypes, because, as she told me, she believes that in a visual medium one must be visibly identifiable.[50] This statement points as much to the limitations of the visual medium as to its strengths or demands. Novaczek's own looks are not classically Jewish (nor easily classifiable as lesbian, for that matter). She often casts her straight-haired, aquiline-nosed, green-eyed self as her starring Jew, or Jewish star (usually through necessity, as her budgets are virtually nonexistent). Yet she has as frequently cast the archetypal Jewess, with corkscrew-curly brown hair, brown eyes, a big nose, olive skin, and hyperanimated facial expressions and hand gestures. A Jew, that is, looks like Novaczek and not like Novaczek. The figure of the black Jewish child takes these associations about Jewish physiognomy a step further, ultimately asserting many things at once: Jews are black; blacks are Jews; and, Jews are neither black nor white. The alliances shift and the ambivalence of racialized Jewishness within the body politic comes to the fore.

Although Novaczek blatantly disregards the unwritten code of Jewish assimilation (most stringently adhered to in England, it would seem), which is to avoid calling attention to one's difference from the dominant (white, Christian) culture, she is not nearly as disruptive in her queer representation. In *Rootless,* she constructs a narrative of two Jewish women friends that has homoerotic overtones, yet their bond is unnamed and remains unexplored. It is rather reminiscent of a visual from another of her films, *Let Them Eat Soup* (1993), where two naked Barbie dolls float in a tub of water, orbiting each other without ever looking or touching. Yet Novaczek has made films where lesbian desire is made explicit (in words, at least), though generally in terms of rejection and loss, eulogizing a relationship or lamenting love gone wrong.[51] As intimated at the beginning of this chapter, queerness and Jewishness don't entirely get on in her work, as much as she might want them to.

What we have seen in Novaczek's work is an ardent commitment to visibility that is nonetheless ambivalent in its representation of the Jewish lesbian. In Gregg Bordowitz's film *Fast Trip, Long Drop,* we see further and more elaborate ambivalences. Even more than Novaczek, and perhaps as a testament to his brash New Yorker persona, Bordowitz proclaims his queer and Jewish affinities and affiliations prominently. Yet it can easily be said that *Fast Trip* is a deeply ambivalent text, and even that its ambivalences are discernable in the formal register. Bordowitz claims to have been inspired by Brechtian notions of defamiliarization, and that the structure of *Fast Trip* mimics the disconcerting and discontinuous experience of channel surfing, alighting briefly and then switching modes, borrowing from a host of televisual styles: from TV talk show to news to public service announcement.[52] Bordowitz was committed to "mobilizing doubt" in the service of what he calls, following Abraham Heschel, "radical wonder." He acknowledges his resistance to easy categorizations, something Bauman would argue is already implicit in the subject matter of the work, yet Bordowitz actively emphasizes that as "soon as an identity claim was advanced" in the film, it would be immediately "canceled by the following assertion."[53] About *Fast Trip*, he writes that "the emotional cues were inconclusive, hybrid. Emotional confusion opens up the possibility for a new landscape of affects, a terrain of unexplored sensations." Hybridity and inconclusiveness are thus, to invoke Bordowitz again, "conceptual motors" for this piece.[54]

Symptomatic ambiguities abound. Is the piece film or video?[55] Is it political commentary or political comedy? Is it documentary or mockumentary? Actors in the film play themselves and other characters, enticing with the codes of documentary veracity only to toy with our expectations when people both are and are not who we expect them to be. Bordowitz's own subjectivity is multiply split, creating layers of ambiguity. He relies at times on an unproblematized "I," who is sick in bed with a fever, has friends, attends HIV-positive support groups, has a mother and stepfather in Long Island, and who claims to want to be "in control of his own narrative," yet he plays several characters, for whom the only consistent throughline is presumably HIV. In the film, Bordowitz (as "himself") comes out as a gay-identified bisexual, refusing to concede to the social demand of choosing between the sexual binaries heterosexual and homosexual except for political expediency. He also plays several personas in the piece, such as the young politician making a parodic stump speech, dressed identically to Bordowitz's younger activist self as seen in archival footage of ACT-UP demonstrations. There is the driving-school Bordowitz, whose friends play his interchangeable driving instructor as they spout pretentious pre-scripted lines about God's nonexistence and other metaphysical conundra. By far the most compelling and troubling alter ego in *Fast Trip*, though, is Alter Allesman; for now, suffice to say that there is no shortage of ambiguity in the film's makeup.[56]

In terms of visibility politics, *Fast Trip, Long Drop* emerges out of the AIDS-activist movement, for which visibility was more than a central tenet, it was a fine art. No oppositional activist movement in history has placed more emphasis on developing a coordinated visual presence, verging on what corporate PR people call *branding* (complete with ACT-UP's clearly identifiable logo), generating everything from posters, pins, and stickers to videos, street theater, billboards, subway, bus campaigns, and art shows, all combining to create what Douglas Crimp referred to as "AIDS demo/graphics" of world renown.[57] Bordowitz was one of the early members of the AIDS video-activist collective Testing the Limits, and after leaving the collective continued his video activism through his role first as the associate producer and later as the producer of *Living With AIDS,* a weekly cable television show committed to "giving a face" to AIDS. However, *Fast Trip* departs from many of the conventions and carefully conceived messages of AIDS-activist video. It is in fact an antidote to the heady optimism and forthright claims of those earlier agitational works. It is not visibility but complexity that Bordowitz insists upon. When his former AIDS-activist video partner, Jean Carlomusto, reviews footage they had shot from countless ACT-UP demonstrations, she articulates the dawning recognition that the footage has begun to feel more like a funeral dirge than a call to action. In this passage, Bordowitz affirms the existence and relevance of the actions (and their videotaped incarnation) but subtly shifts the tense of the address. No longer a present-tense demand for action and activism, the footage becomes, upon viewing, a past-tense reminiscence, the material record of a bitter chapter in history. Visibility is relegated to an account recorded for posterity, not an activist sign of the changing of the times. And, rather than looking upon the material as a source of pride and achievement, our gaze finds a pall of morbid nostalgia, seeing only the faces of the living dead staring back at us.

Beyond its divergence from what had already become an established genre of AIDS-activist films,[58] and its repositioning of the role of visibility within that movement, this film has a complicated relationship also toward Jewish visibility. Jewishness can be said to be at the symbolic center of this film, which makes all the more surprising how little it is explicitly articulated. Jewishness is a backdrop—whether as signs and symbols on Allesman's shelves (menorahs, photographs, book titles), or as the visual wallpaper of the generic shtetl stock footage—to the foregrounded action. Ultimately it is less visibility than aurality that identifies the film as Jewish.[59] To modify this claim slightly, it is rather in the interstices between the aural and the visual that Jewishness most fully emerges. Bordowitz clearly went for a particular Jewish sound when he asked the Klezmatics to score the film. As in *Complaints,* though in a more premeditated and integrated way, music is the key element giving *Fast Trip, Long Drop* its Jewish "flair." Bordowitz commissioned the New York–based Klezmatics to write and perform the score, and it is their signature brand of politically charged klezmer music that suffuses the entire project.[60] Known for their reappropriation of early-twentieth-century Bundist songs,[61] the Klezmatics were one of the first contemporary bands to revive and recast klezmer music as not only fun and hip ("Jewish Jazz") but also socially and politically engaged. The Klezmatics were a perfect fit for Bordowitz, who attempts to update Jewish tropes and thematics, drawing them into a contemporary context and thereby transforming them. Hearing the Yiddish language lament against police brutality on the sound track, written about the excesses of czarist forces but presented over visuals of AIDS-related street actions of the film's present day, aurally and auratically links these political struggles as intergenerational comrades-in-arms. The ACT-UP demonstrations and vigils become the direct descendants of the noble labor strikes and anti-czarist actions. The fusion of identities, politics, and temporalities occurs largely in the relationship between the aural and the visual registers. Neither register on its own can fully sustain this precarious yet meaningful convergence.

Further, the Klezmatics, in league with Bordowitz, intentionally queer the meanings of these historical songs, allowing them to admit into the ranks of revolutionaries those who may have previously been excluded. With one-third of their members being out gays and lesbians, the Klezmatics have eagerly sought ways to introduce gay themes into Jewish songs from the past. For instance, in their rendition of the rousing Jewish socialist song "Ale Brider" ("We're All Brothers"), they not only add a verse that is inclusive of women ("We're all sisters like Rachel, Ruth, and Esther") but sing a stanza in Yiddish, "We're all gay, like Jonathan and King David." When we hear them perform an ecstatic rendition of the Yiddish song "Give Me a Kiss" over footage of an ACT-UP kiss-in demonstration where men kiss men and women kiss women, the singer (the Klezmatics' out gay lead singer, Lauren Sklamberg) seems to give his imprimatur to the newfound application of this song. The Klezmatics are, after all, known in Jewish musical circles as the queer klezmer group.[62]

Of course this is all very Jewish and queer–positive, but now we come full circle to where the convergences of queer, Jewish, and AIDS meet up with more insidious legacies. Jewishness, as envisioned in this video, emerges as a legacy of suffering and resistance, creating tailor-made parallels for Bordowitz's contemporary scenario. The typhus epidemic that claimed his great uncle in the shtetl becomes a precursor for the AIDS epidemic; hence the Jewish experience in Eastern Europe gives meaning and context to Bordowitz's own current condition.[63] So, too, the entrenched Eastern European Jewish imaginary of pogroms, poverty, police brutality, devastating diseases, and the political activism waged in the face of all this lends its moral authority (as if any were needed) to Bordowitz's experience of AIDS and AIDS activism. Also, subterranean to this narrative is the unspoken correlation between the neglect, prejudice, and greed that propelled the Nazi genocide of the Jews (and of homosexuals, among others), and the epidemic of silence, governmental and societal indifference, and corporate avarice that has fueled the contemporary AIDS crisis. Jewishness and Jews are quickly abstracted, becoming an emblem of persecution with which the person with AIDS can indignantly identify. Jewish suffering becomes the model for suffering per se. Jewish perseverance against all odds becomes the inspiration for Bordowitz to move forward in this seemingly endless contemporary political and corporeal battle. Jewish stigmatization (though never explicitly mentioned) becomes akin to the stigmatization experienced by People with AIDS (PWAs), creating more than just a link between the ages. Rather, this legacy becomes the Jewification of suffering and resistance, thereby both particularizing (the suffering Jew) and universalizing (the Jew *as* suffering) the Jewish *everyman*—a word that is the meaning of Allesman's name. Alter (ego) Allesman is not only the eternally suffering Jewish everyman, he is also a modern-day incarnation of the diseased Jew.

I see the weaving of queerness and Jewishness through the trope of suffering, and particularly of disease, as a reemergence of a troubling, if provocative, legacy—that of the pseudoscientific discourses of the turn of the previous century that virtually conflated diseased sexuality and Jewishness. These earlier framing tropes of illness, sexual "perversion," and Jewishness have endured, though it is important to recognize the ways they have been transformed in the process of changing epistemological and political paradigms. In Bauman's words, "Frames may be put together solidly enough to survive the change of social formations and cultures—but it is social formation and culture that each time paints the picture inside the frame."[64] Indeed, we may even say that the frame, or frame of reference, has shifted as well; consider the ways in which *Fast Trip, Long Drop* engages with and syntagmatically displaces—reframes— the meanings and implications of these nineteenth-century discourses.

▶

Of Alter Egos and Alterity: Jewish-Queer Pathologies

In the preceding analyses I explored the implications of ambivalence *as* a trope in queer Jewish autobiographical films. Now I will focus on the use of an ambivalent trope *within* a queer Jewish autobiographical film. The cultural trope to which I refer is the old canard of the pathologized queer Jew, as invoked by Bordowitz's character Alter Allesman. But, with such a potent past and such ready roles, it remains ultimately unclear who invokes whom. There is the distinct possibility that the trope may invoke Bordowitz's self-representation at precisely the same time we may imagine Bordowitz to be hailing it. To rephrase this in a way centrally thematic to this entire study: do we call up our cultural ghosts, or do they call on us? Is not the latter likely, where in the process of being called upon (to represent, to represent ourselves, to represent ourselves in certain ways, using certain, very specific tropes), we are interpellated into the body of (cultural) knowledge we think of as our (contested) self? So, here, I think of Alter Allesman as Bordowitz's ghost of *shtetlakh* past, shamelessly (though not entirely unproductively) reclaiming a place in Jewish self-representation after having been banished to what most had hoped would be the dustbin of anti-Semitic history.

The history of this particularly knotty trope has been well documented and investigated by contemporary scholars. There have been several studies tracing the linkages between European views of Jews and of homosexuals.[65] In nineteenth- and early-twentieth-century Europe, Jews and sexual inverts, as they were called, were intimately and irremediably linked through discourses of pathology and the body.[66] Both Jews and so-called inverts were considered prone to specific diseases; both were believed to have innately impaired senses of morality; both were considered antithetical to gender standards of the time; and both were considered to have had a predisposition toward mental and physical illnesses (neurasthenia, neurosis, hysteria, syphilis).[67] In the confused, if hyperrationalist, narrative of the day, these identities could not be easily separated. In fact, at least in terms of the image of the Jew, the pathology was thought to include (though not universally) a tendency toward sexual perversion and effeminacy, two presumed defects of the so-called invert. In general, the tropes that recur with most frequency in these analyses are: the sickly Jew, the pathological Jew, the vice-ridden Jew, the feminized Jew, the perverse and inappropriate Jew, and the castrated Jew. The associations are broad, but they all lend themselves immodestly to a reading of the Jewish male as sickly, effeminate, neurotic, possibly even psychotic, and inevitably sexually "other."

Enter Gregg Bordowitz, a full century later: A gay-identified Jewish man with an incurable disease whose filmic alter ego, Alter Allesman, almost seems lifted from a page torn out of that pathologizing past. What we shall see, however, is that in the context of contemporary discourses of representation, sexuality, psychology, race, and disease, this character is no longer the depraved pariah he once was. Instead, he has been transformed into an articulate spokesman for the disenfranchised, "the burnt out, the broken-hearted . . . and the profoundly confused," as one of Bordowitz's many alter egos pledges in a pseudo–stump speech performed toward the end of the film. Put another way, he suddenly has all the attributes of a postmodern poster boy.

Even though the trope seems familiar, its deployment has changed. No longer framed within stigmatizing discourses of the Jew and the invert, it finds its frame itself inverted. To be sure, the image of the PWA

(Person with AIDS) is still subject to stigmatized representation, yet in Bordowitz's film, as in Oz, these stigmatizing discourses seem to have no power. Bordowitz goes to great lengths to highlight his control over the image and his desire to posit a different audience than the one normally assumed—that is, the one composed of those people who have been discursively posited as normal. Instead, he names (and in so naming, constitutes) an audience of his peers and coconspirators. He is no one's case study, no specimen to be dissected under the penetrating gaze of the phrenologist or the criminologist. In a reappropriative gesture that indicates some modicum of control over his medium, Bordowitz reframes the debate, choosing a pointedly contrarian representational strategy (though how much control he has is never finally decidable, and, as indicated, we may wonder if this representational strategy has not in fact chosen him). The questions of degree and agency aside (large and unwieldy questions, to be sure), Bordowitz's reappropriative reframing does reclaim tremendous discursive authority for the position he occupies.[68]

Why, then, would Bordowitz seek to evoke such a discomfiting and indeed ambivalent figure as Alter Allesman? Bordowitz's own claims that this alter ego enabled an articulation of aspects of his self that he was afraid to show are insufficiently incisive. Of course, it is true that any alter ego might create such a distancing device, yet the character of the cranky, sickly, queer Jew has something of the *vorschrift* about it: prewritten, prescribed, and all too available for the asking. Here, we may find Arendt's discussion of the nineteenth-century Jewish (and queer) social conundrum of either pariah or parvenu instructive. Since for Arendt the precarious social status of the nineteenth-century Jew indeed teetered vertiginously between that of the social pariah and the ignominious parvenu, the only viable recourse for any self-respecting and politically engaged Jew was to take up the oppositional mantle of the "conscious pariah."[69] This is precisely the figure, I want to argue, that Bordowitz (re)claims, embodied in his perverse and acerbic alter ego, Allesman.

The conscious pariah, mind you, was never envisioned as a wholesome or loveable character. He was by nature difficult, ornery, prepared to be reviled, yet he spoke his conscience and took a stand wherever hypocrisy or complacency lurked, a description that I believe suits Allesman well. Allesman's character may allow for a modicum of sympathetic identification at moments—in his struggle with the disease, his resistance to false optimism, his search for meaning—yet overall he is repugnant in his self-pity, his slovenliness, and, most of all, his homicidal fantasies. Determined to be nobody's hero, he eschews every opportunity for positive representation. His particular style of "unheroic conduct"—philosophical, bookish, unmanly—bears some of the markings of Jewish masculinities as elaborated by Daniel Boyarin.[70] Boyarin draws a portrait of the sedentary, serious, studious "sissy" as the idealized Jewish male in rabbinic Judaism. This supposedly feminized Jewish male is a figure that inspired great consternation among assimilating Jews of late-nineteenth and early-twentieth-century Western Europe. Boyarin very persuasively argues that the modernizing projects of Theodor Herzl, Max Nordau, and Sigmund Freud were all in the service of civilizing Jewish masculinities—i.e., ceding to a Christian/dominant valuation of masculinity (virile, aggressive, strong, militaristic, etc.) and moving aggressively away from the limp, stooped, and studious Jew. Along with the disfigured and feminized image of the Jewish man, Allesman recalls the stigmatizing discourses of pathology to which Herzl and the early Zionists were also responding. That pathological Jewish man is hunched and cranky, uncooperative and angry. He is also sexualized in perverse ways. In particular, as Allesman, his murderous fantasy announced on the spoof cable television show, *Thriving with AIDS*, strikes at the core of the deepest, most intransigent fear of the population at large: that a "carrier" dreams of spreading the deadly virus with malicious intent. Pleasure is displaced onto the new goal of knowingly infecting a partner. Eros turns all too quickly and cynically into thanatos. Desire is unleashed as the murderous threat it has long been feared to be. The pathological queer Jew takes on the mantle of diseased and depraved vector—a role that is to be understood as preordained for him.

Until now we have been talking about nineteenth-century European stereotypes of the pathological sickly Jew, yet America also has its own

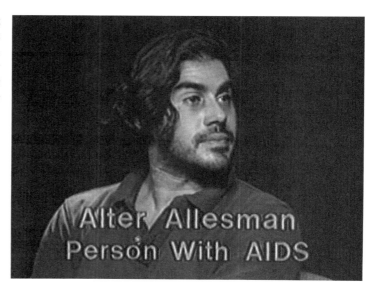

Gregg Bordowitz as Allesman, the sickly Jew, in *Fast Trip, Long Drop*.

precedents of the psychopathic and sexually perverse Jew.[71] Two legal trials in early-twentieth-century American history provide disturbing yet relevant prototypes for Bordowitz's Allesman. In 1913, Leo Frank, a Jewish factory manager and former president of the Atlanta chapter of B'nai B'rith, was falsely accused of the murder of a young shop girl known as "little Mary Phagan." In his trial, it was suggested by the prosecutor that Frank was a sexual pervert, paradoxically accused of being both a homosexual and a pedophile who preyed on young girls. He was convicted and given the state's harshest penalty, though his death sentence was commuted. A rowdy crowd outside the trial allegedly shouted "Hang the Jew." And when it was revealed that his execution was not to be carried out by the state, a mob stormed the prison hospital where Frank was recovering from having his throat slashed by a fellow inmate, kidnapped him, and lynched him in front of Mary Phagan's home, one hundred miles away.[72]

The Frank case was a nationwide scandal, though it did not cause nearly the stir of the case of two murderous homosexuals that haunted the headlines eleven years later. In 1924, Nathan Leopold and Richard Loeb, two wealthy, young Jewish geniuses (so the legend goes), plotted and executed what they believed to be the perfect murder, except that Leopold dropped his easily traceable, one-of-a-kind glasses at the scene of the crime. The trial lawyer representing the two young men was none other than the celebrated defense attorney Clarence Darrow, who constructed his case around their mental instability and indeed their psychological abnormality.[73] In the end, he managed to avert the death penalty for his clients, yet the image of the deranged, young, wealthy, Jewish perverts further etched itself in the public imaginary.[74] From Leopold and Loeb, Bordowitz, in the guise of Allesman, borrows the commingling of homosex and homicide, along with an apparent contempt for cultural norms and ethics that is based on a sense of intellectual, if not moral, superiority.

A key difference between Bordowitz's character and Leopold and Loeb is the actual versus the discursive intent to kill. Where Leopold and Loeb decided to test their theory of the perfect murder on a living specimen, Allesman poses his desire to fuck a man for the sole purpose of infecting him with HIV as "just a fantasy." Allesman is not so much depraved as defiant. He is fully able to distinguish between fantasy and actuality, and his only real transgression is the willingness to articulate a socially repellent desire. His speech act punctures a bloated silence that surrounds and threatens to subsume the sexuality of any person living with HIV in this phobic society. The words are perhaps the articulation of what might even be seen as a deep-seated social wish, imagined and sought by a panic-ridden public determined to find a contemporary correlate to "Typhoid Mary"—an AIDS fairy?—wantonly distributing retributive retrovirus to a public guilty of severe, indeed murderous, indifference. In the scene in question, Allesman volunteers to play the demon conjured by society's guilty conscience.[75] Allesman/Bordowitz is a conscientious objector in the war of representation, equally hostile to the pernicious images of PWAs in the mainstream corporate media and to the "positive images" that form the retort of the alternative AIDS educational media. Notably, in the scene described above, Allesman articulates an array of silence-breaking taboos, from refusing to accept the role of suffering martyr to insisting that it is not his burden alone, as a PWA, to fight AIDS. He calls the general audience to task for their detached apathy, while simultaneously directing his address to the vastly neglected audience of people infected with the virus. Here, Bordowitz, via Allesman, attains the status of a conscious pariah, willing to risk social status and cultural acceptance by stating things outright that are otherwise being repressed. This conscious pariah is at home nowhere, and is dangerously intent on disrupting comfortable assumptions and normative values, however alienating that may ultimately prove. He is prepared to be seen as radically other—or perhaps it is best to say here: Alter.

Of all the characters in Bordowitz's video (and there are several), Alter Allesman is the most crucial for understanding the resistance to conformity that this video hopes to represent. When I suggest that he is Bordowitz's alter ego, I mean not only that he ventriloquizes Bordowitz's political agenda, but that he vocalizes the uncontainable and inassimilable feelings and beliefs that modify, alter, and otherwise inform Bordowitz's performance and text. Allesman is a figure who refuses to be repressed and who will not be made to compromise or conform to accepted standards of ethics and morality that would effectively defuse the disruptive power that the AIDS epidemic and the PWA pose to the status quo. He is modeled as a Jew from the old school—another repressed figure—not a Zionist or a *muskeljuden,* not a well-adjusted analysand, but a long-suffering autodidact whose iconoclasm and perversity stem as much from his prodigious intellect as from his inherently outsider status.

To an historicization of the AIDS epidemic already firmly rooted in the cognitive mappings of earlier ages (consider the myriad historical associations from past epidemics: the distorted and misogynist image of the diseased and contagious woman, the plague as god's punishment, etc.), Bordowitz reintroduces the figure and specter of the Jew—a highly sexualized, pathologized revenant. Bordowitz revives this image only to let it wreak havoc upon commonly held assumptions and civilities that had become stifling in their political correctness. This figure, unlike his

nineteenth-century counterpart, is no longer dependent on prevailing social mores, nor does he feel the need to assimilate or acquire the trappings
of dominant masculinities in order to take his place at the image-making
table. Allesman (and, by analogy, Bordowitz) displays a keen awareness of
the power of the film medium and an ability to manipulate it for his own
purposes, as he cannily beckons the camera toward him and arrogates for
himself the privileged mode of direct address. The desire for control of the
medium bridges the conceptual gap between the disempowered, sickly,
pathologized Jew and the turbo-powered, media savvy, image-making
Jew. Bordowitz ultimately embodies neither of these tropes, yet he draws
heavily on both, shaking them up so that neither is finally recognizable its
previous form. His "sickly Jewish" impotence is challenged through his
command of the medium, though the running theme of randomness and
chance in the film tends to undermine any illusion of mastery or control
either over image-making or over life itself.

Bordowitz's film pushes many boundaries (of taste, ethics, genre,
format), and he performs a sometimes harrowing tightrope act between
articulating that which is difficult but necessary to posit and that which
crosses some invisible line of social acceptability. The promotional poster
for *Fast Trip* (and, for that matter, the cover photo for Bordowitz's book)
features a still from the video of a corpulent white man (dressed in 1940s
style) precariously balancing a baby in one hand, while standing pre-
cipitously on the ledge of a skyscraper. This "modern" man defies fate,
tests luck and limits, holds "the future" in his hands, and presumably

Bordowitz's
vertiginous
balancing act
literalized in
the figure of
the "precipice
man."

survives to tell the tale. Bordowitz, with his multiply represented selves, his complex sexuality, his genre bending, and, most of all, his willingness to articulate socially repellent fantasies, may well be the contemporary manifestation of this precipice man. His risky reappropriation of tropes that, a century before, had Jews and homosexuals running for cover (either the cover of the closet or the trappings of "proper" masculinity offered by the "hard Jew" of Zionism) is a clear testament to the changed context in which these tropes are now deployed. I say this not to toll the bell of progress, but to suggest that cultural tropes are eventually open to resignification. How long it takes, and in which direction the resignification may move, is entirely unpredictable. However, in diagnosing the fate of what many have thought was a hopeless case, the image of the pathological Jew, the prognosis looks surprisingly promising. The conscious pariah as a disruptive figure may yet have its day.

In this chapter, I have sought ways to analyze a set of dissimilar first person films made by lesbian and gay Jews, all of whose films display a certain ambivalence with regard to one or other of these two complex identities. In the process, I have frequently found myself reading these films against their own (ambiguous) grain. Reading for silences, indeterminacies, ambivalences, entails, at best, a kind of interruption, at worst, a violence. Such reading is always a matter of digging where one is not wanted, insisting when one has not been asked, effectively disrupting a story. One can justify this as the work of interpretation, or even simply analysis—the pursuit of the not said—yet there is also something unwelcome in the venture. It seems to me that the very prolificness of queer Jewish first person film owes something to ambiguity. That is, this ambivalence is perversely generative and deserves to be, if not protected, at least respected as a composite response to divergent visibility strategies and pernicious pathologizing discourses that remain active, if mutable, in contemporary representational practices. Better to resist the urge to reconcile the irreconcilable, and to allow for the "explosive energy" of fruitful contradiction, as Zimmerman suggests, rather than to artificially attempt an integration of these complex and competing identities at the expense of such expressive forms. I recommend embracing this manifest ambivalence as a site of productivity, an excess not to be suppressed. So I end with a modification of the sagacious statement by Beauvoir with which I began this chapter: we must not attempt to dispel the ambivalences of queer Jewish first person filmic representation, but accept and learn from the resounding ambiguities of its realization.

Conclusion:

A Limit Case for Jewish

Autoethnography

I would like to conclude by looking at one last Jewish autobiographical film made by a filmmaker/theorist, one that precluded the possibility of autocritique in that the filmmaker did not survive to write about it. *In Her Own Time* (1985) by Barbara Myerhoff (codirected by Lynne Littman) is a prototypical Jewish autobiographical film, preceding most of the films discussed in this study and pioneering many of the salient themes of this book. The first person Jewish films of this study are primarily distinguished by three characteristics. First, in the service of contemporary self-representation, each deploys, often unwittingly, a cultural narrativity that revives and remakes historical tropes both by and about Jews. Second, the unity of the author/subject is always, in some way, at issue in the work, challenging the monologics of the unitary self and prominently displaying a crisis of authorship inherent in all autobiography. And the third defining feature of the first person Jewish films discussed in these pages is their generic ambiguity: they operate on the borders of documentary, fiction, and experimental filmmaking, often too between autobiography and biography, and in so doing, challenge the already suspect integrity of documentary and autobiography as discrete generic categories.

I have chosen to look at Myerhoff's film as the final film examined here because it deftly condenses these three key aspects of my project even as it may at points raise more problems for my arguments than it solves. Myerhoff was an avowed storyteller, specializing in Jewish cultural narratives, a cultural anthropologist who innovated some of the theoretical paradigms that have enabled me to formulate my first criterion. She believed in storytelling as an indispensable mode of cultural transmission. Her ethnographic work highlighted the power of narrative to endow members of a given culture with a sense of belonging and, more important, the sense of being "active participants in their own history."[1] She describes these self-conscious tellings, in performative terms, where life history narratives allow people to be "knowing actors in a historical drama they script. They 'make' themselves, sometimes even 'make themselves up.'" Believing, like Walter Benjamin, that the self is a project to be built, Myerhoff acknowledges that "it is an artificial and exhilarating undertaking, this self-construction."[2] Here, Myerhoff writes about others, but we may apply her ideas about the cultural performativity of subjectivity to her own self-representation/construction as well. Jewish cultural narratives evoke and inscribe her subjectivity even as she defines herself against them.

To briefly summarize, *In Her Own Time* is Myerhoff's final film, made at a time when she was diagnosed with, and quickly afflicted by, incurable lung cancer. The film had originally been planned as another of her ethnographic films, the most famous of which had been about an elderly Jewish community in Venice Beach, California *(Number Our Days)*, which won an Academy Award in 1976. *In Her Own Time* was to be a study of the unlikely community of Hasidic Jews of the Fairfax section of Los Angeles, the men dressed in their black suits and hats, the women in wigs and stockings, among the blond surfers and mini-skirted hipsters of Los Angeles. Her signature reflexive approach already inclined her toward first person narration, yet *In Her Own Time* goes further into the autobiographical than any of her previous work. Here Myerhoff the ethnographer subjects herself to the machinations of culture, ritual, and belief systems that are simultaneously her own (she is, after all, Jewish) and not her own (being, up until that point, a nonpracticing, secular, atheist Jew). Her illness becomes the catalyst for an encounter with religious Judaism that promises healing in the spiritual if not the somatic sense. This is an encounter of the self *as* other, as she negotiates the alien arcana of her own religious and cultural heritage.

Myerhoff stages her historical drama of illness and identity through and against an explicitly religious Jewish context (Chabad Lubavitcher Hasidim of Fairfax), and in the process she allows us to glimpse what the other films of this study have implied yet elided, that the Jewish autobiographical subject is split within itself as a Jew: there is no unity within that identity; no home to which to return. Jewishness, like any other ethnicity or identity, is not monolithic and provides an unstable yet uncommonly fecund grounding for these self-representational endeavors. To rephrase an assertion made in chapter 3, there is no doing without these identifications even as they continue to paradoxically place and displace us.[3]

This fact informs the second aspect of the films that constitute this study: the non-unitary subject. More than a postmodern device, a context and a history (of alienation from tradition, assimilation, secularization) informs these filmmakers' choices to represent themselves, through their varied prismatic lenses, as fragmented, multiple, divided, ambivalent. The relationship to Jewishness is itself an atomized identity in contemporary Jewish first person film; it is multiple, changing, elusive, contradictory, confounding, inspiring, and persistent. The other element of this non-unitary self-representation is the vexed question of authorship. If the first person Jewish films of this study denote, in part, a fractured and frag-mented authorial positionality, one enacted variously through surrogacy, indirection, or bifurcation, then *In Her Own Time* adds a new element, posthumous authorship, into the mix. In this sense, this film, by no means one of the more formally innovative films of the study, takes autobiography to its furthest extreme. The other films may complicate notions of author-ship in diverse ways, but none raises the question as a matter of life and death in quite the way that *In Her Own Time* does.

When Barbara Myerhoff set out to make an ethnographic film about her fieldwork with the Chabad of Fairfax, she did not intended to focus on herself.[4] She tells us in voice-over at the beginning of *In Her Own Time,* "This is not the film that I started out to make." She implies that she had envisioned a more traditional ethnography, taking "the kind of professional distance that every social scientist wants to bring to the subject," though there is reason to doubt this assertion, considering her prior challenges to that very objectivist paradigm.[5] Had she not been confronted with the devastating diagnosis of lung cancer midway through her fieldwork with this Lubavitcher community, she would no doubt have employed her, by then signature, reflexive style, where she as the ethnographer/filmmaker would include aspects of her process and of her interactions with the subjects of the study. Myerhoff was one of the in-novators of reflexive anthropology in America, and, at the time, one of its best-known practitioners. She cowrote the introduction to *A Crack in the Mirror,* the collection of essays that consolidated reflexivity's influence in the field.[6] In fact, she took reflexivity beyond what some of her fellow ethnographers had envisioned, by conducting fieldwork within her own (extended) community.[7] Myerhoff was a prescient leader in her field, help-ing to (re)direct anthropology's (and her) considerable cultural insights and energies inward toward autoethnographic studies.

As suggested earlier, *In Her Own Time* takes this inward direction further. Myerhoff's cancer diagnosis becomes the catalyst for what was to be a very unusual ethnographic engagement. In deciding to make her con-dition the organizing principle and framing device of *In Her Own Time,* she transforms the work from autoethnographic (a study of one's own culture) to ethnoautobiographic (a culturally grounded study of oneself).

Her work fits well within anthropologist Michael Fischer's definition of ethnic autobiography, of which he writes, "Contemporary ethnic auto-biographies partake of the mood of meta-discourse . . . of using the narrator as an inscribed figure within the text whose manipulation calls attention to authority structures, of encouraging the reader to self-consciously participate in the production of meaning."[8] In his article, Fischer concerns himself with others' ethnic autobiographies, only fleetingly including ethnic autobiographical details of his own. Myerhoff's film goes well beyond Fischer's anecdotal ethnographer's ethnic autobiography. In her characteristically understated, unassuming way, Myerhoff ventures where few in her field had gone before.

Generically, *In Her Own Time* does little to dislodge documentary certainties, though it does allow us to explore aspects of documentary's boundaries that give the genre its fabled factual edge over fiction. As much a documentary about Jewish culture and practices, it also documents the last months of a dying woman, Myerhoff herself, and as such, incontestably anchors documentary's indexical relationship with the real—in this case, the irrefutable imminence of the filmmaker's death. Then, it pushes the limits even further and posits a self-representation that defies death.

I was drawn to this film in part because of its obvious resonances with the Jewish themes of this project, but what makes it the film with which I want to conclude is the way it takes the questions of authorship, selfhood, and Jewish identity inscribed into first person filmmaking to their logical extreme. The autobiographical self posited in her film does not merely question the coherence of the subject, it questions the existence of the subject. In this film, the "death of the author" is no post-structuralist axiom; it is the very condition of the film's production.

As a result, this (ethnic) autobiography produces an unlikely authorial conundrum: how do we ascribe authorship to this text? Practically speaking, Myerhoff both is and is not the author of this text. It is clearly her autobiographical story and her first person voice-over narration (occasionally augmented with supplementary third person voice-over). Even though Lynne Littman is credited as the film's director, Myerhoff is posited diegetically as the filmmaker and is also understood professionally as such, in collaboration with Littman. Effectively and by design, *In Her Own Time* gives the impression of Myerhoff's authorial control until the end. We are made to believe at the outset that it is Myerhoff who has decided to focus on her health in relation to this community, Myerhoff who chooses to film such painful, intimate, and delicate situations as receiving her cancer diagnosis, or her purification immersion in the mikvah (ritual bath), and Myerhoff who decides to have herself interviewed two weeks before her death. Clearly she needed to agree, and perhaps these filmings were even done at her instigation, but the impression given by the film is more than that. Myerhoff is not only our conduit into the community, and our "heroine" who takes us along on her emotional journey; she is the authorial voice as well, and she speaks to us at times with a hindsight she could not possibly have had.

We've seen temporal decussation performed syntagmatically in several of these films, where intergenerational looks are exchanged and impossible simultaneities are effected, as with Abraham Ravett's sibling rivalry with his long dead stepbrother and stepsister, Alan Berliner's mother and sister's transhistorical beachpaddle game, and Michelle Citron's eight-year-old and forty-eight-year-old selves gazing at each other. *In Her Own Time* effects this chiasm grammatically in the voice-over, where she speaks in the present tense as if she herself is past. For instance, she tells us that the film had to be more personal than objective because "to do anything except something that touched my own life *was time I did not have*." There is something strangely proleptic about this line. I appreciate that she situates the pursuit of objectivity as a luxury, not a necessity. However, it is the tense of the address that is unsettling. By the time she tells us that there "was time I did not have," it sounds as if her time has already run out. If these words are not actually spoken from a place outside mortal time, they are yet spoken with an awareness and acceptance of an imminent time when her time will have run out. This is an eerie reminder that death haunts this film—that, in fact, we are listening to the voice of death. The "time" of the title may well refer, then, to a private time, an infinite amount of time that she *does* have, though perhaps in a different temporality, which is to say: time immemorial. Her first person voice-over employed in the film can be read in two possible ways: (1) it maintains the compelling yet misleading conceit that she lives to tell her tale; or (2) it (she) speaks to us from another dimension—Myerhoff *as* the Jewish uncanny.[9] Either way, she, and consequently the film, pushes the boundaries of narrative ontology. The authorial self here is beyond fractured or fragmented; it is in effect evanescent.

In Gregg Bordowitz's film, the filmmaker ponders, imagines, and even stages his own death; Myerhoff actually dies by her film's end (it ends with the years of her birth and death, 1935–1985). Someone else has finished this film; someone else is in fact credited as filmmaker; yet the film addresses us for the most part in the first person, from the world beyond.[10] I know of no other documentaries that have attempted this device, let alone managed to sustain it.[11] Even fiction films have rarely been so bold as to speak from beyond the grave. In fact, in fiction films, the convention is firmly adhered to that first person voice-over implies that the narrator has survived her or his harrowing circumstances long enough to retell them. The paradigmatic exception to this rule, *Sunset Boulevard* (Billy Wilder, 1950, though of course there are others), still stands as a rarity, and owes at least some of its freshness and startling effect to this iconoclasm.

Death has always been a limit case for documentary. It is what has steadfastly reassured documentary theorists of the irreducible difference between documentary and fiction. When an actor dies in a fiction film, we can generally be certain that as soon as the camera has stopped rolling, she or he will rise again (Brandon Lee excepted). When a documentary subject dies, on or off the screen, we are forced to admit that somewhere, beyond symbolic representation, a real life has been lost. Documentary theorists have had an almost ghoulish enthusiasm for this distinction.[12] It is the one thing that has been said to indisputably affirm documentary's more than symbolic affinity with indexical reality. When we watch Myerhoff become enfeebled before our eyes, we know that this is not the result of a six-hour make-up session and movie magic. In fact, we may sorely wish for some movie magic to resuscitate her health. Myerhoff herself wishes for miracles in a scene where she writes to the legendary Lubavitcher Rebbe, Menachem Schneerson, but none are to be had. Instead we are faced with the grim reality and immediacy of her mortality and the remarkably disorienting experience of witnessing what amounts to an auto-epitaph. This film is even more directly prosopopoetic than Chantal Akerman's *D'Est*. It epitomizes Paul de Man's assertion that "the dominant figure of the epitaphic or autobiographical discourse is . . . the prosopopeia, the fiction of the voice-from-beyond-the-grave."[13]

Of course, Lynne Littman is the silent (but formally credited) partner in the filmmaking process, but the effacement of Littman's presence and contribution exposes the limits of the reflexive film project. With all its pretense to reflexivity, the film reveals nothing about one of its most striking attributes, the question of authorship. There is only so much "behind the scenes" that is or can be revealed, and the decision of how to contend with authorship remains beyond the scope of this reflexive project. The authorship of the film is in contention, and it is a battle pitched from the other side. These two "authors" are not literally fighting each other for control, of course; rather, the origin or source of the authorial voice is intentionally obscured. There is no clear author of this text: the credited filmmaker is invisible and self-effacing, yet the apparent filmmaker has died before she could have authored the work. The viewer is left with an unsettling, though provocative, uncertainty. This uncertainty, to be clear, is more conceptual than logistical. Surely we know that Littman finished the film, and we can ascertain, with a minimum of acuity, that her authorial strategy was to foreground Myerhoff's presence and words. The result could be written off as a simple case of what Michael Renov has called assisted autobiography—that is, an autobiographical film that was finished by another due to extenuating circumstances.[14] But this film is, nonetheless, made by a ghost on whose reputation the film rides, and whose remarkable insight and commanding presence lend authority and weight to the piece. The same could of course be said of a luminary brought in to participate in a film without exercising an iota of authorial control. Not so of Myerhoff. She is not the correspondent or the expert witness. She is the subject, object, and author of a film she did not live to complete, and the film's conceit is that she nonetheless orchestrated its direction.

When the credits roll, with Littman listed as sole director, is she acting in Myerhoff's place? Has there been an omission, if not an error? Can it be said that this film is made pseudonymically—in which case, whose name identifies the real filmmaker? When one looks the film up on the notoriously inaccurate Internet Movie Database,[15] Myerhoff is listed merely as "actress," clearly an injustice to her role in the making of the film. More commonly and in most biographical descriptions, Myerhoff is hailed as a filmmaker and the films attributed to her (and not always in collaboration with Littman) are *Number Our Days* and *In Her Own Time*.[16] Regardless of the correct or accurate accreditation, it is fair to say that this film creates an unresolvable crisis of authorship.

The name of the author is a diegetic concern of the film as well: who is Barbara Myerhoff in and to this film? One of the rituals to which Myerhoff subjects herself in the film is a renaming ceremony. A charismatic rabbi in the Fairfax Lubavitcher community (Reb Naftali) suggests that she have her name changed, in a service traditionally performed for the ill and dying. The belief is that if one's (Hebrew) name is changed (according to the proper ritual), the angel of death will look for the old name to call on when death beckons. Myerhoff undergoes this "magical" transformation that at first seems simplistic to her ("You change my name, you change my destiny"), but which quickly appeals to her desire for renewal, to "begin again." In a further surrender of control, she lets the rabbi choose her new name. By the end of the ceremony, she seems visibly moved and expresses her hope that, as a result of this symbolic renaming, she will feel physically better by the afternoon. Needless to say, she does not.

This is not the only instance of name changing in this study. As noted in chapter 4, Bordowitz's alter ego, Alter Allesman, is actually the name that Bordowitz's great-uncle was given when he was, as a child, dying of typhus in Poland. The concept is related to the renaming ritual in Myerhoff's film, where the new name is supposed to distract the angel of death from its originally intended object. The name Alter Allesman was apparently commonly given to young boys who were ill, as a message to the angel of death that he should take "any old man" rather than a child who has yet to live his life. Bordowitz takes this name as his own without benefit of ritual or sanction, yet with an awareness of tradition and a sincere desire to circumvent, by whatever means necessary, his own premature demise. Thus it seems that the alter egos and performative displacements of the self seen in these films have a culturally motivated rationale. We see here an interpretive, manipulable approach already embedded in Jewish culture toward identity, at least as far as identity is inscribed in a name. The soul may not be transferable, in the Jewish tradition, but the way we call and know ourselves is, and this idea resonates well with the mutability of identity seen in many of the films of this study.[17]

Myerhoff's film functions in part as a precursor to these other films, but, in at least one respect, it is an example of the path not taken. Unlike what occurs in any of the other films considered here, or in fact in any other Jewish first person film that I have seen, in this film the filmmaker chooses to perform at least a partial return to religious Judaism. Although Myerhoff asserts mid-film that she feels unable to fully embrace these traditions and that there is a "membrane" separating her from full acceptance of halakhic Judaism, by the end of the film she concedes that the membrane has gotten thinner (in direct proportion to her own emaciation, it would seem), and that she can no longer conceive of her life without this spiritual/religious dimension. She stages a collision between secular and religious Judaism, essentially from her wheelchair,[18] and in it we can see precisely what is gained and at what cost by a full embrace of the secular world. What is gained in independence, access to (nonreligious) education, sexual freedom, and participation in a multicultural world, comes at the expense of cohesive community, an unambiguous sense of belonging, the reassurance that can be provided by age-old rituals, and an enduring belief in a power greater than oneself.[19]

The homecoming that Myerhoff enacts to her own culture's religious precepts is instructive. The rituals and rules are as foreign to her and as much in need of explanation as the Huichol rituals that she studied as a graduate student years before. The languages spoken (Yiddish, Hebrew, Russian) must be translated for her benefit. She is visibly ill at ease with the rites she is asked to perform, and perhaps even more skeptical of them than she would be of a culture to which she had no ties and against which she had not, in effect, rebelled. This return is painful, not only for her but for those of us in the audience who have chosen not to make such a return. It is not hard to sympathize with her desperation and to wonder what we would do in her circumstances, yet for avowedly secular, not to mention feminist and/or gay or lesbian viewers, her path spells a betrayal of much of what we have fought for and hold dear—and of what we may have come to believe that she, as a secular fellow traveler, also believed.[20] The contradictions are present for Myerhoff, but not insurmountable in the way that Bonnie Zimmerman has suggested they are for Jewish lesbians, for instance.[21] Myerhoff is also clearly attracted to these ancient rituals, even as they chafe with her modern, assimilated, liberated, secularly educated self-definition. She reflexively holds up to us a mirror that is indeed cracked. There is a stark demonstration of the rupture between traditional and modern secular Judaism that, despite her eleventh-hour declarations to the contrary, seems indeed too great to repair. In addition, the film posits a direct challenge to the explanations and justifications given, or implied, in the other films for sometimes cynical compromises and rationalizations of how to maintain a Jewish identity in the absence of (or even in opposition to) religious observance. In this regard, and in spite of itself, the film has disturbingly reactionary inclinations.[22] Myerhoff's religious experiment can be seen as a repudiation of the best efforts to negotiate a truce with this sometimes unyielding heritage.

From beyond the grave, and in advance of much of the ethnoautobiographical endeavors considered here, Myerhoff seems to warn: it is of no avail; your compromises will not save you. Yet we cannot help but note, a bit defensively, that her "return" did not save her. Perhaps it was the membrane (what Derrida would have suggestively called the hymen), that thin barrier she felt between herself and total embrace of orthodoxy, that was her downfall. Perhaps she simply did not go far enough.

Be that as it may, in the absence of compelling evidence to dissuade us from our path, we, the filmmakers of this study, have proceeded to make our ambivalent, contradictory, secular work that not only attempts to represent an increasingly common and valid experience of contemporary Ashkenazi Jewishness, but also constructs the terms in which it can be represented. And these terms are not, it turns out, entirely new, nor thoroughly alienated from tradition. To revisit Baal Shem Tov's famous parable about the rabbi who used to pray in front of a specific tree in a particular forest, and his descendants who have progressively forgotten the tree, the forest, and even the words to the prayer, we are still telling Jewish stories, even if not the traditional ones in the traditional way. We narrate our Jewishness in all its permutations, and Jewishness, in turn, is enhanced by our embellishments. As untraditional as it may be, this work exists still implicitly *in relation to* tradition, even if at times from a considerable remove. Nor is tradition monolithic; it would be more appropriate to speak of *traditions.* At this point in Jewish history, there are many traditions from which to draw on, religious orthodoxy being only one. The films of this study show that Jewish tradition can be conceptualized historically, politically, aesthetically, denominationally, secularly, and even ambivalently.

Fischer has written that ethnic autobiography can be seen as the mode of expression best suited to understanding postindustrial, late-twentieth-century and early-twenty-first-century society.[23] This may be so, not only as a result of the inadequacy of traditional sociological models, (which, Fischer argues, cannot accommodate the complicated cultural configurations and expressions of ethnicity that define experiences of ethnicity in pluralist, advanced capitalist, societies), but also because in the absence of mimetically transmitted cultural traditions that require a cohesive, relatively unassimilated, ethnic cultural context to survive, ethnicity is something that each individual must negotiate for herself or himself.[24] If ethnic identity is self-exploration and a self-conscious attempt at self-definition, then the autobiographical mode is uniquely well-suited for such a negotiation. Fischer is aware of this when he says that, at this point in modern or postmodern society, ethnicity is "something reinvented and reinterpreted in each generation by each individual and that it is often something quite puzzling to the individual, something over which he or she lacks control [or mastery]. Ethnicity is [no longer] something that is simply passed on from generation to generation, taught and learned."[25] Nor is it ever entirely invented anew. It is a pastiche of excavation and pilfering, recontextualizion and translation.[26] In a Jewish context, the ability to find the new within the old, *khidush,* is a venerated activity, revealing the postmodern first person filmmakers of this book to be an integral part of an old tradition, even as they question, challenge, and oppose many of its tenets. Can Jewish culture withstand the autocritique? Surely it must, for the autocritique is already well underway.

However, these films hold our interest well beyond their modest, if lively, contribution to Jewish cultural representation; as memory migrates intergenerationally, identity interpenetrates familially, and historical tropes return in new guises, transformed by their new context. Fischer's assertion that each individual reinterprets and reinvents ethnicity anew must be modified, as the films of this study provocatively display the ways that the postindustrial, postmodern representation of the self, too, is always reinscribed into preexisting cultural narratives during the interpretive process. Speaking culturally in the first person means being neither fully autonomous from, nor finally fully determined by, cultural terms and tropes, but being, rather, some productive admixture of the two. These films boldly reveal what Michael Renov has called "the essential plurality of what we call the first person singular."[27] Grammatically, then, as the title suggests, filmically speaking in the first person Jewish is to speak in the first person plural of an ethnically inscribed yet infinitely variable identity.

Notes

Introduction

1. Benjamin, "A Berlin Chronicle," 26.
2. Egan, "Encounters in Camera."
3. See Levinas, *Otherwise Than Being, or Beyond Essence*. Judith Butler has written, "The 'I' has no story of its own that is not also the *story of a relation—or set of relations—to a set of norms*. . . . *The subject forms itself in relation to a set of codes, prescriptions and norms*. . . . There is no making of oneself *(poesis)* outside of a mode of subjectivation *(assujettisement)* and, hence, no self-making outside of the norms that orchestrate the possible forms that a subject may take" (my emphasis), in *Giving an Account of Oneself*, 7–8 and 17, respectively.
4. One of the first articles ever written on autobiographical nonfiction film focused on avant-garde films. See "Autobiography in Avant-Garde Film," by P. Adams Sitney, 199–246.
5. Michael Renov makes reference to the "repression of subjectivity" in the introduction to *The Subject of Documentary*, xviii.
6. As a point of clarification, it is important that the reader understand that not all contemporary autobiographical film fits the description of "the new autobiography." There are many auto-biographical films being made that do not construct subjectivity "as a site of instability" and in fact strive to represent it as a unified, coherent, narrative certainty, however much this may remain an illusion.
7. Renov, "The Subject in History," 110.
8. According to Leigh Gilmore, the literary memoir also boomed in the 1990s. See "Limit Cases," 128. First person films have proliferated nowhere so much as in the United States and Canada but the practice has also become more widespread elsewhere.
9. Renov, "The Subject in History," 107–8.
10. A secondary set of films will also be discussed that address Jewish subjectivity from an auto-biographical perspective but that I do not analyze in the same detail. These films include *Below the New* (1999), by Abigail Child; *One of Us* (1999), by Susan Korda; *A Letter without Words* (1998), by Lisa Lewenz; *Paper Bridge* (1987), by Ruth Beckermann; *Chantal Akerman by Chantal Akerman* (1996); *Tomboychik* (1993), by Sandi DuBowski; *A Healthy Baby Girl* (1996), by Judith Helfand; *Divan* (2003), by Pearl Gluck. Still other films are referenced along the way. For a filmography of Jewish diasporic first person documentaries, see my filmography in the present volume.
11. Renov names it thus in "The Subject in History," 104–19. Renov is hardly the only one to use this "new" designation. The "new documentary" has also been hailed by theorists, including Linda Williams, "Mirrors without Memories," 9–21, and Stella Bruzzi, *New Documentary*. Examples of this "new autobiography" can be seen in some films of Marlon Fuentes, Cheryl Dunye, Elia Suleiman, Mona Hatoum, Kidlat Tahimik, Marilou Mallet, Marlon Riggs, Richard Fung, Gurinder Chadha, Su Friedrich, Rea Tajiri, Sadie Benning, David Achkar, Frances Negrón-Mutaner, and Karim Aïnouz.
12. Norman Kleeblatt, the curator of the New York Jewish Museum's 1996 exhibition "Too Jewish?" writes in the preface of the show's catalogue, *Too Jewish?* "While multicultural exhibitions have abounded in the years since 1989, there has been little focus on Jewish artists or Jewish subject matter. The interrogation of this absence—and of what makes Jewish artists less marginal

than other groups—was integral to the formulation of this exhibition." The cultural climate, and new provocative works by Jewish artists, forced "me to confront my own cultural difference as a Jew and to figure out how different my 'otherness' was from the 'otherness' of any number of diverse minorities." Kleeblatt, *Too Jewish?*, x.

13. Such a postmodern representational approach has been identified also in the written narratives by children of survivors. Efraim Sicher writes, "In common with many postmodern texts, second generation narrative draws attention to the fragmentation of self, to the relativity of truth, to the fluidity of memory and to the impossibility of ever fully knowing." "The Future of the Past," 80–81.

14. It was coined by Mary Louise Pratt in *Imperial Eyes*, 7, and has been used to great effect by Catherine Russell in the concluding chapter of *Experimental Ethnography*, 275–314.

15. Russell, *Experimental Ethnography*, 276.

16. Bakhtin, "Discourse in the Novel," 293.

17. The original quote is: "The 'talking head' must always belong—at some level—to a body politic." See Chon Noriega, "Talking Heads, Body Politic," 211.

18. "Culture," as Raymond Williams declared a quarter of a century ago, is one of the most complicated terms in the English language. As he and others have asserted, it has come to stand in for virtually everything humans do. In my usage, of course, I am unable to avoid significant slippage as my invocation has nothing pure, homogeneous, or authentic about it, and in fact I do mean for *culture* to stand in for many things. Culture has been usefully derided and demystified by many social scientists and theorists, most famously by Raymond Williams in *Culture and Society* and in Alfred Kroeber's and Clyde Kluckhohn's study *Culture*. For overviews of more contemporary debates within anthropology and cultural geography, see Susan Wright's "Politicization of 'Culture,'" 7–15, and Don Mitchell's "There's No Such Thing as Culture," 102–16, respectively.

19. Don Mitchell, citing Donna Haraway, describes culture as "infinite regress" ("There's No Such Thing as Culture," 107). I have relied heavily on Susanna Egan's description of the "general category of autobiography" in this discussion ("Encounters in Camera," 598).

20. Noriega, "Talking Heads, Body Politic," 207–28. Doris Sommer coined the phrase in reference to Latin American women's written testimonies; see, "Not Just a Personal Story," 107–30.

21. Hannah Arendt usefully differentiates Jewishness from Judaism (the religion) in this way: "Jewish origin, without religious . . . connotation, became everywhere a psychological quality, [and] was changed into 'Jewishness.'" This Jewishness devoid of its traditional historical significance has become an idiosyncrasy, which at times verges on obsession; as Arendt notes, "The more the fact of Jewish birth lost its religious, national and social-economic significance, the more obsessive Jewishness became; Jews were obsessed by it as one may be by a physical defect or advantage, and addicted to it as one may be to a vice." *Origins of Totalitarianism*, 83–85.

22. For an interesting discussion of the universalizing of the Jew, see Paul Eisenstein, "Universalizing the Jew." For some of the best-known philosophical allegorizations of the Jew, see Karl Marx, "On the Jewish Question"; Jean-Paul Sartre's *Anti-Semite and Jew*; Jean-François Lyotard's *Heidegger and "the jews."*

23. Elizabeth Bruss makes such a claim, with the backing of Walter Benjamin, Frank McConnnell, and Stanley Cavell; see her "Eye for I," 318, n. 30.

24. J. Butler, *Bodies That Matter*, 228.

25. For a fascinating discussion of the stereotype in relation to the Jew, see Gilman, *Jewish Self-Hatred*. For another important discussion of the stereotype, see Bhabha, "The Other Question," 66–84.

26. Stuart Klawans, "iCinema," in *Nation*, October 18, 2004.

27. With my detailed description, it should be obvious that such a film exists: *A Letter without Words*, by Lisa Lewenz. Although this film is not one of the primary texts of my study, I do include it in secondary discussions and in the filmography. The reasons for not choosing to analyze this film in depth have nothing to do with the Jewishness of the filmmaker, but rather with an overly simplified address of the first person in the film's narration (see my fifth criterion). There are other films, included in my filmography, made by filmmakers with only a Jewish father, such as by Mark Wexler, whose famous filmmaking father, Haskell Wexler, is Jewish, and whose mother is not.

28. The least formally innovative film of this study, *In Her Own Time*, is the one film that most directly negotiates the terms of religious practice. Films such as *Hiding and Seeking* (2003), by Menachem Daum and Oren Rudovsky, and *My Brother's Wedding* (2003), by Dan Akiba, are important first person films in many ways but are, not surprisingly, conservative in their aesthetic approach. There are notable exceptions, however, including *Divan* (2003), by Pearl Gluck, a playful treasure hunt mystery that cleverly weaves in the complexity of leaving the Hassidic fold while still retaining strong, if ambivalent ties to it; and works by Anat Zuria in Israel—I mention

especially *Purity* (2002) since it is a first person film—whose films are visually arresting and surprisingly nonconformist on many levels, made by an intriguing ultra-orthodox filmmaker with a nascent feminist sensibility.

29. Berliner has made a film about his maternal grandfather (who began as a cotton exporter in Egypt), *Intimate Stranger* (1991), but this is a much more distant, almost clinical, portrait that does not begin to develop the personal voice with the same intensity and passion of Berliner's later films.

30. There have, of course, been more than a few first person films made by Sephardic and Mizrahi Jews to date: *Love Iranian-American Style* (2005) and *Najib* (2000), by Tanaz Eshaghian; *Adio Kerida*, by Ruth Behar (2002); *I Miss the Sun* (1983), by Mary Halawani; *Nana, George, and Me* (1998), by Joe Balass; *Nana: A Portrait* (1972), by Jamil Simon. As this book was going to press, two very interesting new first person documentaries by Mizrahi diasporic Jews had been released: *The Rabbi's Twelve Children*, by Yael Bitton (Switzerland, 2007), and Nadia Kamel's *Salata Baladi* (Egypt, 2007). Although Simone Bitton's fascinating film *Wall* came out in 2004 and was co-produced by France, I consider it to be an Israeli film and, as such, not appropriate for this study.

31. Quoted from Barbara Kirshenblatt-Gimblett's presentation at "Eye and Thou II," sponsored by New York University, March 24–25, 2001.

32. Stratton, *Coming Out Jewish*, 300.

33. Renov refers to Vertov's wife and brother as "the delegates of his projected subjectivity." Renov discusses these films, among others, as prototypes of contemporary autobiographical documentaries. See *The Subject of Documentary*, xviii. A longer discussion of the origins of autobiographical documentary in America can be found in the first chapter of Jim Lane's *Autobiographical Documentary in America*, 11–32.

34. Of course, some of the best-known practitioners of Direct Cinema were Jewish (Frederick Wiseman, the Maysles brothers). I don't mean to imply here that Jews are somehow unable to maintain the illusion or artifice of objectivity that their non-Jewish counterparts can. Certainly countless Jewish scientists, doctors, journalists, and documentarists attest otherwise. Yet it is worth noting that the Maysles, in particular, and from very early on, infused their direct cinema with a personal, engaged quality far from the journalistic tenets espoused by Robert Drew in his three rules of the "school of storm and stress": (1) I am determined to be there when news happens; (2) I am determined to be as unobtrusive as possible; (3) I am determined not to distort the situation. Of course no Direct Cinema practitioners could ever fully succeed in the task as Drew defined it, and the resultant infractions have been duly noted in the scholarly writings on the subject, notably by Jeanne Hall (see her "Realism as a Style in Cinema Verité"), but I have yet to see an elaborated argument about how the Maysles' exceptional work radically deviated from those norms even as they claimed to pursue them. The clearest example of their interactive, psychological, and most certainly not disinterested approach is their film *Grey Gardens* (1976).

35. Together they made *Happy Mother's Day* (1963).

36. The concept of the feminist theory film is elaborated in Kaplan's *Women and Film*, 125–41.

37. Citron, *Home Movies and Other Necessary Fictions*.

38. She can be said to be yet another instance of Naomi Seidman's "parenthetical Jew," who allies herself with political causes and cultures that may or may not include an aspect of her own identity, but neglects to include, or intentionally excludes, reference to her Jewishness. She may reveal her Jewishness (if at all) as an aside, at times literally marked off in parentheses. Although Seidman only concerns herself with a small sampling of feminist (Jewish) theorists (Nancy K. Miller, Eve Kosofsky Sedgwick, and Judith Butler—all of whom have since been quite explicit about their Jewishness) the phenomenon is evident among filmmakers as well. Jewish filmmaking, perhaps unlike recent queer and/or feminist theory by Jews, has begun to come out of the parentheses. Ambivalence is still pervasive, a fact that is detailed throughout this thesis, but Jewishness has gone from being an incidental aside to a theme in and of itself, ranging from major to minor. See Seidman, "Fag Hags and Bu-Jews," 254–68.

39. Beginning in 1996, the National Foundation for Jewish Culture (NFJC) in the United States established a documentary film fund that has since funded numerous autobiographical Jewish films. The initial seed money for this fund came from a $450,000 grant from Steven Spielberg's Righteous Persons Foundation. This targeted Jewish documentary fund has supported such Jewish first person films as: *Treyf, A Healthy Baby Girl, The Return of Sarah's Daughters, One of Us, A Letter without Words, The March, Divan, King of the Jews, My Architect,* and *Hiding and Seeking*. It is important to point out that the fund only provides partial funding, leaving these filmmakers to raise the bulk of their budgets elsewhere. The NFJC funds nonautobiographical documentaries as well. See http://www2.jewishculture.org/disciplines/media_arts/. To my knowledge, no such targeted Jewish documentary fund exists in Europe. Most of the films discussed at length in this study, with the exception of *Treyf*, did not benefit from NFJC funding.

40. Fischer, "Ethnicity and the Post-Modern Arts of Memory," 197.

41. Benjamin, "Thesis on the Philosophy of History," 255, 263.

42. F. Ginsburg, "The Parallax Effect," 17.
43. Ibid.
44. Renov coins the term *domestic ethnography* in his essay "Domestic Ethnography and the Construction of the 'Other' Self," 216–29.
45. Kirshenblatt-Gimblett, "Kitchen Judaism," 75–105.
46. This is Jacques Derrida's neologism; see *Circumfession*, 213.
47. Trinh T. Minh-ha, *When the Moon Waxes Red*, 74.
48. This argument is encapsulated in Bauman's article "Allosemitism," 143–56.
49. The term is actually borrowed from Bernard Lazare. See Arendt, *Origins of Totalitarianism*, 65, n. 26.
50. Renov used this term in a presentation at "Eye and Thou II," New York University, March 2001. Another, more famous example of the assisted autobiography is Tom Joslin's and Peter Friedman's *Silverlake Life* (1993), though the conceit of Joslin finishing the film postmortem is never indulged and it is explicit within the film that it is Peter Friedman who finishes it.
51. Derrida does so in relation to Nietzsche's preface to *Ecce Homo*, in "Otobiographies," 1–38, and in discussion with Eugene Donato, ibid., 54–59. De Man does so in his brief but influential essay "Autobiography as De-Facement," 67–81.

1. Memory Once Removed

1. Finkielkraut, *Imaginary Jew*.
2. "On *D'Est*," by Chantal Akerman, 22.
3. Benjamin, "N," 49.
4. Benjamin, "A Berlin Chronicle," 28.
5. Ibid., 26.
6. Benjamin, *Moscow Diary*.
7. Benjamin, "N," 43.
8. These seemingly random tropes have distinct motivations, according to Akerman, some feminist, others related to Jewish thematics, and still others classifiable in formalist terms. There is some overlap in these categories: for instance, obsessiveness and repetition resonate as Jewish concerns, certainly as psychoanalytic ones, and also adhere to certain formalist constraints.
9. *Jewish*, in this book, as in common usage, at times refers to culture, at other times specifies the religion and its traditions, and at still others may imply an identity position occupied by individual Jews. In general, however, I try to use *Judaism* (sometimes modified by *rabbinic* or *traditional*) when discussing religious and traditional concerns. When referring to cultural aspects or expression, I tend to use the term *Jewishness*, which, following Arendt among others, I use to entail an active engagement with Jewish identity. I feel compelled to clarify that with this usage I am in no way implying an inherency or innate tendency of Jews to any particular type of Jewishness or to Jewishness at all. Any meaningful discussion about Jewish identity must rest not on essentialist conceptions of Jewishness, but rather on culturally constructed and historically fluctuating definitions of what Jewishness may be.
10. Akerman is well aware of this parable and chose to begin her film *American Stories* by recounting it in voice-over. She identifies herself as that character in this scene.
11. Janet Bergstrom has noted its recurrence in Akerman's *News From Home* (1976) and *Meetings with Anna*. Bergstrom, "Invented Memories," 109.
12. Ibid. This statement echoes Jonathan and Daniel Boyarin's concept of Jewish diasporic identity, in which "displacement of loyalty from place to memory of place" occurs. See Boyarin and Boyarin, "Diaspora," 719.
13. David, "*D'Est*," 62.
14. Halbreich and Jenkins, introduction to *Bordering on Fiction*, 8–9. Akerman reads only the second half of the commandment (Exodus 20, 4–7), omitting 1–3. It has been suggested that the installation engages in the deconstruction of the process of filmmaking itself, beginning with the edited film, moving into disparate clips, and ending with the abstract concept that subtends the project. See Kristine Butler's review of the installation in *Post-Modern Culture*.
15. Schama, *Landscape and Memory*, 12.
16. Although the images are not, strictly speaking, abstract, the portrait of the place as a whole emerges in shapes and patterns and registers viscerally, more than rationally or linearly as would a more representational portrait.
17. With regard to this notion of respectful distance from the subject and the look (or point of view) of the camera, Akerman has very distinct opinions. In an interview she gave about her film *Jeanne Dielman*, she commented on the shooting style: " 'You always know who is looking; you always know what the point of view is, all the time. It's always the same. But still, I was looking with a great deal of attention and the attention wasn't distanced. It was not a neutral look—

that doesn't exist anyhow. For me, the way I looked at what was going on was a look of love and respect. Maybe that's difficult to understand but I really think that's it. I let her live her life in the middle of the frame. I didn't go in too close, but I was not very far away. I let her be in her space. It's not uncontrolled. But the camera was not voyeuristic in the commercial way because you always knew where I was. You know, it wasn't shot through a keyhole.'" Akerman, "Chantal Akerman on *Jeanne Dielman*," 119.

18. Michael Tarantino has placed the look in *D'Est* "somewhere between a glimpse and a gaze," in "The Moving Eye," 53–54. Ivone Margulies refers to the look in this film alternately as a "gliding gaze," and a "mix of interest and estrangement," in, respectively, *Nothing Happens*, 203, and "Echo and Voice in *Meetings with Anna*," 62.

19. Benjamin, "Theses on the Philosophy of History," 257.

20. Benjamin, "N," 51–52.

21. Hartman, "Benjamin in Hope," 347.

22. As quoted in Margulies, "Echo and Voice," 61–62.

23. Clearly the New York Jewish Museum was well aware of the Jewish connection that this film and Akerman have with the region in question when it mounted the "Bordering on Fiction: Chantal Akerman's *D'Est*" exhibition in 1997. In the program notes, the museum refers to Akerman's family history and to the Holocaust, although her personal details are generally described as a contribution to Akerman's interest in this region, not as the motivation that subtends this interest. Akerman was approached with the idea to do a project on the "coming together of the European Community," and apparently it was she who introduced the component of anti-Semitism into the proposal. "She proposed a look at what was left out of this union as well, and at the concomitant rise of nationalism and anti-Semitism." See Halbreich and Jenkins, *Bordering on Fiction*, 8.

24. Benjamin, "Theses on the Philosophy of History," 263.

25. Margulies, "Echo and Voice in *Meetings with Anna*," 62.

26. Margulies, *Nothing Happens*, 202. Margulies always refers to the history of both parents, yet Akerman is famously concerned with the (everyday) history of one parent in particular, the mother. See her "Chantal Akerman on *Jeanne Dielman*." And her introductory monologue in the film refers only to the town "where my mother comes from," leading me to refer to this history as the history of the mother. That said, it is important to remember that Akerman's monologue refers, however obscurely, to "a letter written to the father."

27. Amy Taubin, *Village Voice*, May 12, 1998, 123.

28. Hirsch is quick to point out, of course, that survivor memory is not unmediated, but "that it is more directly connected to the past." She distinguishes postmemory from Kaja Silverman's notion of heteropathic memory, "a way of aligning the 'not me' with the 'me' without interiorizing it, or . . . 'introducing the "not me" into my memory reserve.'" The distinction is precisely a temporal one, where heteropathic memory depends solely on a spatial or cultural distance (an empathy between "the me and the not me") that need not be connected through familial or group relation. With postmemory, the memory effect is generationally created. Hirsch, "Projected Memory," 8–9.

29. Ibid., 9.

30. Ibid., 8.

31. Dominick LaCapra laments the absence of archival footage in Claude Lanzmann's *Shoah* (1985), considering its omission a structuring absence, and suggesting that "his method of confining himself to present words and sites derives its effect from its relation to what is omitted" (*History and Memory after Auschwitz*, 108). While I do not share LaCapra's longing for the historical images, I have to agree that both *Shoah* and *D'Est* do derive much of their power from that which is *not* seen—from, that is to say, a palpable sense of the losses of the Holocaust. These are not the only autobiographical films treating the themes of European Jewish history to eschew the use of archival footage of the Holocaust. Neither Ruth Beckermann's *Paper Bridge* (1987) nor Susan Korda's *One of Us* (1999), about the effects of the reunification of Berlin on her perception of her family's Holocaust memories, rely on a single frame of archival footage from World War II.

32. Benjamin, "Theses on the Philosophy of History," 255.

33. Ibid.

34. Akerman, "On *D'Est*," 17.

35. Ibid., 18.

36. Ibid., 34.

37. Ibid., 20; emphasis mine. I return to this notion of indirectness.

38. Ibid., 22.

39. Margulies, "Echo and Voice in *Meetings with Anna*," 62.

40. Schama, *Landscape and Memory*, 6–7.

41. An example of a text that attempts to create this type of filmic match is Abigail Child's video *Below the New* (1999) about life in Moscow after the fall of the Soviet Union. Child, another

Jewish experimental filmmaker, literalizes this imbrication by superimposing cinematic images of the prior era (official processions, images of Stalin, peasants dancing, etc.) onto video images of the present (also processions, marching bands, people in the streets, folkloric dancers, avant-garde jazz musicians, etc.). The title of Child's work references the past that lies immediately below the surface of "the new." At one point, Child intercuts two scenes of fireworks, one from the past and one from the present, with intervening shots of spectators from both eras. These explosions evoke the flashes from the past that Benjamin refers to, but are perhaps a bit too literal. Like Akerman, Child is also a Jewish experimental filmmaker whose film is a personal exploration of post-Soviet life, yet her approach to the subject could hardly be more dissimilar to Akerman's.

42. See Yerushalmi, *Zakhor*, 120–21, n. 7.

43. Ibid., 17.

44. Jonathan Rosen has gone as far as to suggest similarities between the nonlinearity of the Talmud and the interactivity of the Internet. See his *The Talmud and the Internet*.

45. Predictably, I prefer the telescopic metaphor to Yerushalmi's accordion, for the former's visual, and hence filmic, implications. For a further discussion of time in the Book of Genesis, see Graves and Patai, introduction to *Hebrew Myths*, 18.

46. Yerushalmi refers to this type of historical abbreviation as "capsule history" (*Zakhor*, 12).

47. Ibid., 51.

48. Ibid., 46–48.

49. Ibid., 50. Emphasis mine.

50. The Hebrew word *shoah* also means "destruction" or "ruin."

51. Pierre Vidal-Naquet mentions other historical collapses when he references the Jewish day of mourning known as Tisha B'Av (the ninth day of the month of Ab in the Jewish calendar). "Does not the mourning of the Ninth of Ab," he writes, "commemorate the fall of the first temple as well as the second? To this double commemoration could easily have been added the Spanish catastrophe of 1492, even the massacres in Poland and the Ukraine in the seventeenth century." Vidal-Naquet, *The Jews*, 60.

52. Benjamin, "N," 60.

53. Margulies, *Nothing Happens*, 7.

54. Benjamin, "Theses on the Philosophy of History," 264.

55. Yerushalmi means the Jewish people, not the state, when he says Israel. Yerushalmi, *Zakhor*, 9.

56. Harold Bloom, in his introduction to *Musical Variations on Jewish Thought*, by Revault d'Allonnes; italics are Bloom's.

57. Yerushalmi, *Zakhor*, 10.

58. In *Nothing Happens*, Margulies expounds upon Akerman's uses of cliché, defined thus: "Suggesting a condensation of thematic redundancy and serial reproduction, the term 'cliché' refers to a platitude, a phrase flattened out by repeated use." Margulies, *Nothing Happens*, 84. Later she defines cliché as "an image known before it is seen," 203. Both in Akerman's work and in traditional Jewish forms of remembering, cliché becomes a mnemonic mode whose very familiarity and repetitiveness form crucial aspects of its efficacy.

59. Margulies, "Echo and Voice," 61.

60. In regard to Akerman's relation to selective memory, it is worth noting that she only recounts a limited number of details about her family history, and she does so over and over again. As Janet Bergstrom aptly states, "What is striking about the many interviews Akerman has given over the past thirty years is not the autobiographical element per se, but rather how few of the events from her past she has spoken about repeatedly." Bergstrom, "Invented Memories," 99.

61. As far as I am aware, Benjamin is not an intentional or conscious point of reference for Akerman.

62. Benjamin, *Moscow Diary*, 6.

63. Yet it cannot be said that Eastern Europe or the Soviet Union resist interpretation or theoretical speculation any more or less than does any geopolitical region. Additionally, other writers and filmmakers have indeed attempted to analyze the Eastern European situation in considerable depth over the years. Thus what emerges in this comparison is an affinity between Benjamin's and Akerman's approaches to the subject, more than any inherent resistance of the subject to interpretation.

64. Asja Lacis was the woman to whom Benjamin's *One Way Street* is dedicated, and with whom he was visiting in Moscow. Lacis is credited, among other things, with introducing Benjamin to Brecht and to Marxist theory.

65. For a discussion of this prejudice in France, see Alain Finkielkraut, "The Jew and the Israelite," 47–80. Sander Gilman identifies the pejorative attitude toward Eastern Jews in Freud (whose family was originally from Galicia). Gilman tells us that Freud, in a letter to his friend and colleague Wilhelm Fleiss, dated April 27, 1898, "refers to his brother-in-law Moriz Freud (a distant cousin who married his sister Marie) as a 'half Asian' who suffers from 'pseudologica fantastica.'

He is a 'half-Asian' because he is an Eastern Jew (he comes from Bucaharest), and the 'disease' he is said to suffer from is, in fact, the psychiatric diagnosis for those mythomaniac patients who lie in order to gain status. For Freud it is the damaged, comic discourse of the Eastern Jew which approximates the anti-Semitic image of the lying Jew" (Gilman, *Difference and Pathology*, 272, n. 26).

66. Benjamin, letter to Buber (February 23, 1927), excerpted in Gershom Scholem's preface to *Moscow Diary*, 6.

67. This does not imply that bodies exist above or outside of history, merely that history is readable on and through the body, though not always in ways that are easily apparent. With regard to "looking elsewhere," Akerman herself has indicated this preference. In an interview conducted by Jean-Luc Godard in 1979 (translated and quoted in Bergstrom's essay), Akerman states: "Instead of showing a 'public' event because it is so sensational, or full of lots of things, I will tell the story of *something small nearby*." Bergstrom, "Invented Memories," 94; emphasis mine.

68. In his outstanding study of Benjamin's "corpus of autobiography," to which my analysis is deeply indebted, Gerhard Richter develops a theory based on the uselessness of the body in Benjamin's work, which can be extended to the entirety of Benjamin's theoretical corpus. The body, seen by Richter as being in perpetual retreat, is rendered "useless for political mobilizations"—this in opposition and resistance to the fascist mobilizations of body for political purposes. Richter, *Walter Benjamin and the Corpus of Autobiography*, 85.

69. Margulies, *Nothing Happens*, 203.

70. With regard to Akerman's long takes, Margulies has asserted that "with little in the way of action, [they] elicit a hyperacute perception, in which one recognizes both the image's literal and its representational aspects," *Nothing Happens*, 44.

71. Akerman, "On *D'Est*," 21.

72. We may be familiar with Akerman's face, either from pictures of her in articles and reviews, or from earlier work. She has appeared in several of her own films: *Saute Ma Ville* (1968); *L'Enfant aimé ou je joue a être une Femme Mariée* (1971); *Je tu il elle* (1974); *L'Homme a la valise* (1983); *Sloth* (1986); *Mallet-Stevens* (1986); and, more recently, *Chantal Akerman by Chantal Akerman* (1996).

73. Akerman, "On *D'Est*," 20.

74. Levinas, *Totality and Infinity*, 24.

75. Ibid., 52.

76. de Man, "Autobiography as De-Facement," 75.

77. Ibid., 69.

78. Ibid., 76.

79. Richter, *Walter Benjamin and the Corpus of Autobiography*, 113.

80. David, "*D'Est*," 62–63.

81. Akerman deftly constructs an auteurist autobiography here, creating an intertextual interplay between the "present" images in *D'Est* and her filmic past. As we have seen, this is her chosen autobiographical strategy, seen in its most elaborated form in *Chantal Akerman by Chantal Akerman*.

82. Akerman, "On *D'Est*," 17.

83. LaCapra, *History and Memory after Auschwitz*, 129.

84. Ibid., 133.

85. W. J. T. Mitchell, "Holy Landscape," 219–20.

86. Kalman Bland has written extensively on the problem of interpretation of the Second Commandment. He contends that it is only in the modern era that the Second Commandment has been interpreted all-inclusively and that, prior to the eighteenth century, the prohibition was understood to be restricted to visual representation of God. Ultimately, Bland argues that there is no necessary Jewish resistance to visual culture, much less a blanket prohibition against visual representation. See Bland, *The Artless Jew*. Bland is not the first to take this position. A notable precursor (there are others) is Cecil Roth in his book *Jewish Art*.

87. It is particularly interesting that, if Bland is correct, the belief in Jewish aniconism gained credibility precisely at the historical moment when European Jews were struggling with issues of visibility, and when Jewish Enlightenment (Haskalah) leaders such as Moses Mendelsohn were advocating for what amounts to a closeted, or nonvisible, Jewishness.

88. Bloom, introduction to *Musical Variations on Jewish Thought*, 15.

89. Bland, *The Artless Jew*, 18.

90. Avrum Kampf makes this argument; see Bland, *The Artless Jew*, 52.

91. Margulies notes this defiance in Akerman's video *Lettre de Cinéaste* (1984), saying that "she verbally asserts her 'defiance' of the Jewish proscription of image-creation ('Thou shalt not make . . . any graven image, or any likeness of anything that is in heaven . . . or is in the earth . . . '

Exodus 20:4). She is, after all, an image-maker." The quote is from "Echo and Voice," 66. Margulies herself does not question the breadth or applicability of this prohibition.

92. Bergstrom, "Invented Memories," 94.

93. Richter, *Walter Benjamin and the Corpus of Autobiography*, 34. In the interview with Godard mentioned above, Akerman and Godard differ on this point; Godard begins with the image and Akerman with the word.

94. Bloom, introduction to *Musical Variations on Jewish Thought*, 20.

95. Clearly Akerman is not referring specifically to the Freudian primal scene of the child witnessing his or her parents engaged in sexual intercourse. However, it is fair to say that the elements of fear of loss, and of annihilation, experienced by the child (Akerman, in this case) through her perception of her parents' experience retains some significant elements of Freud's interpretation of the original "Wolfman" scenario.

96. Yerushalmi, *Zakhor*, 15–16.

97. Ecclesiastes 3:15.

98. See Yerushalmi's "Postscript: Reflections on Forgetting," in *Zakhor*, 105–17. Bloom writes on forgetting in his introduction to *Musical Variations on Jewish Thought*, 18.

99. This model of repression is also operative in Freud's conceptualization of mourning as well as of melancholia, a connection that will become increasingly relevant to my argument.

100. Freud, "The Uncanny," 220. Susan Shapiro writes about the Jew in the nineteenth- and twentieth-century European imaginary *as* the uncanny. See her "The Uncanny Jew," 63–78.

101. Bloom, introduction to *Musical Variations on Jewish Thought*, 5.

102. Ibid., 16. Whether or not this is an accurate reading of the Second Commandment is not at issue here. The *perception* of the commandment as a prohibition, and the transformation of that perception into an anxious repression "in our time" is what concerns Bloom.

103. Žižek, *Looking Awry*, 8–12.

104. In fact, she can look squarely into the faces of others, faces both present and absent, faces that represent herself and her (m)other, and this looking turns into another form of evacuation, the evacuation of self.

105. From Benjamin, "One-Way Street," 480.

106. Akerman, "On *D'Est*," 20.

107. Culbertson, "Embodied Memory, Transcendence, and Telling," 191.

2. Reframing the Jewish Family

1. All but one of the films considered in detail in this chapter are about Jewish American families, so my analysis of the Jewish family here is largely limited to an American context.

2. Walker, *Trauma Cinema*, 16.

3. Renov, "Domestic Ethnography and the Construction of the 'Other' Self," 218. Renov joins the two words *complication* and *co-implication* in his neologistic compound *co(i)mplication*. For Renov, domestic ethnography includes any and all family autobiography, including any by parents about their children. Significantly, nearly all Jewish family autobiographies are made from the child's perspective. One notable exception is Menachem Daum's and Oren Rudovsky's *Hiding and Seeking* (2003).

4. Citron, "Fleeing from Documentary," 175. In Citron's case, this has certainly been true. See *Parthenogenesis* (1975), *Daughter Rite* (1979), and *Mother Right* (1983).

5. Bachelard, *The Poetics of Reverie*, 21.

6. Tellingly, Lacan does not insist that it is the mother holding the infant; in fact he even suggests that the infant can be a mechanical prop, a "trotte bébé." See Jacques Lacan, "The Mirror Stage as Formative of the *I* Function," 4.

7. See Miller's "Putting Ourselves in the Picture," 51.

8. To be born Jewish by halakha (Jewish law) requires Jewish matrilineal descent. Of course, this requirement has been contested and reconsidered by recent Jewish revisionist movements, such as the reconstructionist movement, which considers those born of Jewish fathers and non-Jewish mothers also to be legitimately Jewish.

9. For an extended discussion of the concept of disidentification, see Muñoz, *Disidentifications*.

10. See Kirshenblatt-Gimblett's presentation "The 'New Jews,'" 3–4.

11. This is Jeffrey Shandler's phrase, quoted in ibid., 4.

12. For an interesting discussion of Jewish descent vs. Jewish assent, see Michael Krausz's essay "On Being Jewish," 264–76. In this essay, Krausz makes a worthwhile distinction when he says "The question of Jewish descent addresses the question, How are we to *identify* someone as a Jew as opposed to a non-Jew? The question of Jewishness by assent addresses the question, How are we to characterize someone's Jewishness" (267). See also the "American Jewish Identity Survey," by Egon Mayer et al.

13. "American Jewish Identity Survey," 10.

14. Kirshenblatt-Gimblett, "The 'New Jews,'" 2–3.

15. I would also readily include a discussion of a film made by a filmmaker whose origins are uncertain but who proclaims a Jewish identity for the purposes of the film. Had time permitted, I would have liked to discuss the conundra implied by this very position in Jamie Kastner's film *Kike Like Me* (2007). Kastner's Jewishness is at issue in the film in that he models his project on Elia Kazan's film *Gentleman's Agreement* (1947), in which Gregory Peck's Christian-born character masquerades as a Jew to confront latent anti-Semitism. Kastner "poses" as a Jew in myriad circumstances and uncovers troubling anti-Semitism at nearly every turn. However, unlike *Gentleman's Agreement*, this film at no point indicates, from outset to conclusion, the truth of Kastner's origins (which ultimately seems immaterial but is interesting nonetheless).

16. Derrida, *Circumfession*, 213.

17. One explicit exception to this is *A Healthy Baby Girl*, which states in no uncertain terms that the highly personal family drama of a DES-affected family is to be understood in its broader sociopolitical context, wherein millions of families like Helfand's are in similar or worse situations. At one point, when faced with a tough question, by a lawyer who will represent Helfand's suit against the pharmaceutical company, as to why she wants to film these "private" moments, Helfand powerfully and articulately declares (before breaking down in tears) that the videotaping "is forcing me to deal with the fact that my disease is public and political. I also want my parents to know that this is not their disease and this is not my disease. This isn't a private thing we have to keep in our house, it's not gonna fester here. There's nothing to be ashamed of, you know. My mother is one of three million women; I'm one of nine million children. This is a very public crisis."

18. A film such as *Put the Camera on Me* (2004), by Darren Stein and Adam Shell, is one such video. The filmmakers had an extraordinary amount of home and amateur footage of their days as preteens in suburban Los Angeles, but the final film is only slightly more than a glorified home movie, holding the most interest for those caught in the original films' frames and, perhaps, for scholars of amateur filmmaking or suburban Jewish American life, but the filmmakers seem so convinced of their brilliance they neglected to imagine that others might not be as taken by the self-indulgences of a group of sadistic, suburban American kids.

19. Miller, "Putting Ourselves in the Picture," 52.

20. *Daughter Rite* is, as mentioned in the introduction, a prototype of the Jewish autobiographical film even though it effects a nearly total erasure of Jewish signifiers. In chapter 4, I interrogate further the absence or ambivalence of Jewish indicators in several films, *Daughter Rite* being perhaps the most extreme example.

21. An interesting exception to this patriarchal point of view is the 16 mm footage shot by Lisa Lewenz's German Jewish grandmother in interwar Berlin. This is not typical home movie footage, by any stretch of the imagination. Lewenz's grandmother films the intellectual elite of Berlin society along with the family, and the fact that we know it was a woman behind the camera, shooting on a semiprofessional camera (unlike the point-and-shoot 8 mm and super-8 cameras introduced a few decades later) gives an entirely different feel to the footage. We know the point of view is anomalous, which lends it an air of exception, quite the opposite of the normalized gaze of the super-8-toting or video-camera-wielding father. See *A Letter without Words* (1998).

22. Citron attests to this when she says "Through filmmaking I receive my childhood wish. I become the father standing behind the ground-glass wall of the camera's lens." *Home Movies and Other Necessary Fictions*, 111.

23. Miller, "Putting Ourselves in the Picture," 51.

24. Quoted in Bachelard, *The Poetics of Reverie*, 126.

25. A film was made precisely on this topic: *Mamadrama: The Jewish Mother in Cinema* (2001, Australia), by Monique Schwartz.

26. Prell, *Fighting to Become Americans*, 145. Prell analyzes the comic routines and fictional descriptions by popular midcentury writers and comedians such as Philip Roth, Myron Cohen, Dan Greenberg, Henny Youngman, Milton Berle, and Harry Goldman. Their litany of complaints has become the jeremiad of the modern Jewish male.

27. Ibid., 150.

28. As we see later in this chapter, Oxenberg's mother does, in *Thank You and Goodnight*, at points perform the guilt-tripping Jewish mother role quite convincingly.

29. On the mother as repository and primary inculcator of Jewish cultural values, see also Hyman, *Gender and Assimilation in Modern Jewish History*, 161–63.

30. Prell, *Fighting to Become Americans*, 163. See the entire chapter on "The Devouring Jewish Mother," as well (142–76). Haym Soloveitchik argues that, at roughly the same time that most American Jews moved toward further assimilation and secularization, orthodox Jews were

becoming (in direct opposition to this tendency) more rigorous in their practice. See Soloveit-chik, "Rupture and Reconstruction," 78–82.

31. There is a somewhat outdated, and to some degree discredited, theory that has resonances here. In 1938, Marcus Lee Hansen developed a theory of a generation-based process of ethnic identification in American society. In his essay "The Third Generation in America," he proposed that, in general, second-generation Americans tended to reject their ethnic identities in favor of Americanizing and third-generation Americans took an active interest in their immigrant past. This is what Hansen called the "principle of third-generation interest," characterized by the phrase "What the son wishes to forget, the grandson wishes to remember." This principle (which Hansen, as a second-generation son of immigrants yet interested in these themes, was living proof *against*) became known as Hansen's Law, Hansen, "The Third Generation in America," 495. For an extensive discussion and refutation of Hansen's Law, see Sollors, *Beyond Ethnicity*, 214–21.

32. Quoted in Sollors, *Beyond Ethnicity*, 215.

33. Such salvage projects were undertaken in written form starting in the 1970s, inspired by feminism to give voice to women of all ages and experiences. In one book, *Jewish Grandmothers*, editors Sydelle Kramer and Jenny Masur conducted oral histories with ten Jewish grandmothers, explicitly to challenge the stereotype and to show Jewish immigrant (mostly) women in their diversity. It is interesting to note that in this written collection from a quarter of a century ago, an effort is made to challenge the stereotype, whereas in the films of the past decade-and-a–half, the grandmother has reverted back to type. What the film projects all seem to share is a romanticized notion of cultural authenticity, and the need, as the editors assert, to preserve these voices that "offer us all a heritage" (xv).

34. Let me draw your attention to one exceptional film, made by the Rosenbergs' granddaughter, Ivy Meeropol, *Heir to an Execution: A Granddaughter's Story* (2004, USA). This film clearly features a most unusual Jewish grandmother, one who stands as an anomaly in every possible way. Ethel Rosenberg, as is well known, was among the many Jewish Communists active in New York City in the 1940s and 1950s, and the image of her as a committed activist stands in stark contrast to other representations of Jewish grandmothers in this collection of first person films. However, both at the time of the trial and in the narrative of the film, great pains were taken to represent her as a caring and devoted mother, rather than to emphasize her political activities. Needless to say, she was ruthlessly denied the opportunity to fulfill her role as a grandmother.

35. This topic is taken up more extensively in the following chapters. Suffice it to say here that Oxenberg is one of the first out lesbian filmmakers, having made two lesbian films in the early 1970s: *Not One of Them* (1974) and *A Comedy in Six Unnatural Acts* (1975).

36. Alan Berliner had a child in 2004, but that is well after he made *Nobody's Business*, the primary text of his that I consider here.

37. Notably, *Hiding and Seeking* (2004), by Menachem Daum, and the much shorter and funnier *Orders of Love* (2004), by Jeremy Benstock, come to mind. *First Person Plural* (1988–96), by Lynne Hershmann, and *Joyce at 34* (1972), by Joyce Chopra and Claudia Weill, both at least mention the filmmakers' children. Interestingly, Jonathan Caouette decided, on the advice of his high-powered producers not to include anything about his son in *Tarnation*, as such an inclusion was considered too confusing. The producers apparently feared that it would complicate matters too much to have a film about a gay man and his dysfunctional family introduce the "unlikely" fact of his progeny. Caouette's ex-girlfriend is quoted in *LA Weekly* as saying "We were in the original version . . . but, when Jonathan showed that to Stephen Winter and John Cameron Mitchell, they felt like the story of me and our son was too big to be just another subplot." Scott Foundas, *LA Weekly*, October 15–21, 2004. One wonders if a more in-depth treatment of Jewish-ness within this narrative might also have been considered "too big" (that is, too difficult to explain within the narrow demands of linear narrative).

38. Miller, "Putting Ourselves in the Picture," 64.

39. Bachelard, *The Poetics of Reverie*, 20.

40. Ibid., 107.

41. In the distributor's summary of the film, the cardboard character is referred to as Scowling Jan, but, as she represents a range of emotions, and since there is no indication that Oxenberg herself preferred that name, I have chosen to use the diminutive of Jan. http://www.nvr.org/vidforum_content.php?pro=health&sec=vid&subsec=com&start=P&end=Z&sid=&filmid=12.

42. Citron, *Home Movies and Other Necessary Fictions*, 22.

43. Citron discusses this form of complex family dynamics, dynamics that emerge through the process of making autobiographical films. She states that "autobiographical work risks exposing that which the culture [and the family] wants silenced." She considers that such films "can be dangerous to others." Citron, "Fleeing from Documentary," 273.

44. The conflation of disease with racial difference is, of course, a well-documented cultural phenomenon. It is the subject of Sander Gilman's two books *Difference and Pathology* and *Disease and Representation*. It is a running subtext in Gregg Bordowitz's *Fast Trip, Long Drop* (see my analysis in chapter 4), and is even more explicitly considered in an altogether different cultural context, that of a Japanese American, in the wonderfully inventive *Halving the Bones* (1995, USA), by Ruth Ozeki.

45. Derrida, *The Ear of the Other*, 57–58.

46. See Derrida, *Circumfession*, 213.

47. The first interview in an Akerman documentary is in *Sud* (1999), where, toward the end of the film, and somehow reluctantly, she interviews people in the American South about the lynching of a black man. Her next documentary, *From the Other Side* (2002), about the U.S.–Mexican border, includes several interviews. Even though this film is shot with her characteristic distance from the subject, and with prime lenses that forbid zooms, the interviews lend a more traditional documentary style than exists in her earlier nonfiction work, such as *D'Est*, *News From Home* (1976), or *Hotel Monterey* (1972).

48. In a footnote about Ravett's later film, *The March* (1999), Jeffrey Skoller seems to concur: "*The March* can be seen as part of a stylistically similar series of films that Ravett has made to explore his struggle to know about his parents' experiences of the Shoah, and *the impact this history has had on his family*, especially *Everything's for You* (1989)" (emphasis mine). See Skoller, *Shadows, Specters, Shards*, 201, n. 19.

49. Barthes, *Camera Lucida*, 65. Barthes makes the distinction between History with a capital *H*, which happened before he was born, and history with a small *h*, in which he is included. As we saw in chapter 1, Akerman makes a similar distinction. However, in both cases, the distinction warrants but does not receive further explanation. In critical studies (feminist theory, cultural studies, postcolonial studies, and related disciplines), History with a capital *H* might imply hegemonic master narratives, of the sort that need to be contested; history with a small *h* might then be the unofficial, nonhegemonic, counternarrative that challenges but does not attempt to supplant the master narrative. There are many ways to conceive of this capitalization of history, but one wonders if any ultimately stands up to scrutiny.

50. Naming is always a delicate matter, with complex representational psychological ramifications and interpretations. In a reading that turns Freud's theories of hysteria back onto Freud himself, Ann Pellegrini analyzes the (unconscious) process of Freud naming his most famous hysterical patient, Dora. See Pellegrini, "Whiteface Performances," 115–18.

51. The name is pronounced the same way in Hebrew or in Yiddish. Ravett chooses the common transliterated spelling of the name, *Chaim*, though the YIVO standard for Yiddish transliteration would have it spelled *Khayim*.

52. On Yom Kippur, the Day of Atonement, the holiest day of the Jewish calendar, there is a series of prayers that entail repeated recitations.

53. The extra time is for the audio tails on either end, on which we hear Ravett and his mother's voice while watching black film leader.

54. Ravett also features repetition within his oeuvre. The film *Half Sister* includes part of an interview with Ravett's mother, a part that reappears in *Toncia* in its unedited version. Again, we have repetition with a difference.

55. Hirsch, *Family Frames*, 9.

56. This childhood in perpetuity is echoed in Oxenberg's film with regard to her dead sister. She asks, in the voice of her childlike alter ego, "Will Judy remain seven years old? Will she never learn algebra?"

57. An eruv is a dividing line used to delineate the space of a Jewish community within which boundaries it is acceptable, according to Jewish law, to perform certain tasks on the Sabbath that are forbidden outside of its physical remit. Here, the term is used to denote a relational space.

58. Hirsch, *Family Frames*, 9.

59. Ibid.

60. Sander Gilman writes frequently about *Mauscheln* as a Jewish corruption of the German language, or, in his words, "the language ascribed to the Eastern Jew who attempted to speak German." See his illuminating chapter, "The Jewish Voice," in *The Jew's Body*, 10–37 (quote from page 21). In Hasidic communities in Brooklyn, there is even a certain pride in maintaining a discernible Jewish accent, though of course this is rare among non-Hasidic Jews. See Fader, "Literacy, Bilingualism in a Hasidic Community," 261–83.

61. Compare this relative lack of cultural translation with Judith Helfand's discussion of shiva in *A Healthy Baby Girl*. Shiva comes up in a highly unorthodox context, after Helfand has had a radical hysterectomy; she is mourning what amounts to the foreclosure of any future progeny; yet she openly discusses the Jewish rituals of mourning with her parents, in part to convey to

them the depth of her grief and in part to convey to the audience the terms of the mourning ritual to which she has referred.

62. *Shiva* (Hebrew for "seven") refers to the seven days of mourning from the day of death, when the immediate family gathers under one roof and grieves together.

63. I am grateful to Barbara Kirshenblatt-Gimblett for this phrase.

64. Finkielkraut, *Imaginary Jew*.

65. This is not as antithetical a phrase as it may appear. Many Jewish households have paintings of rabbis or shtetl life on the walls. I remember a painting, of a man in a yarmulke studiously peeling an apple, hanging on my grandmother's living-room wall. A friend's grandmother had little, dancing Hasid porcelain figurines on her coffee table. For a discussion of Jewish iconography and the myth of Jewish aniconism, I refer you to Bland's *The Artless Jew*, discussed at some length in chapter 1.

66. Stratton, *Coming Out Jewish*, 300.

67. In Stuart Hall's terms, we could say "decoding"; see "Encoding/Decoding," 128–38.

68. Stratton, *Coming Out Jewish*, 300.

69. The word derives from the Hebrew word for "pepper," *pilpel*, and the method implies a spicing or seasoning of the Talmud through passionate disputation.

70. On Jews and civility, see Stratton, *Coming Out Jewish*, 285, 288, 307–10. See also Cuddihy, *The Ordeal of Civility*.

71. Berliner, "The Reluctant Witness," 33.

72. Hirsch, *Family Frames*, 10.

73. Ibid., 8.

74. "*Complaints of a Dutiful Daughter* and 'The Jewish Question,'" paper presented at the first "Eye and Thou" symposium on Jewish autobiographical film and video, held at the University of Southern California, October 24–26, 1998.

75. Ibid.

76. It is also true that the context in which this paper was given demanded that Ginsburg find something explicitly Jewish about the film, beyond the few explicitly Jewish indicators discussed in the following chapter.

77. Another, very interesting film to attempt this filmic repair is Ivy Meeropol's *Heir to an Execution*. As the granddaughter of Ethel and Julius Rosenberg, Meeropol declares outright , at the end of this moving inquest, that the making of the film was an endeavor to recover the Rosenbergs for her family, to bring them back into the fold.

3. A Treyf Autocritique of Autobiography

1. The Yiddish word *treyf* means unkosher and refers specifically to that which is forbidden by Jewish dietary laws. The word derives from the Hebrew *trefa*, "to rip or tear." In the film, we take some liberties with the term, expanding it for our purposes. When I use it capitalized and italicized, I am referring to the title of my film. Otherwise, I use the term as an adjective that describes an oppositional, insider/outsider stance.

2. The writings of Michelle Citron and Gregg Bordowitz are two noteworthy examples of works by autobiographical filmmakers who have amply and engagingly availed themselves of this opportunity of autocritique. See Citron's *Home Movies and Other Necessary Fictions* and Bordowitz's *The AIDS Crisis Is Ridiculous*, especially chapters 4–6 and 13. Also see Negrón-Mutaner's "When I Was a Puerto Rican Lesbian," 511–26.

3. See Derrida's *Ear of the Other*.

4. The heading for this section refers to a quote from Bakhtin on the split subjectivity of the autobiographical author–creator. The complete quote is as follows: "Even if the author–creator had created the most perfect autobiography, or confession, he would, nonetheless, have remained, in so far as he had produced it, outside of the universe represented within it. If I tell (orally or in writing) an event that I have just lived, in so far as *I am telling* (orally or in writing) this event, I find myself already outside of the time-space in which the event occurred. To identify oneself absolutely with oneself, to identify one's 'I' with the 'I' that I tell, is as impossible as to lift oneself up by one's hair" (quoted in Todorov's *Mikhail Bakhtin*, 106). Bakhtin does not even consider the possibility of an autobiographer also performing a metacritique of the work— surely a doubly impossible proposition.

5. This argument of course is subject to infinite regress, our very selves being alter to ourselves and subject to the narrative imperative.

6. In a very succinct example taken from Rousseau's *Neuchatel preamble*, as translated in Olney's *Memory and Narrative*, Rousseau says, "In giving myself over both to my remembrance of the past impression and to my present feeling, I will depict *doubly* the state of my mind, that is both at the moment the event happened to me and at the moment I describe it; my *style*, which

is uneven yet natural—now energetic and now leisurely, now subdued and now extravagant, now grave and now gay—will itself form a part of the *story*." 168, emphasis mine. Paul Jay has claimed an even earlier and less likely proponent of the discontinuous and fragmentary (or what he, according to de Man, calls the *disappropriated*) subject, in St. Augustine. See Jay, "Being in the Text," 1046–48.

7. Olney, *Memory and Narrative*, 207–8.

8. Nietzsche, *The Will to Power*, 267.

9. J. Butler, *Bodies That Matter*, 123. In an earlier assertion, she claims, "My position is mine to the extent that 'I'—and I do not shirk from the pronoun—replay and resignify the theoretical positions that have constituted me, working the possibilities of their convergence, and trying to take account of the possibilities that they systematically exclude. No subject is its own point of departure; and the fantasy that it is one can only disavow its constitutive relations by recasting them as the domain of a countervailing externality." See her "Contingent Foundations."

10. J. Butler, in *Giving an Account of Oneself*, essentially declares the necessary failure of the "I" from "I"'s perspective, since the "I" can never give an adequate account of its own becoming. See in particular her discussion on "The 'I' and the 'You,'" 65–82.

11. Elizabeth Bruss, in her troubling and troubled article on filmic autobiography, "'Eye' for I," 296–320, insists that filmic autobiography is less viable than its written counterpart, in part due to the temporal disjuncture involved. Her argument is effectively refuted by Rachel Gabara in her essay "Mixing Impossible Genres," 335–37.

12. In his extraordinarily erudite and compelling close reading of a broad range of anti-authorial criticism, Seán Burke explores this conundrum with the delicacy and precision of a theoretical neurosurgeon. See Burke's *The Death and Return of the Author*, especially 53–56.

13. Autobiography in and of itself (written as well as filmic) raises this specter of the infinitely repeating self. Louis Renza wrestles elegantly with this problem of the proliferating auto-biographical "I" in his article "The Veto of the Imagination: A Theory of Autobiography," 278–79. His questions are resoundingly similar to mine when he states: "To persist in the autobiographical project, the autobiographer must come to terms with a unique pronominal crux: how can he keep using the first-person pronoun, his sense of self-reference, without its becoming in the course of writing something other than strictly his own self-referential sign—a defacto third-person pronoun?" He claims quite rightly that autobiography entails an imper-sonating effect of the self, and that any "autobiographical intentionality depends on just such diacritical retention of the 'I.'"

14. For a further discussion about the limits of the utility of the experiential narrative, see Scott, "The Evidence of Experience," 773–97. Scott rightly problematizes the expectation that experi-ential narratives are inherently counterhegemonic, an assumption made all too uncritically by many feminist and queer theorists (among others). To summarize, she contends that "experi-ence" has been used against political and cultural dissidents more often than it has worked for them, and that we must beware of relying too heavily on its redemptive prospects. Nonetheless, I believe experiential narratives can be mobilized strategically to great effect, even if they are only to be conceived of as a powerful rhetorical device.

15. How this may differ in the case of autocritique in written autobiography is not the subject of this chapter, though it may be interesting to point to a handful of autobiographical works writ-ten by theorists that are simultaneously autobiographical and autocritical, or what Nancy K. Miller has called "autocritography." See Miller's, *Bequest and Betrayal*, Barthes's *Roland Barthes by Roland Barthes* and *Camera Lucida*, Derrida's *Circumfession*, and Kuhn's *Family Secrets*. For Miller's defense of "autocritography," see her article "But enough about me, what do you think of my memoir?" 421–36.

16. The double vision that I claim as exceptional in *Treyf* is so only in that the two perspectives most elaborately represented are those of the filmmakers. However, many autobiographical films do include other characters whose participation contributes to a multiperspectival subjectivity. It is through this relationality (as I discuss in my introduction) that the subject is constituted, at times to the point of appropriating other's memories, mannerisms, and narratives as the subject's own (see chapter 1 for an extended discussion of appropriated postmemory). Also, there are a number of first person films that list two directors, yet the second is almost always the silent/invisible partner; see, for example: *In Her Own Time* (1985), Barbara Myerhoff and Lynne Littman; *Hiding and Seeking* (2004), Menachem Daum and Oren Rudovsky; *Silverlake Life* (1992), Tom Joslin and Peter Friedman; *Born into Brothels* (2004), Ross Kauffman and Zana Briski.

17. I use the term *strategic* in a similar vein, much as, for instance, Gayatri Spivak uses *strategic essentialism*, wherein the use is invoked despite an awareness of the pitfalls of such a strategy yet with a knowledge that such strategies can be effective, even necessary, for certain political interventions to take place. See Spivak's *In Other Worlds*, 205.

18. Trinh T. Minh-ha, *When the Moon Waxes Red*, 74.

19. Beauvoir, *Ethics of Ambiguity*, 78.
20. This was based on a series of considerations having to do with the actual biographical details of our lives, Cynthia's having lived in Jerusalem for ten years before our relationship, and my struggle to reconcile my early Zionist education and indoctrination with my adult political beliefs, positions that turned out to be irreconcilable.
21. There is a small, though not insignificant, collection of books and articles by Jewish critics of Zionism that preceded the making of *Treyf*. See Edward Corrigan's article "Jewish Criticism of Zionism" for extensive references. Some of the publications mentioned are: Noam Chomsky's *The Fateful Triangle: The United States, Israel, and the Palestinians* (1983); Marc H. Ellis's *Towards a Jewish Theology of Liberation: The Uprising and the Future* (1989); Roberta Strauss Feuerlicht's *The Fate of the Jews* (1983); Georges Friedmann's *The End of the Jewish People* (1967); Maxim Ghilan's *How Israel Lost Its Soul* (1974); Alfred M. Lilienthal's *What Price Israel?* (1953); Norton Mezvinsky's *The Character of the State of Israel* (1972); Cheryl Rubenberg's *Israel and the American National Interest* (1986); and Michael Selzer's *The Wineskin and the Wizard* (1970). There are also edited volumes: *Zionism Reconsidered,* ed. Michael Selzer, and *Zionism: The Dream and the Reality—A Jewish Critique,* ed. Gary V. Smith.
22. See http://www.jfrej.org/.
23. The year 2001 saw, following on the beginning of the Al Aqsa Intifada (September 2000), the birth of several Jewish anti-occupation groups, including JATO in New York (http://www.jatonyc .org/) and Not in My Name in Chicago (http://www.nimn.org/). There was a Jewish Unity for a Just Peace (JUNITY) conference held in Chicago in May 2001 that brought together many of the U.S. Jewish voices against the occupation. See Alisa Solomon's article in the *Village Voice,* "Not in My Name," May 16–22, 2001.
24. Kushner and Solomon, eds., *Wrestling with Zion.* See also Farber, *Radicals, Rabbis, and Peacemakers.*
25. Varadharajan, *Exotic Parodies,* xxi.
26. See the letter from Arendt to McCarthy, October 3, 1963, in *Between Friends,* 151. Arendt answered her critics indirectly in an essay titled "Truth and Politics."
27. In the realist debates of the 1970s, we would most certainly have been denounced for this "bourgeois" strategy. For a discussion of the realist debates, see Kaplan's "Realist Debate in the Feminist Film," 125–41.
28. Metz, *The Imaginary Signifier.*
29. People of my generation and older, raised in the United States before home video, have generally been exposed to the visual images (in mirrors, photos, home movies) well before ever hearing our recorded voices, hence the defamiliarized effect of the voice in contrast with the very familiar aspect of our visual image. Those growing up with home video and telephone answering machines may be much more accustomed to, indeed identified with, the sound of their recorded voices.
30. This has been a tried and tested approach of political documentary, especially popular with feminist filmmakers. Consider such venerable examples as: *The Woman's Film* (Newsreel Collective, 1971); *Growing Up Female* (Julia Reichart and Jim Klein, 1970); *Union Maids* (Julia Reichart and James Klein, 1976); *With Babies and Banners* (Lorraine Gray, 1977); *The Life and Times of Rosie the Riveter* (Connie Field, 1980); and countless more, including a film I worked on called *Women and Children Last* (Amber Hollibaugh and Gini Reticker, 1996). The strategy is to interview a range of participants, preferably from a variety of ethnic backgrounds, who all testify to essentially the same narrative, which corroborates the point of view, or voice, of the filmmaker.
31. I am thinking of such forebears as Ross McElwee or Joyce Chopra, but even more contemporary first person filmmakers, such as Jonathan Caouette, Morgan Spurlock, and many others have garnered attention only through their first person films, not before. Michael Moore was a fairly well-known journalist before he began making films, but only within a very limited left-wing circle. His first person films were what propelled him to international fame. For most first person filmmakers, Michael Moore and Nick Broomfield notwithstanding, fame or personal recognition seems a secondary concern.
32. My insistence on strategy and strategic mobilization of the first person narrative leans perhaps too heavily on a notion of conscious intentionality, yet, as any psychoanalytically inclined critic can attest, there is always more to any representation than the artist's intention. Perhaps it is better to leave to others to identify the forces at work upon our self-representation in *Treyf*. Here, it seems, we meet one of the palpable limits of autocritique.
33. I invoke the term *propaganda* knowingly and by no means derogatorily. I do not subscribe to the belief that only pernicious political motivations deserve to be called propaganda, but rather that any film or text that intends to persuade, promote, or publicize (that is, propagate) a particular

political cause or point of view is worthy of the term. Like John Grierson, I take propaganda to be a vocation, not an accusation.

34. This discussion is in no way meant to conflate truth with morality or factuality. I am only arguing that the film's truth value resides in the degree to which it resonates as plausible or believable to the spectator, not the degree to which the spectator agrees with the positions taken nor the degree to which the positions taken are verifiably correct.

35. What could be said to visually or iconographically characterize secular Jewish life? Bagels and lox? At one desperate moment in the production, we filmed radical queer Jewish circus performer Jennifer Miller literally juggling bagels. Fortunately, that scene was cut (though Miller was, as always, brilliant).

36. The authoritative Jewish voice cited here is only authoritative within a limited sphere. The voice is readable as Jewish by American Jews raised in a religious community, or by those who have encountered such communities. It is decidedly *not* a credible voice of authority outside of this context. The nasal timbre, the sing-song tone, the dentated *d*s and *t*s are all indicators of this so-called Jewish voice. For an in-depth discussion of the Jewish voice, see Gilman's *The Jew's Body*, 10–37.

37. It is also interesting to track the ways in which these very credentials render us suspect in certain leftist activist contexts.

38. Two films that address this position are Sandi DuBowski's *Trembling before G-d* (US, 2001) and Ilil Alexander's *Keep Not Silent* (Israel, 2004).

39. Of course there are signifiers of legitimacy that go beyond what is said—for instance, in our case, our race and class indices, which gain us tacit acceptance within American middle-class Jewish culture. Had one or both of us not had white skin, for instance, our status would immediately be questioned and even the indisputable proof of matrilineage or education would not necessarily gain us acceptance or the privileges, such as they might be, of "membership."

40. See Nichols' "Voice of the Documentary," 48–63.

41. Even though this is a Bakhtinian concept, Bakhtin himself is contradictory on the point. He alternately declares all language to be dialogic ("The dialogic orientation of discourse is a phenomenon that is, of course, a property of any discourse," he says in "Discourse in the Novel," 279), while nonetheless consigning some modes of expression, even some writing styles, to the exclusively monologic (as he does, for instance, with Tolstoy's prose as opposed to Dostoevsky's, or the rhetorical articulations of a military order). On Tolstoy's monologism, see Bakhtin's *Problems of Dostoevsky's Poetics*, 69–71.

42. Unfortunately, even were we to have carefully delineated the two voices, the problem would not simply disappear. Two unitary voices can even help to perpetuate the illusion of an integrated, whole, subjectivity: two complete, discrete "universes" speaking to one another, and with one another, across the intersubjective void.

4. Ambivalence and Ambiguity in Queer Jewish Subjectivity

1. Unpublished interview with the author, September 28, 2000.

2. Philip B. Roth's *I Was a Jewish Sex Worker* (1996) is a flagrant exception, in that it is explicitly Jewish and quite explicitly sexual. He also made a film called *A 25-Year-Old Gay Man Loses His Virginity to a Woman* (1990), and the woman is the well-known New York sex worker turned performance artist, Annie Sprinkle, another queer Jew. Sprinkle's own videos could not be more sexually explicit, though they are explicitly silent on the subject of her Jewishness.

3. Clearly, this should not lead to the presumption that the risks of public identification either as a Jew or as queer are the same, or are the same everywhere. It is simply to suggest that the risks for these particular filmmakers would seem scant yet their evasions and ambiguities persist. Also, to be clear, in several of these films generally one of the two identities is proudly proclaimed at the awkward expense of the other.

4. See Zimmerman's essay, "The Challenge of Conflicting Communities," 213–15.

5. Ibid., 213.

6. Ibid., 209. This is not to imply any kind of Jewish exceptionalism in this regard; in fact, it very much brings Jewish lesbian (if not gay) experience in line with that of other cultures. Additionally, I am not suggesting that these contradictions make a queer Jewish identity untenable. Rather, along with Zimmerman, I believe that the contradictions make for a dynamic, complex, and nonunitary identity that is in line with the concept of postmodern nonunified subjectivity. In his book *Unheroic Conduct*, Daniel Boyarin would seem to be arguing the opposite in regard to (gay) men. He believes that traditional, rabbinic Judaism is not at all incompatible with certain queer identifications. Although his scholarship is impressive and his arguments persuasive, his thesis may have more valence in theory than in practice, and sheds precious little light on Jewish gendering for women.

7. See Sedgwick's section on the Esther story in chapter 1 of *Epistemology of the Closet*, 75–83. For less theoretical, more historical and experiential, writings on the subject, see *Nice Jewish Girls*, ed. Beck, and *Twice Blessed*, ed. Rose and Balka.

8. Zimmerman, "The Challenge of Conflicting Communities," 212. Although these parallels are certainly compelling, I am not sure how obvious they have been, even to many who occupy the identity positionalities in question.

9. In my reading of this phenomenon, I remain wary of teleological tendencies that would place this late-twentieth-century self-representational work in a direct evolutionary line from nineteenth-century discourses. Michel Foucault, in fact, cautions us that genealogical analyses, to which my study aspires in part, are not to be confused with a search for origins (Foucault, "Nietzsche, Genealogy, History," 142). I have attempted to avoid casting my inquiry in originary terms, even as I trace resemblances and reconfigurations of tropes popularly ascribed to Jews and homosexuals in the last century and recently reprised in self-representational strategies by queer Jews. I heed Eve Kosofsky Sedgwick's warning, as well, to resist the temptation to reduce our definitional understandings of homosexuality (let alone queerness), and in this case Jewishness, into a "coherent definitional field." Sedgwick argues that such a tendency attenuates our potential understandings of a varied and rich interpretive arena, and forecloses the possibility of mapping out a "space of overlapping, contradictory, and conflictual definitional forces." Sedgwick, *Epistemology of the Closet*, 45. A note on my use of *queer*: *queer* is a term that only found its way into common usage toward the end of the twentieth century, but I find it a more useful term than *homosexual*, on the whole. This is a testament to the particular historical moment in which I enter these debates. Be that as it may, I find the inclusivity of the term attractive, in that it not only describes men and women in a single word (whereas *homosexual* denotes male, and *gay/lesbian* requires a double articulation), but it also extends to include bisexuals and transsexuals as well as those who identify with the social positioning of sexual renegades regardless of their own sexual practices, although surely there are, at times, further competing and contradictory pressures that each of these identities brings to bear on a given matter. In addition to the term *queer*'s inclusivity, there is the added attraction of the defiant stance that it proclaims by reappropriating what had previously been an insult. For the definitions of *queer* to which I subscribe, see Warner, *Fear of a Queer Planet*, vii–xxxi; Sedgwick, "Queer and Now"; and de Lauretis's "Queer Theory," iii–xviii. However, for the most part, my use of the term *queer* refers specifically to a range of homosexual performances and identities, and does not attend to transgender in any detail. I look forward to the opportunity to analyze a transgender Jewish first person documentary.

10. Sedgwick has also noted and analyzed the ways end-of-the-twentieth-century Jews, gays, and lesbians share the conundrum of visibility. Although some Jews are readily identifiable as such, most, like most gay men and lesbians, cannot be visually detected unless they self-identify. Sedgwick says, "Ethnic/cultural/religious oppressions such as anti-Semitism are more analogous [to gay oppression] in that the stigmatized individual has at least notionally some discretion—although importantly, it is never to be taken for granted how much—over other people's knowledge of her or his membership in the group: one could 'come out as' a Jew or a Gypsy in a heterogeneous urbanized society more intelligibly than one could typically 'come out as,' say, female, Black, old, a wheelchair user, or fat" (*Epistemology of the Closet*, 75).

11. Bauman, "Allosemitism," 144.

12. Ibid., 148.

13. Ibid., 153.

14. Ibid., 145.

15. Gilman, *Difference and Pathology, Disease and Representation, The Jew's Body*, and *Freud, Race and Gender*; D. Boyarin, *Unheroic Conduct*; Geller, "The Aromatics of Jewish Difference," 203–56, "'A Glance at the Nose,'" 427–44, "(G)nos(e)ology," 243–82, and "The Unmanning of the Wandering Jew," 227–62; Pellegrini, *Performance Anxieties*; Itzkovitz, "Secret Temples," 176–202.

16. I know of one autobiographical film that broaches religion and lesbianism, specifically the issue of how difficult it is to reconcile the two, but the filmmaker herself is not a lesbian and is instead referring to an old friend of hers who left orthodox Judaism and was studying to become a reconstructionist rabbi, having found it too paradoxical and contradictory to remain orthodox and lesbian. This film is *The Return of Sarah's Daughters* (1997), by Marcia Jarmel. Although autobiographical, this film does not challenge any of the formal or conceptual definitions of documentary or autobiography, nor does it problematize the representation of "self" in what I see as interesting ways; hence its exclusion from this study.

17. Sedgwick calls our attention to the etymology of the word *queer* that implies a sense of torquing or twisting; see *Tendencies*, xii.

18. Beauvoir, *The Ethics of Ambiguity*, 78.

19. Included in this subgenre would be: *Bubbeh Lee and Me*, by Andy Abrahams Wilson (1998);

Nana, George, and Me, by Joe Balass (1998); *Tomboychik,* by Sandi DuBowski (1993); *Revisions* (1994), by Chana Pollack; *Past Perfect* (2001), by Cynthia Madansky; and (the grandmother of them all) *Thank You and Goodnight* (1991), by Jan Oxenberg. We may even include, though somewhat tangentially, *Chantal Akerman by Chantal Akerman* (1996).

20. This salivary salvage impulse (food as cultural metonymy) persists in another Jewish lesbian film, Chana Pollack's brief but memorable experimental film *Revisions,* which features the filmmaker's grandmother, in silent, optically altered Super 8, making matzoh balls in her kitchen.

21. Although this American-born grandmother never uses the word, *nakhes* would be the appropriate Yiddish term for this kind of pleasure, since *nakhes* implies a struggle or uncertainty that has been overcome, making the pleasure particularly sweet. In this case the struggle is against Jan's encroaching spinsterhood and the uncertainty of her sexuality.

22. I use the term *anti-aesthetic* in the spirit of Hal Foster's definition, as "a practice, cross-disciplinary in nature, that is sensitive to cultural forms engaged in a politic (e.g. , feminist art) or rooted in a vernacular—that is, to forms that deny the idea of a privileged aesthetic realm." See H. Foster, "Postmodernism," in his *Anti-Aesthetic,* xv.

23. This parable is the famous one (mentioned in chapter 1), attributed to the Baal Shem Tov, about successive generations losing first the place where family prayers were said, then the words, but never the intent. I shall refer to this as the parable of the forest and the tree.

24. This mode of translation (adherence to the spirit but not the letter) has typically been associated with Christianity, whereas Jewish translation of scripture has often been disparagingly referred to as text-bound— that is to say, too literal. For a discussion of this matter, see Lawrence Venuti's introduction to Derrida's essay "What Is a Relevant Translation?" 171–72.

25. The Hebrew *khozer/et b'tshuva* (literally, "one who returns to the answer") is the phrase commonly used to designate a renewal of religious and traditional commitment in the formerly lapsed or assimilated Jew. The return to orthodox Judaism is thematized in Barbara Myerhoff's film *In Her Own Time.*

26. Daniel Itzkovitz considers ways in which these two closet identities inform one another, especially in the context of early-twentieth-century American culture. See his "Secret Temples," 193–95.

27. Foucault, *Discipline and Punish,* 200. Lacan made a very similar statement ten years before *Discipline and Punish* came out. In *Four Fundamental Concepts of Psycho-Analysis,* he claimed "In this matter of the visible, everything is a trap," 93.

28. Phelan, *Unmarked,* chapter 1, "Broken Symmetries: Memory, Sight, Love," 1–33.

29. Again, my reference point here is Europe and, to a lesser degree, America. My position may have no bearing on the history of visibility and assimilation among Sephardic and Mizrahi Jews, as their collective and individual histories attest to different struggles. *Mizrahi* means "eastern" in Hebrew, but refers to Jews of North African and Middle Eastern, not Eastern European, origin.

30. The San Francisco Jewish Film Festival tends to set the standard that many other, smaller Jewish film festivals follow in terms of programming. It is widely considered the mother of Jewish film festivals. The Jewish film festival circuit rivals only the gay and lesbian film festivals in sheer ubiquity throughout the United States. There are no other identity-based film festivals that approach the number of either queer or Jewish film festivals. In Europe and elsewhere, gay and lesbian festivals far outnumber Jewish film festivals.

31. Ginsberg, *"Complaints of a Dutiful Daughter* and 'The Jewish Question,'" paper presented at "Eye and Thou," University of Southern California, October 1998.

32. Ibid.

33. Riv-Ellen Prell refers to this phenomenon as the "aroma of difference" when discussing the de-Judaicization of *The Goldbergs* in the transition from radio to television. See Prell, *Fighting to Become Americans,* 171. Of course there are identifiably Jewish musical styles and tropes, just as there are traditional songs and tunes that could easily be used to signify Jewishness, such as "Hava Nagila" or, for that matter, a klezmer tune, to give the most obvious examples. Consider the aural Jewishness of Gregg Bordowitz's *Fast Trip, Long Drop,* with its Klezmatics score. Yet what remains surprising here is the idea that one can simply add a little musical flavoring, like spice to a tasteless soup.

34. Moses Mendelsohn proposed the democratic principle that it was possible to "be a Jew on the inside and a man [sic] on the outside." Ironically, it was Mendelsohn, the man most responsible for bringing Jewish thought into the light of modernity, who was responsible for promoting the idea of, in effect, keeping Jewishness hidden from view (that is, in the dark). He essentially proposed the closet as the apotheosis of assimilatory strategies. For an interesting discussion of this Enlightenment project of assimilation, see Finkielkraut, *Imaginary Jew,* 57–80. For a much more extensive discussion, see Marrus, *The Politics of Assimilation.*

35. As discussed in the introduction, a Jewish text is not entirely dependent on the identifications of

its author, but rather depends on how it is read. To repeat a quote from Barbara Kirshenblatt-Gimblett in an unpublished presentation, ultimately "Jewish film is what happens when it encounters an audience" ("The New Jews").

36. Blackwell, "Deborah Hoffmann Documentarian," 14. Hoffmann's editing credits include Marlon Rigg's *Ethnic Notions* and *Color Adjustment* and Rob Epstein's *The Times of Harvey Milk*. Her film *Long Night's Journey into Day* (2000), made in collaboration with Frances Reid, was nominated for an Academy Award.

37. Ibid.

38. Hoffmann says, "It's so revealing that my mother could have this deep-seated [homophobic] prejudice, which the Alzheimer's makes you realize is based on nothing." Ibid.

39. Arendt, *The Origins of Totalitarianism*, 80. It is interesting to note that Arendt chooses to ignore Proust's quite virulent remarks about both Jews and homosexuals. Be it from internalized self-hatred or not, Proust referred to Jews and homosexuals each as "the accursed race." And as Daniel Boyarin points out, both of these conditions constitute, for Proust, "incurable diseases." D. Boyarin, *Unheroic Conduct*, 215. For an elaborated discussion on the relationship between homosexuality and Jewishness in Proust, see Freedman, "Coming out of the Closet with Proust," 334–64.

40. Arendt, *The Origins of Totalitarianism*, 82.

41. Of all the films discussed in this book, *Rootless Cosmopolitans* may have the most tenuous link to documentary, using (nonprofessional) actors and few recognizable documentary techniques. However, its claim to fiction is equally tenuous, with the actors essentially playing themselves with different names, and each character representing an aspect of Novaczek's personality (again, as in *Cheap Philosophy*), multiply split. In addition, there are audio interviews in the film, and observational footage, and so the film is arguably no more or less documentary than the mock documentary *Daughter Rite* or the clumsily staged, episodic *American Stories*, each of which has its rightful, if awkward, place in this study.

42. The Lurianic Kabbalah, a school of Jewish mysticism attributed to the sixteenth-century rabbi Isaac Luria, has an intricate cosmology, at the center of which, stated plainly, are the shards of the universe, each containing a holy spark, that shattered in the moment of creation. This theory is known as *Shevirat HaKelim*, the breaking of the vessels. These shards must be re-assembled or repaired to make the world whole again *(tikkun olam)*. I do an injustice to the poetic and spiritual complexity of the idea here. Perhaps the most well-respected lay analysis of the Kabbalah is Gershom Scholem's *Kabbalah*; see also his *Major Trends in Jewish Mysticism*.

43. Stratton, *Coming Out Jewish*, 20.

44. Admittedly, Jews have embraced white identity in great numbers. In the United States the 1950s have been identified as the period in which Jews became accepted, and accepted themselves, as white. See Brodkin, *How Jews Became White Folks*, 138–74. See also Kun, "The Yiddish Are Coming," 356–59. In America, Jews self-identified in nonwhite racial terms very clearly in the late nineteenth and early twentieth centuries. See Goldstein, "'Different Blood Flows in Our Veins,'" 29–55. Brodkin argues that, regardless of self-identification, "the Jews' whitening and unwhitening were not of their own making" (175). It is unlikely that the same conditions were replicated in England, where Novaczek lives and works. The choice to racially identify as white in the United States occurs against a strict black/white binary, whereas in Europe racial categorization had long been primarily that of Aryan and Semite (see Goldstein, 37). Only relatively recently has the internal dialogue about national identity in European countries admitted (however grudgingly) other racial categories; see Gilroy, "There Ain't No Black in the Union Jack." However, it may be worth noting that, in contemporary Britain, South Asians and people of African descent are both referred to as black. It is from within this context that Novaczek's work emerges.

45. For another take on British Jewish assimilatory strategies, see Stratton, *Coming Out Jewish*, 20, 38, 61–63.

46. In our unpublished interview, Novaczek narrated her life story in terms that concisely reveal her identification as nonwhite or even mixed race (half Sephardic and half Ashkenazi): "I'm brought up in London in the sixties, seventies, eighties. I was born in 1956. I also have a Turkish sister, I grew up in a single-parent family; I went to Christian, so-called, secular schools, where I didn't go to the religious assembly in the morning or eat pork at the mealtimes, so guess who I ended up with? The Muslims, the non–pork eaters who were often Indian, whatever. And my gang at school, there were the white white kids, the black black kids, and then in the middle were the mixed-race kids, the Indians, the Greeks, the Italians, the Jews, although we didn't really talk about [this] much, and the black people who didn't want to be part of the black groups and the white people who didn't want to be part of the white groups. So that's very very interesting and it always made me feel like there's lots of stuff going on. And that's the only culture I want to be in. Half of my friends are mixed race. It could be because I'm technically mixed race but that's a really complex story. It's too complex to go into."

47. The Jew as mixed race, or *mischling*, a nineteenth-century invention, was a common phantasm of the Nazi imaginary. See Gilman, *The Jew's Body*, 101–2, 175–76
48. Ibid., 175.
49. Stratton, *Coming Out Jewish*, 61.
50. Unpublished interview with the author.
51. I am thinking here of two shorts made in 1995, *Drive She Said* and *50/50*.
52. For Bordowitz's discussion of his strategy, see the section on *Fast Trip* in "More Operative Assumptions" in his *The AIDS Crisis Is Ridiculous*, 249–58.
53. Ibid., 254.
54. Ibid., 253.
55. *Fast Trip* was one of the early video-to-16-mm transfers to call itself (in the promotional materials) a *film*.
56. About the splitting of himself into characters, Bordowitz acknowledges only two: himself (in documentary and scripted scenes) and Alter Allesman. "Splitting myself into two characters enabled me to act out versions of myself that I was afraid to show. I obviously had a desire to reveal them, but I needed a fictional ruse, a distancing device to remove myself from the pain and anguish I felt at the time. Inventing a double was a way to provoke skepticism in the audience about the veracity of the claims coming out of the author's mouth. Doubt can be productive; it forces people to wrestle with truth." Bordowitz, *The AIDS Crisis Is Ridiculous*, 251–52.
57. Crimp with Rolston, *AIDS DemoGraphics*.
58. Some of the best-known videos of this movement are: *Testing the Limits*, by the Testing the Limits Collective (1987); *Seize Control of the FDA*, by Gregg Bordowitz and Jean Carlomusto (1988); *Doctors, Liars, and Women*, by Jean Carlomusto and Maria Maggenti (1988); *Target City Hall*, by DIVA TV (1989); and *Stop the Church*, by Robert Hilferty (1990).
59. It is interesting to note that nearly all discussions and considerations of passing privilege the visual over the aural register as the key to successful mimesis—yet in all passing the aural element is crucial.
60. Bordowitz tells us that he knew he would use klezmer music before he knew anything else about the tape. Yet he refers to decision as an "intuitive" unconscious choice (Bordowitz, *The AIDS Crisis Is Ridiculous*, 250–51). For an excellent overview of the Klezmatics' career, philosophy, and politics, see Seth Rogovoy, "The Klezmatics Revitalize Their Roots." Also see London, "An Insider's View," and Svigals, "Why We Do This Anyway." For an overview of the new klezmer movement, and a critique of this reputed revival, see Kirshenblatt-Gimblett, "Sounds of Sensibility."
61. The Bund was the name of the Jewish socialist party.
62. The word used for *gay* in Yiddish, *freylekh*, is also the word used to describe certain upbeat, fast tempo (2/4), klezmer tunes, thereby making this particularly festive and celebratory form of klezmer *gay*. There are other queer klezmer groups by now, such as Eve Sicular's Isle of Klezbos, but the Klezmatics were the first to make this link.
63. As mentioned, Bordowitz's great-uncle Berle died in the typhus epidemics that swept the Jewish *shtetlakh* (villages) of Eastern Europe in the early twentieth century. Apparently, the name Berle was given to trick the Angel of Death when Berle was critically ill with typhus as a child was Alter Allesman. The custom of changing a dying person's name to trick fate comes up as well in Barbara Myerhoff's *In Her Own Time*, discussed in the conclusion of this book. It is no stretch to imagine Bordowitz renaming himself, in deference to the custom, toward similar ends. On the Jew as the quintessential victim, see Derrida, "The Question of the Book," 75.
64. Bauman, "Allosemitism," 144–45. Derrida's "Parergon" is also relevant here, in terms of both delimiting differences (the frame delimits where art ends) and inciting ambiguity (is the frame part of the picture or distinct from it?). Both functions (delimiting difference and inciting ambiguity) are performed by the Jew in Western culture, according to Bauman. See "Parergon," 37–82.
65. See the works of Daniel Boyarin, Sander Gilman, Jay Geller, Daniel Itzkovitz, and Ann Pellegrini already cited in this chapter.
66. For a view of the topic in an American context, see Goldstein, "'Different Blood Flows in Our Veins,'" 29–55.
67. See Gilman, *Freud, Race, Gender*, 93–168. Unfortunately, my discussion here will not substantially disrupt the masculinist assumptions of either the nineteenth-century discourses or the late-twentieth-century scholarship on the subject. Even though it would be a highly worthwhile project to challenge these assumptions, and one that has been taken on by very few, notably by the intrepid Ann Pellegrini in her *Performance Anxieties*, *Fast Trip Long Drop*, the film that prompted me to raise these simultaneities, did not lend itself well to a cross-gender/feminist analysis. However, I would like to take up such a project in relation to other films in the future.
68. As discussed in my introduction, not everyone is convinced of the radical implications of reappropriative gestures. See J. Butler, *Bodies That Matter*, 228.

69. Arendt credits Bernard Lazare for this term. See Arendt, *Origins of Totalitarianism*, 65, n. 26. Lazare's article in which the "conscious pariah" makes its appearance was "The Jew as Pariah."

70. D. Boyarin, *Unheroic Conduct*.

71. What tends to be missing from the American version of the anti-Semitic stereotype is the diseased body. The image of the diseased Jew seems *not* to have been effectively exported from Europe to America. The image of the psychologically disturbed and medically "treatable" homosexual, did, unfortunately, survive the geographical transfer.

72. Recorded in "The Lynching of Leo Frank," chapter 94 of *Chapters in American Jewish History*. Itzkovitz also discusses this case in his "Secret Temples," 178.

73. One sign of the disturbance was that they had both read Nietzsche, according to the defense. On the history of Nietzsche-influenced murder cases, see Gilman's "The Nietzsche Murder Case," 59–75.

74. On the sexually criminal Jew in the American national imaginary, see Itzkovitz, "Secret Temples," 176–79, 185–92. Two feature films have been made based on this case, Alfred Hitchcock's *Rope* (1948) and Tom Kalin's *Swoon* (1992).

75. Gilman argues persuasively that the tropes of the diseased carrier (such as Typhoid Mary) were derived from images of the syphilitic of the sixteenth century, yet had, since the advent of penicillin, been floating without a referent and so were available for the next deadly sexually transmitted disease, which happened to be AIDS. See Gilman, *Disease and Representation*, 252.

Conclusion

1. Bordowitz uses almost the exact same words, toward the end of *Fast Trip, Long Drop*, to describe his desire for agency and instrumentality in the face of his own mortality. He says, "Before I die, I want to be the protagonist of my own story, the agent of my own history."

2. Myerhoff, "Life History among the Elderly," 100. For the Benjamin quote, see *One-Way Street and Other Writings*, 14.

3. See J. Butler, *Bodies That Matter*, 123.

4. Initially, she had intended to do a study on the religious life of the diverse communities and congregations located in Fairfax. There was always going to be a film component, but originally this was to be produced by her colleague at the University of Southern California, the late Timothy Asch. Littman was apparently brought onto the project when Myerhoff was already sick, and, according to one article, she agreed to do the film only if Myerhoff was to be at its center. Littman and Myerhoff had collaborated on an earlier film, *Number Our Days*, which won an Academy Award in 1976 for best short documentary. See Frank, "The Ethnographic Films of Barbara G. Myerhoff," 211–14. See also Kirshenblatt-Gimblett's foreword to Myerhoff's *Remembered Lives*, xi–xiv. *Number Our Days* is a moving film about a Jewish retirement community in Venice, California, that focuses on a long-neglected subculture within American society and treats its elderly subjects not only with affection but also with the serious attention they deserve both as repositories of cultural knowledge and as members of a complex community in their own right. *Number Our Days* is also the title of Myerhoff's book, published after the film was released, about the same community.

5. Both quotes are from the opening voice-over of *In Her Own Time*. It remains an open question as to whether such objectivity is indeed the desire and goal of "every social scientist." Gelya Frank finds Myerhoff's statement "disingenuous." According to Frank, "She had already made the turn to reflexive ethnography in *Number Our Days*. This move was ratified and intensified by the Fairfax project." Frank believes that Myerhoff had already "traveled far beyond the paradigm from which the language of 'professional distance' comes." Frank, "Ethnographic Films of Barbara G. Myerhoff," 227–29, n. 19.

6. On the importance of reflexivity to Myerhoff's work, see Prell, "The Double Frame of Life History in the Work of Barbara Myerhoff," 241–58.

7. It is important not to overstate her innovations here, however. Myerhoff was not alone in this movement "homeward," as it were. The 1981 collection of essays *Anthropologists at Home in North America*, edited by Donald Messerschmidt, reveals that others had been making inroads in this direction as well.

8. Fischer, "Ethnicity and the Post-Modern Arts of Memory," 232.

9. On the Jewish uncanny, see Shapiro, "The Uncanny Jew." The notion of the Jewish uncanny can be traced to the myth of the Wandering Jew, which originated in German chapbooks in the seventeenth century. It describes a person who is not quite dead yet is not alive, or rather is "a dead man who has not yet died" (63).

10. Lynne Littman's voice is also heard (though unattributed, more like an omniscient voice of God) when explanation is deemed necessary that Myerhoff must have not provided before her untimely death. The tone of these third person voice-overs is rather monotone and unobtrusive.

An effort is made to support or elucidate Myerhoff's words, not to override them or displace their authority in any way.

11. There is one film, however, that is exclusively shot by a cameraman who died while filming. *Death in Gaza* (2004) is credited as directed by James Miller, though Miller was shot by the Israeli military as he was filming in Gaza and the film was finished by his coproducer, Saira Shah, who narrates the introduction. Shah essentially informs us that, although the film is not the one James Miller would have made, every inch of footage was shot by him—a fact in effect positioning us to watch the succeeding images as if through the eyes of a dead man. This produces an uncanny spectatorial position though somewhat different from the positioning produced by *In Her Own Time*. Another notable difference is that Miller's is never posited as the authorial voice.

12. On death and the documentary, see Nichols, *Representing Reality*, 80–81, 110–11. Also see Sobchack, "Inscribing Ethical Space," 283–300.

13. de Man, "Autobiography as De-Facement," 77.

14. Renov, paper presented at "Eye and Thou II," New York University, March 24–25, 2001.

15. The URL is http://us.imdb.com/Name?Myerhoff,+Barbara.

16. See Prell's entry for Myerhoff in *Jewish Women in America: An Historical Encyclopedia*, vol. M–Z, 958–60; Frank, "The Ethnographic Films of Barbara G. Myerhoff"; also see the entry on Myerhoff on the Jewish Women's Archive web site: http://www.jwa.org/archive/.

17. For a fascinating, if solipsistic, first person filmic meditation on a Jewish name, see Berliner's *The Sweetest Sound*.

18. Incidentally, we learn from Frank that Myerhoff did not need the wheelchair but that Littman suggested she use it to "conserve her energy during a long hot summer day of filming" (Frank, "Ethnographic Films of Barbara G. Myerhoff," 222).

19. Lest we forget, there are people confronting these issues on a daily basis and attempting to create a community where these values are not mutually exclusive. We also see this collision in Dan Akiba's film *My Brother's Wedding* (2003), though Akiba himself is not the one who undergoes the religious transformation.

20. Frank quotes Littman and Deena Metzger in saying that Myerhoff did not identify as a feminist; see Frank, "Ethnographic Films of Barbara G. Myerhoff," 229 n. 31. Frank seems as disturbed as I about Myerhoff's feminist transgressions; see 217–18.

21. Zimmerman asserts "that certain influences and traditions cannot be harmonized smoothly, that being lesbian [or gay] is a decisive break with [Jewish] tradition that cannot be repaired easily, and that contradiction is a fruitful, if difficult, state in which to live" (quoted in chapter 4 of the present volume). See Zimmerman, "The Challenge of Conflicting Communities," 209.

22. This disappointingly conservative, antifeminist turn is somewhat reminiscent of aspects of Alan Berliner's film *Nobody's Business* that relate to his attempt to defend and repair the sanctity of his nuclear family.

23. Fischer, "Ethnicity and the Post-Modern Arts of Memory," 195.

24. For an in-depth discussion of Jewish mimesis and what Soloveitchik calls "self-evident Judaism," i.e., Jewishness that is unself-consciously passed down from one generation to the next and does not need to be formally taught, see Soloveitchik, "Rupture and Reconstruction," 64–130.

25. Fischer, "Ethnicity and the Post-Modern Arts of Memory," 195.

26. I do not use *pastiche* in the Jamesonian sense of something evacuated of meaning and political significance. See Jameson, *Postmodernism*, 17.

27. Renov, "The Subject in History," 117.

Bibliography

Adorno, Theodor. *Negative Dialectics*. Trans. E. B. Ashton. New York: Continuum Press, 1997.

Akerman, Chantal. "Chantal Akerman on *Jeanne Dielman*." *Camera Obscura* 2 (Fall 1977): 118–21.

———. "On *D'Est*." In *Bordering Fiction: Chantal Akerman's "D'Est,"* ed. Kathy Kalbreich and Bruce Jenkins. Minneapolis: Walker Art Center, 1995.

Anderson, Benedict. *Imagined Communities*. New York: Verso, 1991.

Anzaldúa, Gloria. *Borderlands, La Frontera: The New Mestiza*. San Francisco: Aunt Lute Books, 1987.

Appiah, Kwame Anthony. *In My Father's House*. Oxford: Oxford University Press, 1992.

Appiah, Kwame Anthony, and Henry Louis Gates, eds. *Identities*. Chicago: University of Chicago Press, 1995.

Arendt, Hannah. *Between Friends: The Correspondence of Hannah Arendt and Mary McCarthy, 1949–1975*. Ed. Carol Brightman. New York: Harcourt, Brace, 1995.

———. *The Origins of Totalitarianism*. New York: Meridian, 1963.

———. "Truth and Politics." In *Between Past and Future: Eight Exercises in Political Thought*. New York: Penguin, 1968.

Ashley, Kathleen, Leigh Gilmore, and Gerald Peters, eds. *Autobiography and Postmodernism*. Amherst: University of Massachusetts Press, 1994.

Aufderheide, Patricia. "Public Intimacy: The Development of First Person Documentary." *Afterimage* 25, nos. 16–18 (July/August 1997).

Bachelard, Gaston. *The Poetics of Reverie*. Boston: Beacon Press, 1971.

Bakhtin, Mikhail. "Discourse in the Novel." In *The Dialogic Imagination*. Austin: University of Texas Press, 1981.

———. *Problems of Dostoevsky's Poetics*. Minneapolis: University of Minnesota Press, 1984.

———. *Rabelais and His World*. Bloomington: Indiana University Press, 1984.

———. *Speech Genres and Other Late Essays*. Austin: University of Texas Press, 1986.

Barker, Philip. *Michel Foucault: Subversions of the Subject*. New York: St. Martin's Press, 1993.

Barthes, Roland. *Camera Lucida: Reflections on Photography*. Trans. Richard Howard. New York: Hill and Wang, 1981.

———. *Roland Barthes by Roland Barthes*. London: Macmillan, 1977.

Bartov, Omer. *The "Jew" in Cinema*. Bloomington: Indiana University Press, 2005.

Battaglia, Debbora, ed. *The Rhetorics of Self-Making*. Berkeley and Los Angeles: University of California Press, 1995.

Bauman, Zygmunt. "Allosemitism: Premodern, Modern, Postmodern." In *Modernity, Culture, and "the Jew,"* ed. Bryan Cheyette and Laura Marcus. Stanford, Calif.: Stanford University Press, 1998.

———. *Modernity and the Holocaust*. Ithaca, N.Y.: Cornell University Press, 2000.

———. *The Zygmunt Bauman Reader*. Ed. Peter Beilharz. London: Blackwell, 2001.

Beauvoir, Simone de. *The Ethics of Ambiguity*. New York: Citadel Press, 1948.

Beck, Evelyn Torton, ed. *Nice Jewish Girls: A Lesbian Anthology*. Watertown, Mass.: Persephone Press, 1982.

Benjamin, Walter. "A Berlin Chronicle." In *Reflections*. New York: Harcourt Brace Jovanovich, 1978.

———. *Illuminations*. New York: Schocken Books, 1968.

———. *Moscow Diary*. Ed. Gary Smith. Cambridge, Mass.: Harvard University Press, 1986.

———. "N: Re the Theory of Knowledge, Theory of Progress." In *Benjamin, Philosophy, Aesthetics, History*, ed. Gary Smith. Chicago: University of Chicago Press, 1989.

————. "One-Way Street." In *Selected Writings*, vol. 1, *1913–1926*, ed. Marcus Bullock and Michael W. Jennings. Cambridge, Mass.: Harvard University Press, 1996.

————. *One-Way Street and Other Writings*. London: Verso, 1979.

————. *Selected Writings*. Vol. 1, *1913–1926*. Ed. Marcus Bullock and Michael W. Jennings. Cambridge, Mass.: Harvard University Press, 1996.

————. *Selected Writings*. Vol. 2, *1927–1934*. Ed. Michael W. Jennings, Howard Eiland, and Gary Smith. Cambridge, Mass.: Harvard University Press, 1999.

————. "Theses on the Philosophy of History." In *Illuminations*. New York: Schocken Books, 1968.

Bergson, Henri. *Matter and Memory*. New York: Zone Books, 1991.

Bergstrom, Janet. "Invented Memories." In *Identity and Memory: The Films of Chantal Akerman*, ed. Gwendolyn Foster. London: Flicks Books, 2000.

Berkovitz, Jay. "Jewish Scholarship and Identity in Nineteenth-Century France." *Modern Judaism* 18, no. 1 (1998): 1–33.

Berliner, Alan. "The Reluctant Witness." *Independent* (Association of Independent Film and Video Makers), May 1997, 29–49.

————. *The Sweetest Sound*. 2001. http://www.alanberliner.com.

Bernstein, Richard. *Hannah Arendt and the Jewish Question*. Cambridge, Mass.: MIT Press, 1996.

Bhabha, Homi, ed. *Nation and Narration*. New York: Routledge, 1990.

————. "The Other Question: Stereotype, Discrimination, and the Discourse of Colonialism." In *The Location of Culture*. New York: Routledge, 1994.

Blackwell, Erin. "Deborah Hoffmann, Documentarian: *Complaints of a Dutiful Daughter*." *Independent* (Association of Independent Film and Video Makers), March 1995.

Bland, Kalman. *The Artless Jew: Medieval and Modern Affirmations and Denials of the Visual*. Princeton, N.J.: Princeton University Press, 2000.

Bloom, Harold. Introduction to *Musical Variations on Jewish Thought*, by Olivier Bevault d'Allones, trans. Judith L. Greenberg. New York: Braziller, 1984.

Boni, Sylvain. *The Self and the Other in the Ontologies of Sartre and Buber*. Washington, D.C.: University Press of America, 1982.

Bordowitz, Gregg. *The AIDS Crisis Is Ridiculous*. Cambridge, Mass.: MIT Press, 2004.

Boyarin, Daniel. *Unheroic Conduct: The Rise of Heterosexuality and the Invention of the Jewish Man*. Berkeley and Los Angeles: University of California Press, 1997.

Boyarin, Daniel, and Jonathan Boyarin. "Diaspora: Generation and the Ground of Jewish Identity." *Critical Inquiry* 19 (Summer 1993): 693–725.

————. *Jews and Other Differences: The New Jewish Cultural Studies*. Minneapolis: University of Minnesota Press, 1997.

————. *Powers of Diaspora*. Minneapolis: University of Minnesota Press, 2002.

Boyarin, Daniel, Daniel Itzkovitz, and Ann Pellegrini, eds. *Queer Theory and the Jewish Question*. New York: Columbia University Press, 2003.

Boyarin, Jonathan. *Palestine and Jewish History: Criticism at the Borders of Ethnography*. Minneapolis: University of Minnesota Press, 1996.

————. *Polish Jews in Paris: The Ethnography of Memory*. Bloomington: Indiana University Press, 1991.

————. *Storm from Paradise: The Politics of Jewish Memory*. Minneapolis: University of Minnesota Press, 1992.

————. *Thinking in Jewish*. Chicago: University of Chicago Press, 1996.

Boym, Svetlana. *The Future of Nostalgia*. New York: Basic Books, 2001.

Brandt, Joan. "Jabès, Deconstruction, and the "Jews." In *Borders, Exiles, Diasporas*, ed. Elazar Barkan and Marie Denise Shelton. Stanford, Calif.: Stanford University Press, 1998.

Braunstein, Susan, and Jenna Weisman Joselit, eds. *Getting Comfortable in New York: The American Jewish Home, 1880–1950*. New York: The Jewish Museum, 1990.

Brenner, David. "Out of the Ghetto and into the Tiergarten: Redefining the Jewish Parvenu and His Origins in *Ost und West*." *German Quarterly* 66, no. 2 (Spring 1993): 176–94.

Brettschneider, Marla. *Cornerstones of Peace: Jewish Identity, Politics, and Democratic Theory*. New Brunswick, N.J.: Rutgers University Press, 1996.

————, ed. *The Narrow Bridge: Jewish Views on Multiculturalism*. New Brunswick, N.J.: Rutgers University Press, 1996.

Brightman, Carol, ed. *Between Friends: The Correspondence of Hannah Arendt and Mary McCarthy, 1949–1975*. New York: Harcourt, Brace, 1995.

Brodkin, Karen. *How Jews Became White Folks and What That Says about Race in America*. New Brunswick, N.J.: Rutgers University Press, 1998.

Bruss, Elizabeth. *Autobiography: Essays Theoretical and Critical*. Ed. James Olney. Princeton, N.J.: Princeton University Press, 1980.

————. "'Eye' for I: Making and Unmaking Autobiography in Film." In *Autobiography: Essays Theoretical and Critical*, ed. James Olney. Princeton, N.J.: Princeton University Press, 1980.

Bruzzi, Stella. *New Documentary: A Critical Introduction.* London: Routledge, 2000.

Buber, Martin. *Between Man and Man.* Boston: Beacon Press, 1955.

———. *Good and Evil.* New York: Charles Scribner's Sons, 1953.

———. *I and Thou.* New York: Simon and Schuster, 1970.

Buck-Morss, Susan. *The Dialectics of Seeing: Walter Benjamin and the Arcades Project.* Cambridge, Mass.: MIT Press, 1991.

Burke, Seán. *The Death and Return of the Author.* Edinburgh: University of Edinburgh Press, 1998.

Butler, Judith. *Bodies That Matter: On the Discursive Limits of "Sex."* New York: Routledge, 1993.

———. "Contingent Foundations." In *Feminists Theorize the Political,* ed. Judith Butler and Joan Scott, 3–21. New York: Routledge, 1992.

———. *Gender Trouble: Feminism and the Subversion of Identity.* New York: Routledge, 1990.

———. *Giving an Account of Oneself.* New York: Fordham University Press, 2005.

Butler, Kristine. "Bordering on Fiction: Chantal Akerman's *D'Est.*" Review. *Postmodern Culture* 6, no. 1 (1995).

Caruth, Cathy. *Unclaimed Experience: Trauma, Narrative, History.* Baltimore: Johns Hopkins University Press, 1996.

Chapters in American Jewish History. Chapter 94. Published in *Forward,* January 1, 1999, by the American Jewish Historical Society. http://www.ajhs.org/publications/chapters/chapter.cfm?documentID=284.

Chomsky, Noam. *The Fateful Triangle: The United States, Israel, and the Palestinians.* Boston: South End Press, 1983.

Citron, Michelle. "Fleeing from Documentary: Autobiographical Film/Video and the 'Ethics of Responsibility.'" In *Feminism and Documentary,* ed. Diane Waldman and Janet Walker. Minneapolis: University of Minnesota Press, 1999.

———. *Home Movies and Other Necessary Fictions.* Minneapolis: University of Minnesota Press, 1999.

Clifford, James, and George Marcus, eds. *Writing Culture: The Poetics and Politics of Ethnography.* Berkeley and Los Angeles: University of California Press, 1986.

Conway, Jill Ker. *When Memory Speaks: Reflections on Autobiography.* New York: Alfred A. Knopf, 1998.

Copjec, Joan, ed. *Supposing the Subject.* London: Verso, 1994.

Corngold, Stanley. *The Fate of the Self: German Writers and French Theory.* Durham, N.C.: Duke University Press, 1994.

Corrigan, Edward. "Jewish Criticism of Zionism." *Middle East Policy Council,* no. 35 (Winter 1990–91). http://www.mepc.org/journal/9012_corrigan.asp.

Crimp, Douglas, with Adam Rolston. *AIDS DemoGraphics.* Seattle: Bay Press, 1990.

Cuddihy, John Murray. *The Ordeal of Civility: Freud, Marx, Levi-Strauss, and the Jewish Struggle with Modernity.* New York: Basic Books, 1974.

Culbertson, Roberta. "Embodied Memory, Transcendence, and Telling: Recounting Trauma, Reestablishing the Self." *New Literary History* 26 (1995): 169–95.

David, Catherine. "*D'Est:* Akerman Variations." In *Bordering on Fiction: Chantal Akerman's "D'Est,"* ed. Kathy Halbreich and Bruce Jenkins. Minneapolis: Walker Art Center, 1995.

de Lauretis, Teresa. "Queer Theory: An Introduction." *Differences* 3, no. 2 (1991): iii–xviii.

Deleuze, Gilles, and Felix Guattari. *Kafka: Toward a Minor Literature.* Trans. Dana Polan. Minneapolis: University of Minnesota Press, 2000.

———. *The Time Image.* Trans. Hugh Tomlinson and Robert Galeta. Minneapolis: University of Minnesota Press, 1997.

de Man, Paul. "Autobiography as De-Facement." In *Rhetoric of Romanticism.* New York: Columbia University Press, 1984.

Derrida, Jacques. *Acts of Literature.* Ed. Derek Attridge. New York: Routledge, 1992.

———. *Cinders.* Lincoln: University of Nebraska Press, 1991.

———. *Circumfession.* Trans. Geoffrey Bennington. Chicago: University of Chicago Press, 1993.

———. *Dissemination.* Trans. Barbara Johnson. Chicago: University of Chicago Press, 1981.

———. *The Ear of the Other.* Lincoln: University of Nebraska Press, 1988.

———. *Jacques Derrida.* Trans. Geoffrey Bennington. Chicago: University of Chicago Press, 1993.

———. *Margins of Philosophy.* Trans. Alan Bass. Chicago: University of Chicago Press, 1982.

———. "Otobiographies: The Teaching of Nietzsche and the Politics of the Proper Name." In *The Ear of the Other.* Lincoln: University of Nebraska Press, 1988.

———. "Parergon." In *The Truth in Painting.* Trans. Geoff Bennington and Ian McLeod. Chicago: University of Chicago Press, 1987.

———. "The Question of the Book." In *Writing and Difference.* Chicago: University of Chicago Press, 1978.

———. *The Truth in Painting.* Trans. Geoff Bennington and Ian McLeod. Chicago: University of Chicago Press, 1987.

———. "What Is a Relevant Translation?" *Critical Inquiry* 27, no. 2 (Winter 2001): 171–72.

———. *Writing and Difference*. Chicago: University of Chicago Press, 1978.

———. *Writing Performances: The Derrida Reader*. Ed. Julian Wolfreys. Lincoln: University of Nebraska Press, 1998.

Donaldson, Laura. *Decolonizing Feminisms: Race, Gender and Empire Building*. Chapel Hill: University of North Carolina Press, 1992.

Douglas, Mary. *Purity and Danger: An Analysis of the Concepts of Pollution and Taboo*. New York: Routledge, 1992.

Eakin, Paul John. *Fictions in Autobiography: Studies in the Art of Self-Invention*. Princeton, N.J.: Princeton University Press, 1985.

Egan, Susanna. "Encounters in Camera: Autobiography as Interaction." *Modern Fiction Studies* 40, no. 3 (1994): 593–618.

Eilberg-Schwartz, Howard, ed. *People of the Body: Jews and Judaism from an Embodied Perspective*. Albany: State University of New York Press, 1992.

Eisenstein, Paul. "Universalizing the Jew: The Absolute as Antidote for Paranoia." *Journal for the Psychoanalysis of Culture and Society* 3, no. 1 (1998).

Elbaz, Robert. *The Changing Nature of the Self: A Critical Study of the Autobiographic Discourse*. Iowa City: University of Iowa Press, 1987.

Ellis, Marc H. *Towards a Jewish Theology of Liberation: The Uprising and the Future*. Maryknoll, N.Y.: Orbis Books, 1989.

Erens, Patricia. *The Jew in American Cinema*. Bloomington: Indiana University Press, 1984.

Erhart, Julia. "Performing Memory: Compensation and Redress in Contemporary Feminist First Person Documentary." *Screening the Past*, no. 13 (December 2001). http://www.latrobe.edu.au/screeningthepast/firstrelease/fr1201/jefr13a.htm.

Ezrahi, Sidra DeKoven, ed. *Booking Passage: Exile and Homecoming in the Modern Jewish Imagination*. Berkeley and Los Angeles: University of California Press, 2000.

Fader, Ayala. "Literacy, Bilingualism in a Hasidic Community." *Linguistics and Education* 12, no. 3 (2001).

Farber, Seth. *Radicals, Rabbis, and Peacemakers: Conversations with Jewish Critics of Israel*. Monroe, Maine: Common Courage Press, 2005.

Felman, Shoshana. "Benjamin's Silence." *Critical Inquiry* 25 (Winter 1999): 201–34.

Felman, Shoshana, and Dori Laub. *Testimony: Crises of Witnessing in Literature, Psychoanalysis, and History*. New York: Routledge, 1992.

Felski, Rita. *Beyond Feminist Aesthetics: Feminist Literature and Social Change*. Cambridge, Mass.: Harvard University Press, 1989.

Felstiner, John. *Paul Celan: Poet, Survivor, Jew*. New Haven, Conn.: Yale University Press, 1995.

Feuerlicht, Roberta Strauss. *The Fate of the Jews: A People Torn between Israeli Power and Jewish Ethics*. New York: Times Books, 1983.

Finkielkraut, Alain. *The Imaginary Jew*. Trans. Kevin O'Neill and David Suchoff. Lincoln: University of Nebraska Press, 1980.

———. "The Jew and the Israelite: Chronicle of a Split." In *The Imaginary Jew*, trans. Kevin O'Neill and David Suchoff. Lincoln: University of Nebraska Press, 1980.

Fischer, Michael M. J. "Ethnicity and the Post-Modern Arts of Memory." In *Writing Culture: The Poetics and Politics of Ethnography*, ed. James Clifford and George Marcus. Berkeley and Los Angeles: University of California Press, 1986.

Foster, Gwendolyn, ed. *Identity and Memory: The Films of Chantal Akerman*. London: Flicks Books, 2000

Foster, Hal. *The Anti-Aesthetic: Essays on Postmodern Culture*. Port Townsend, Wash.: Bay Press, 1983.

Foucault, Michel. *Discipline and Punish: The Birth of the Prison*. Trans. Alan Sheridan. New York: Pantheon, 1977.

———. *Language, Counter-Memory, Practice*. Ithaca, N.Y.: Cornell University Press, 1977.

———. "Nietzsche, Genealogy, History." In *Language, Counter-Memory, Practice*. Ithaca, N.Y.: Cornell University Press, 1977.

———. *Power/Knowledge*. New York: Pantheon Books, 1980.

———. *Technologies of the Self*. Ed. Luther Martin et al. Amherst: University of Massachusetts Press, 1988.

Frank, Gelya. "The Ethnographic Films of Barbara G. Myerhoff: Anthropology, Feminism, and the Politics of Jewish Identity." In *Women Writing Culture*, ed. Ruth Behar and Deborah Gordon. Berkeley and Los Angeles: University of California Press, 1995.

Freedman, Jonathan. "Coming out of the Closet with Proust." In *Queer Theory and the Jewish Question*, ed. Daniel Boyarin, Daniel Itzkovitz, and Ann Pellegrini, 334–64. New York: Columbia University Press, 2003.

Freud, Sigmund. *Group Psychology and the Analysis of the Ego*. Trans. James Strachey. New York: W. W. Norton, 1959.

———. "The Uncanny." In *The Standard Edition of the Complete Psychological Works of Sigmund Freud.* Vol. 17. Trans. James Strachey et al. London: Hogarth Press, 1962.

Friedlander, Saul. *Memory, History, and the Extermination of the Jews of Europe.* Bloomington: Indiana University Press, 1993.

Friedmann, Georges. *The End of the Jewish People.* Trans. Eric Mosbacher. Garden City, N.Y.: Doubleday, 1967.

Gabara, Rachel. "Mixing Impossible Genres: David Achkar and African AutoBiographical Documentary." *New Literary History* 34 (2003): 331–52.

Geller, Jay. "'A Glance at the Nose': Freud's Inscription of Jewish Difference." *American Imago* 49, no. 4 (1992): 427–44.

———. "The Aromatics of Jewish Difference, or Benjamin's Allegory of Aura." In *Jews and Other Differences: The New Jewish Cultural Studies,* ed. Daniel Boyarin and Jonathan Boyarin, 203–56. Minneapolis: University of Minnesota Press, 1997.

———. "(G)nos(e)ology: The Cultural Construction of the Other." In *People of the Body,* ed. Howard Eilberg-Schwartz. Albany: State University of New York Press, 1992.

———. "The Unmanning of the Wandering Jew." *American Imago* 49, no. 2 (1992): 227–62.

Ghilan, Maxim. *How Israel Lost Its Soul.* London: Penguin, 1974.

Gilman, Sander. *Difference and Pathology: Stereotypes of Sexuality, Race, and Madness.* Ithaca, N.Y.: Cornell University Press, 1985.

———. *Disease and Representation.* Ithaca, N.Y.: Cornell University Press, 1988.

———. *Freud, Race, and Gender.* Princeton, N.J.: Princeton University Press, 1993.

———. "Is Life Beautiful? Can the Shoah Be Funny? Some Thoughts on Recent and Older Films." *Critical Inquiry* 26, no. 2 (Winter 2000): 279–308.

———. *Jewish Frontiers: Essays on Bodies, Histories, and Identities.* New York: Palgrave, 2003.

———. *Jewish Self-Hatred: Anti-Semitism and the Hidden Language of the Jews.* Baltimore, Md.: Johns Hopkins University Press, 1986.

———. *The Jew's Body.* New York: Routledge, 1991.

———. "The Nietzsche Murder Case, or What Makes Dangerous Philosophy Dangerous?" In *Difference and Pathology: Stereotypes of Sexuality, Race, and Madness.* Ithaca, N.Y.: Cornell University Press, 1985.

———. "Salome, Syphilis, Sarah Bernhardt, and the 'Modern Jewess.'" *German Quarterly* 66, no. 2 (Spring 1993): 195–211.

———. *Smart Jews: The Construction of the Image of Jewish Superior Intelligence.* Lincoln: University of Nebraska Press, 1996.

Gilman, Sander, and Steven Katz, eds. *Anti-Semitism in Times of Crisis.* New York: New York University Press, 1991.

Gilmore, Leigh. "Limit Cases: Trauma, Self-Representation, and the Jurisdictions of Identity." *Biography* 24, no. 1 (Winter 2001): 128–39.

———. "The Mark of Autobiography: Postmodernisms, Autobiography, Genre." In *Autobiography and Postmodernism,* ed. Kathleen Ashley, Leigh Gilmore, and Gerald Peters. Amherst: University of Massachusetts Press, 1994.

Gilroy, Paul. *The Black Atlantic: Modernity and Double Consciousness.* Cambridge, Mass.: Harvard University Press, 1993.

———. *"There Ain't No Black in the Union Jack": The Cultural Politics of Race and Nation.* Chicago: University of Chicago Press, 1991.

Ginsburg, Faye. *"Complaints of a Dutiful Daughter* and 'The Jewish Question.'" Presented at "Eye and Thou: Jewish Autobiography in Film and Video," University of Southern California, October 24–26, 1998.

———. "The Parallax Effect: Jewish Ethnographic Film." *Jewish Folklore and Ethnology Review* 10, no. 1 (1988): 16–17.

Ginsburg, Terri. *"Entre Nous,* Female Eroticism, and the Narrative of Jewish Erasure." *Journal of Lesbian Studies* 4, no. 2 (2000): 39–64.

Goldberg, David Theo, and Michael Krausz, eds. *Jewish Identity.* Philadelphia: Temple University Press, 1993.

Goldstein, Eric L. "'Different Blood Flows in Our Veins': Race and Jewish Self-Definition in Late-Nineteenth-Century America." *American Jewish History* 85, no. 1 (1997): 29–55.

Golomb, Jacob, ed. *Nietzsche and Jewish Culture.* New York: Routledge, 1997.

Goodwin, James. *Autobiography: The Self Made Text.* New York: Twayne Publishers, 1993.

Graves, Robert, and Raphael Patai. *Hebrew Myths: The Book of Genesis.* New York: Greenwich House, 1983.

Grewal, Inderpal, and Caren Kaplan, eds. *Scattered Hegemonies: Postmodern and Transnational Feminist Practices.* Minneapolis: University of Minnesota Press, 1994.

Halbreich, Kathy, and Bruce Jenkins, eds. *Bordering on Fiction: Chantal Akerman's "D'Est."* Minneapolis: The Walker Art Center, 1995.

Hall, Jeanne. "Realism as a Style in Cinema Verité: A Critical Analysis of *Primary." Cinema Journal* 30, no. 4 (1991): 24–50.

Hall, Stuart. "Encoding/Decoding." In *Culture, Media, Language,* ed. Dorothy Hobson, Stuart Hall, et al. London: Hutchinson, 1980.

Hansen, Marcus Lee. "The Third Generation in America." *Commentary* 14 (November 1952): 492–500.

Hart, Mitchell B. "The Historian's Past in Three Recent Jewish Autobiographies." *Jewish Social Studies* 5, no. 3 (1999): 132–60.

Hartman, Geoffrey. "Benjamin in Hope." *Critical Inquiry* 25 (Winter 1999): 344–52.

———, ed. *Holocaust Remembrance: The Shapes of Memory.* Oxford, England: Blackwell, 1995.

Hirsch, Marianne, ed. *The Familial Gaze.* Hanover, N.H.: Dartmouth University Press, 1999.

———. *Family Frames: Photography, Narrative and Postmemory.* Cambridge, Mass.: Harvard University Press, 1997.

———. "Projected Memory: Holocaust Photographs in Personal and Public Fantasy." In *Acts of Memory: Cultural Recall in the Present,* ed. Mieke Bal et al. Hanover, N.H.: Dartmouth College–University Press of New England, 1999.

Hobson, Dorothy, Stuart Hall, et al., eds. *Culture, Media, Language.* London: Hutchinson Publishing Group, 1980.

Hoberman, J. *Bridge of Light: Yiddish Film between Two Worlds.* New York: Museum of Modern Art/Schocken Books, 1991.

Huhn, Tom, and Lambert Zuidervaart, eds. *The Semblance of Subjectivity: Essays in Adorno's Aesthetic Theory.* Cambridge, Mass.: MIT Press, 1997.

Hyman, Paula. *Gender and Assimilation in Modern Jewish History: The Roles and Representation of Women.* Seattle: University of Washington Press, 1995.

Hyman, Paula, and Deborah Dash Moore, eds. *Jewish Women in America: An Historical Encyclopedia.* New York: Routledge, 1997.

Itzkovitz, Daniel. "Secret Temples." In *Jews and Other Differences: The New Jewish Cultural Studies,* ed. Daniel Boyarin and Jonathan Boyarin, 176–202. Minneapolis: University of Minnesota Press, 1997.

Jabès, Edmond. *The Book of Questions.* Vol. 1. Trans. Rosmarie Waldrop. Hanover, N.H.: Wesleyan University Press, 1991.

———. *The Book of Resemblances.* Trans. Rosmarie Waldrop. Hanover, N.H.: Wesleyan University Press, 1990.

Jameson, Fredric. *Postmodernism, or The Cultural Logic of Late Capitalism.* Durham, N.C.: Duke University Press, 1992.

Jay, Paul L. "Being in the Text: Autobiography and the Problem of the Subject." *MLN* 97, no. 5 (December 1982): 1045–63.

Kamen, Henry. *Inquisition and Society in Spain.* Bloomington: Indiana University Press, 1985.

Kaplan, E. Ann. "The Realist Debate in the Feminist Film: An Historical Overview of Theories and Strategies in Realism and the Avant Garde Theory Film (1971–1981)." In *Women and Film: Both Sides of the Camera.* New York: Methuen, 1983.

———. *Women and Film: Both Sides of the Camera.* New York: Methuen, 1983.

Katz, John Stuart, ed. *Autobiography: Film/Video/Photography.* Toronto: Art Gallery of Ontario, Media Programmes Division of the Education Branch, 1978.

———. "Ethics and the Perception of Ethics in Autobiographical Film." In *Image Ethics: The Moral Rights of Subjects in Photographs, Film, and Television,* ed. Larry Gross, John Katz, and Jay Ruby. New York: Oxford University Press, 1988.

Kaye/Kantrowitz, Melanie. *The Issue Is Power.* San Francisco: Aunt Lute Books, 1992.

Kirshenblatt-Gimblett, Barbara. *Destination Culture: Tourism, Museums, and Heritage.* Berkeley and Los Angeles: University of California Press, 1998.

———. "Kitchen Judaism." In *Getting Comfortable in New York,* ed. Susan Braunstein and Jenna Weissman Joselit, 75–105. New York: Jewish Museum, 1990.

———. "The 'New Jews': Reflections on Emerging Cultural Practices." Presented at Re-thinking Jewish Communities and Networks in an Age of Looser Connections, Wurzweiler School of Social Work, Yeshiva University and Institute for Advanced Studies, Hebrew University, New York, December 6–7, 2005. http://www.nyu.edu/classes/bkg/web/yeshiva.pdf.

———. "On Difference." *Journal of American Folklore* 107, no. 424 (Spring 1994): 233–38.

———. "Sounds of Sensibility." *Judaism* 47, no. 1 (Winter 1998): 49–78.

———. "Spaces of Dispersal." *Cultural Anthropology* 9, no. 3 (1994): 339–44.

Kleeblatt, Norman, ed. *Too Jewish? Challenging Traditional Identities.* New York: Jewish Museum, 1996.

Klepfisz, Irena. *Dreams of an Insomniac: Jewish Feminist Essays, Speeches, and Diatribes*. Portland, Ore.: Eighth Mountain Press, 1990.

Kramer, Sydelle, and Jenny Masur, eds. *Jewish Grandmothers*. Boston: Beacon Press, 1976.

Krausz, Michael. "On Being Jewish." In *Jewish Identity*, David Theo Goldberg and Michael Krausz. Philadelphia: Temple University Press, 1993.

Kroeber, Alfred, and Clyde Kluckhohn. *Culture: A Critical Review of Concepts and Fictions*. New York: Meridian Books, 1952.

Kugelmass, Jack, and Jonathan Boyarin, eds. and trans. *From a Ruined Garden: The Memorial Books of Polish Jewry*. Bloomington: University of Indiana Press, 1998.

Kuhn, Annette. *Family Secrets: Acts of Memory and Imagination*. London: Verso, 2002.

Kun, Josh. "The Yiddish Are Coming: Mickey Katz, Antic-Semitism, and the Sound of Jewish Difference." *American Jewish History* 87, no. 4 (1999): 343–74.

Kushner, Tony, and Alisa Solomon, eds. *Wrestling with Zion*. New York: Grove Press, 2003.

Lacan, Jacques. *Écrits*. New York: W. W. Norton, 2004.

———. *Four Fundamental Concepts of Psycho-Analysis*. Ed. Jacques-Alain Miller, trans. Alan Sheridan. New York: Norton, 1978.

———. "The Mirror Stage as Formative of the *I* Function." In *Écrits*. New York: W. W. Norton, 2004.

LaCapra, Dominick, ed. *The Bounds of Race: Perspectives on Hegemony and Resistance*. Ithaca, N.Y.: Cornell University Press, 1991.

———. *History and Memory after Auschwitz*. Ithaca, N.Y.: Cornell University Press, 1998.

———. *Representing the Holocaust: History, Theory, Trauma*. Ithaca, N.Y.: Cornell University Press, 1994.

———. "Trauma, Absence, Loss." *Critical Inquiry* 25, no. 4 (Summer 1999): 696–727.

Lacoue-Labarthe, Philippe. *Typography: Mimesis, Philosophy, Politics*. Trans. Christopher Fynsk. Stanford, Calif.: Stanford University Press, 1998.

Lacoue-Labarthe, Philippe, and Nancy, Jean-Luc. "The Nazi Myth." *Critical Inquiry* 16 (Winter 1990): 291–312.

Lane, Jim. *The Autobiographical Documentary in America*. Madison: University of Wisconsin Press, 2002.

———. "Notes on Theory and the Autobiographical Documentary Film in America." *Wide Angle* 15, no. 3 (July 1993): 21–36.

Lazare, Bernard. "The Jew as Pariah: A Hidden Tradition." *Jewish Social Studies* 6, no. 2 (1944).

Lejeune, Philippe. *On Autobiography*. Minneapolis: University of Minnesota Press, 1989.

Levin, David Michael, ed. *Modernity and the Hegemony of Vision*. Berkeley and Los Angeles: University of California Press, 1993.

Levinas, Emmanuel. *Difficult Freedom: Essays on Judaism*. Trans. Seán Hand. Baltimore, Md.: Johns Hopkins University Press, 1990.

———. *Otherwise Than Being, or Beyond Essence*. Trans. Alphonso Lingis. Dordecht, Netherlands: Kluwer Academic Publishers, 1991.

———. *Totality and Infinity: An Essay on Exteriority*. Trans. Alphonso Lingis. Pittsburgh, Penn.: Duquesne University Press, 1998.

Lilienthal, Alfred M. *What Price Israel?* Chicago: H. Regnery, 1953.

London, Frank. "An Insider's View." *Judaism* 47, no. 1 (Winter 1998): 40–43.

Lorde, Audre. *Sister Outsider: Essays and Speeches*. Trumansberg, N.Y.: Crossing Press, 1984.

———. *Zami: A New Spelling of My Name*. Trumansberg, N.Y.: Crossing Press, 1982.

Lyotard, Jean-François. *Heidegger and "the jews."* Trans. Andreas Michel and Mark Roberts. Minneapolis: University of Minnesota Press, 1990.

Mannheim, Karl. "The Problem of Generations." *Psychoanalytic Review* 57, no. 3 (1970): 378–404.

Mansfield, Nick. *Subjectivity*. New York: New York University Press, 2000.

Marcus, Laura. *Auto/biographical Discourses*. Manchester, U.K.: Manchester University Press, 1994.

Margulies, Ivone. "Echo and Voice in *Meetings with Anna*." In *Identity and Memory: The Films of Chantal Akerman*, ed. Gwendolyn Foster. London: Flicks Books, 2000.

———. *Nothing Happens: Chantal Akerman's Hyperrealist Everyday*. Durham, N.C.: Duke University Press, 1996.

Marrus, Michael. *The Politics of Assimilation: The French Jewish Community at the Time of the Dreyfus Affair*. Oxford: Oxford University Press, 1980.

Marx, Karl. "On the Jewish Question." In *Early Political Writings*. Cambridge: Cambridge University Press, 1994.

Mayer, Egon, Barry Kosmin, and Ariela Keysar. "American Jewish Identity Survey." Center for Jewish Studies, Graduate Center of the City University of New York, 2003. http://www.culturaljudaism.org/pdf/ajisbook.pdf.

Memmi, Albert. *Portrait of a Jew*. New York: Orion Press, 1962.

Messerschmidt, Donald, ed. *Anthropologists at Home in North America: Methods and Issues in the Study of One's Own Society*. Cambridge: Cambridge University Press, 1981.

Metz, Christian. *The Imaginary Signifier: Psychoanalysis and the Cinema*. Trans. Celia Britton et al. Bloomington: Indiana University Press, 1982.

Meyer, Michael. *The Origins of the Modern Jew: Jewish Identity and European Culture in Germany, 1749–1824*. Detroit: Wayne State University Press, 1967.

Meyers, Diana Tietjens, ed. *Feminists Rethink the Self*. Boulder, Colo.: Westview Press, 1997.

Mezvinsky, Norton. *The Character of the State of Israel*. London: University College, 1971.

Miller, Nancy K. *Bequest and Betrayal*. Bloomington: Indiana University Press, 2000.

———. "But enough about me, what do you think of my memoir?" *Yale Journal of Criticism* 13, no. 2 (2000): 421–36.

———. *Getting Personal*. New York: Routledge, 1991.

———. "Putting Ourselves in the Picture: Memoirs and Mourning." In *The Familial Gaze*, ed. Marianne Hirsch. Hanover, N.H.: Dartmouth University Press, 1999.

Mitchell, Don. "There's No Such Thing as Culture: Towards a Reconceptualization of Culture in Geography." *Transactions of the Institute of British Geography*, n.s., 20, no. 1 (1995): 102–16.

Mitchell, W. J. T. "Holy Landscape: Israel, Palestine, and the American Wilderness." *Critical Inquiry* 26, no 2 (Winter 2000): 193–223.

Morson, Gary Saul, and Caryl Emerson. *Rethinking Bakhtin: Extensions and Challenges*. Evanston, Ill.: Northwestern University Press, 1989.

Moseley, Marcus. "Jewish Autobiography: The Elusive Subject." *Jewish Quarterly Review* (Winter 2005): 16–59.

Muñoz, José. *Disidentifications: Race, Sex, and Visual Culture*. Minneapolis: University of Minnesota Press, 1999.

Myerhoff, Barbara. "Life History among the Elderly: Performance, Visibility, and Re-Membering." In *A Crack in the Mirror: Reflexive Perspectives in Anthropology*, ed. Jay Ruby. Philadelphia: University of Pennsylvania Press, 1982.

———. *Number Our Days*. New York: Touchstone, 1980.

———, et al. *Remembered Lives: The Work of Ritual, Storytelling, and Growing Older*. Ed. Mark Kaminsky. Ann Arbor: University of Michigan Press, 1992.

Naficy, Hamid, ed. *Home, Exile, Homeland: Film, Media, and the Politics of Place*. New York: Routledge, 1999.

Nancy, Jean-Luc. *Being Singular Plural*. Stanford, Calif.: Stanford University Press, 2000.

Negrón-Mutaner, Frances. "When I Was a Puerto Rican Lesbian." *GLQ* 5, no. 4 (1999): 511–26.

Nichols, Bill. *Blurred Boundaries: Questions of Meaning in Contemporary Culture*. Bloomington: Indiana University Press, 1994.

———. *Ideology and the Image*. Bloomington: Indiana University Press, 1981.

———. *Representing Reality*. Bloomington: Indiana University Press, 1991.

———. "Voice of the Documentary." In *New Challenges for Documentary*, ed. Alan Rosenthal. Berkeley and Los Angeles: University of California Press, 1988.

Nietzsche, Friedrich. *The Will to Power*. Ed. Walter Kaufman. Trans. Walter Kaufmann and R. J. Hollingdale. New York: Vintage Books, 1968.

Nora, Pierre. "Between Memory and History: Les Lieux de Memoire." *Representations* 26 (Spring 1989): 7–24.

Noriega, Chon. "Talking Heads, Body Politic: The Plural Self of Chicano Experimental Video." In *Resolutions: Contemporary Video Practices*, ed. Michael Renov and Erika Suderburg, 207–28. Minneapolis: University of Minnesota Press, 1997.

Olney, James, ed. *Autobiography: Essays Theoretical and Critical*. Princeton, N.J.: Princeton University Press, 1980.

———. *Memory and Narrative: The Weave of Life-Writing*. Chicago: University of Chicago Press, 1998.

Parker, Andrew, et al., eds. *Nationalisms and Sexualities*. New York: Routledge, 1992.

Pellegrini, Ann. *Performance Anxieties*. New York: Routledge, 1997.

———. "Whiteface Performances: 'Race,' Gender, and Jewish Bodies." In *Jews and Other Differences: The New Jewish Cultural Studies*, ed. Daniel Boyarin and Jonathan Boyarin. Minneapolis: University of Minnesota Press, 1997.

Perreault, Jeanne. *Writing Selves: Contemporary Feminist Autography*. Minneapolis: University of Minnesota Press, 1995.

Peskowitz, Miriam, and Laura Levitt, eds. *Judaism since Gender*. New York: Routledge, 1997.

Phelan, Peggy. *Unmarked: The Politics of Performance*. New York: Routledge, 1993.

Phelan, Shane. *Getting Specific: Postmodern Lesbian Politics*. Minneapolis: University of Minnesota Press, 1994.

Pratt, Mary Louise. *Imperial Eyes: Travel Writing and Transculturation*. London: Routledge, 1992.

Prell, Riv-Ellen. "The Double Frame of Life History in the Work of Barbara Myerhoff." In *Interpreting*

Women's Lives, ed. The Personal Narratives Group, 241–58. Bloomington: Indiana University Press, 1989.

————. *Fighting to Become Americans: Assimilation and the Trouble between Jewish Women and Jewish Men.* Boston: Beacon Press, 1999.

Rabinowitz, Paula. *They Must Be Represented: The Politics of Documentary.* New York: Verso, 1994.

Rajchman, John, ed. *The Identity in Question.* New York: Routledge, 1995.

Reed-Danahay, Deborah E., ed. *Auto/Ethnography: Rewriting the Self and the Social.* New York: Berg, 1997.

Renov, Michael. "Domestic Ethnography and the Construction of the 'Other' Self." In *The Subject of Documentary,* Minneapolis: University of Minnesota Press, 2004.

————. "The Subject in History." In *The Subject of Documentary,* Minneapolis: University of Minnesota Press, 2004.

————, ed. *Theorizing Documentary.* New York: Routledge, 1993.

Renov, Michael, and Erika Suderburg, eds. *Resolutions: Contemporary Video Practices.* Minneapolis: University of Minnesota Press, 1997.

Renza, Louis. "The Veto of the Imagination: A Theory of Autobiography." In *Autobiography: Essays Theoretical and Critical,* ed. James Olney. Princeton, N.J.: Princeton University Press, 1980.

Revault d'Allonnes, Olivier. *Musical Variations on Jewish Thought.* Trans. Judith Greenberg. Introduction by Harold Bloom. New York: George Braziller, 1984.

Ricoeur, Paul. *Oneself as Another.* Trans. Kathleen Blamey. Chicago: University of Chicago Press, 1992.

Rich, Adrienne. *On Lies, Secrets, and Silence.* New York: W. W. Norton, 1979.

Richter, Gerhard. *Walter Benjamin and the Corpus of Autobiography.* Detroit: Wayne State University Press, 2000.

Rogin, Michael. *Blackface, White Noise: Jewish Immigrants in the Hollywood Melting Pot.* Berkeley and Los Angeles: University of California Press, 1996.

Rogovoy, Seth. "The Klezmatics Revitalize Their Roots." 1999. http://www.berkshireweb.com/rogovoy/interviews/ klezmatics.html.

Rose, Andy, and Christie Balka, eds. *Twice Blessed.* Boston: Beacon Press, 1991.

Rosen, Jonathan. *The Talmud and the Internet: A Journey between Worlds.* New York: Farrar Straus Giroux, 2000.

Rosenstone, Robert. *Visions of the Past: The Challenge of Film to Our Idea of History.* Cambridge, Mass.: Harvard University Press, 1996.

Rosenzweig, Franz. *The Star of Redemption.* Boston: Beacon Press, 1972.

Roth, Cecil. *Jewish Art: An Illustrated History.* New York: McGraw-Hill, 1961.

Roth, Michael S. "Remembering Forgetting: Maladies de la Mémoire in Nineteenth-Century France." *Representations* 26 (Spring 1989): 49–68.

Rothberg, Michael. *Traumatic Realism: The Demands of Holocaust Representation.* Minneapolis: University of Minnesota Press, 2000.

Rubenberg, Cheryl. *Israel and the American National Interest.* Urbana: University of Illinois Press, 1986.

Russell, Catherine. *Experimental Ethnography: The Work of Film in the Age of Video.* Durham, N.C.: Duke University Press, 1999.

Said, Edward. *Culture and Imperialism.* New York: Random House, 1994.

————. "Invention, Memory, Place." *Critical Inquiry* 26, no. 2 (Winter 2000): 175–92.

————. *Orientalism.* New York: Random House, 1979.

Sanchez, María Carla, and Linda Schlossberg, eds. *Passing: Identity and Interpretation in Sexuality, Race, and Religion.* New York: New York University Press, 2001.

Sartre, Jean-Paul. *Anti-Semite and Jew.* Trans. George J. Becker. New York, 1948.

Schama, Simon. *Landscape and Memory.* New York: Vintage Books, 1996.

Scheman, Naomi. *Engenderings: Constructions of Knowledge, Authority, and Privilege.* New York: Routledge, 1993.

————. "Queering the Center by Centering the Queer: Reflections on Transsexuals and Secular Jews." In *Feminists Rethink the Self,* ed. Diana Tietjens Meyers. Boulder, Colo.: Westview Press, 1997.

Scholem, Gershom. *Kabbalah.* New York: Quandrangle Books, 1974.

————. *Major Trends in Jewish Mysticism.* New York: Schocken Books, 1995.

Scott, Joan. "The Evidence of Experience." *Critical Inquiry* 17 (Summer 1991): 773–97.

Sedgwick, Eve Kosofsky. *Epistemology of the Closet.* Berkeley and Los Angeles: University of California Press, 1990.

————. "Queer and Now." In *Tendencies.* Durham, N.C.: Duke University Press, 1993.

————. *Tendencies.* Durham, N.C.: Duke University Press, 1993.

Seidman, Naomi. "Fag Hags and Bu-Jews: Toward a (Jewish) Politics of Vicarious Identity." In

Insider/Outsider: American Jews and Multiculturalism, ed. David Biale, Michael Galchinsky, and
Susannah Heschel. Berkeley and Los Angeles: University of California Press, 1998.
———. *"A Marriage Made in Heaven?" The Sexual Politics of Hebrew-Yiddish Diglossia.* Berkeley
and Los Angeles: University of California Press, 1997.
Selzer, Michael. *The Wineskin and the Wizard.* New York: Macmillan, 1970.
———, ed. *Zionism Reconsidered: The Rejection of Jewish Normalcy.* New York: Macmillan, 1970.
Shapiro, Susan E. "The Uncanny Jew: A Brief History of an Image." *Judaism* 46, no. 1 (Winter 1997):
63–78.
Sicher, Efraim. "The Future of the Past: Countermemory and Postmemory in Contemporary American
Post-Holocaust Narratives." *History and Memory* 12, no. 2 (2001): 80–81.
Silberstein, Laurence J., ed. *Mapping Jewish Identities.* New York: New York University Press, 2000.
Sitney, P. Adams. "Autobiography in Avant-Garde Film." In *The Avant-Garde Film: A Reader of
Theory and Criticism,* 199–246. New York: New York University Press, 1978.
Skoller, Jeffrey. *Shadows, Specters, Shards: Making History in Avant-Garde Film.* Minneapolis:
University of Minnesota Press, 2005.
Smith, Gary S. J., ed. *Benjamin: Philosophy, Aesthetics, History.* Chicago: University of Chicago Press,
1989.
———, ed. *On Walter Benjamin: Critical Essays and Recollections.* Cambridge, Mass.: MIT Press, 1995.
Smith, Gary V., ed. *Zionism: The Dream and the Reality. A Jewish Critique.* New York: Barnes and
Noble, 1974.
Smith, Sidonie. *Decolonizing the Subject: The Politics of Gender in Women's Autobiography.* Minne-
apolis: University of Minnesota Press, 1992.
———. *Getting a Life: Everyday Uses of Autobiography.* Minneapolis: University of Minnesota Press,
1996.
———. *A Poetics of Women's Autobiography: Marginality and the Fictions of Self-Representation.*
Bloomington: Indiana University Press, 1987.
———. *Subjectivity, Identity, and the Body: Women's Autobiographical Practices in the Twentieth
Century.* Bloomington: Indiana University Press, 1993.
———. *Writing New Identities: Gender, Nation, and Immigration in Contemporary Europe.* Minne-
apolis: University of Minnesota Press, 1997.
Sobchack, Vivian. *The Address of the Eye: A Phenomenology of Film Experience.* Princeton, N.J.:
Princeton University Press, 1992.
———. "Inscribing Ethical Space: Ten Propositions on Death, Representation, and Documentary."
Quarterly Review of Film Studies 9, no. 4 (Fall 1984): 283–300.
———, ed. *The Persistence of History: Cinema, Television, and the Modern Event.* New York: Rout-
ledge, 1996.
Sollors, Werner. *Beyond Ethnicity: Consent and Descent in American Culture.* New York: Oxford
University Press, 1986.
Soloveitchik, Haym. "Rupture and Reconstruction: The Transformation of Contemporary Orthodoxy."
Tradition 28, no. 4 (1994): 64–130.
Sommer, Doris. "Not Just a Personal Story Story: Women's Testimonios and the Plural Self." In *Life/
lines: Theorizing Women's Autobiography,* ed. Bella Brodzki and Celeste Schenck, 107–30. Ithaca,
N.Y.: Cornell University Press, 1988.
Soyer, Daniel. "Documenting Immigrant Lives at an Immigrant Institution: YIVO's Autobiography
Contest of 1942." *Jewish Social Studies* 5 no. 3 (1999): 218–43.
Spivak, Gayatri Chakravorty. *In Other Worlds: Essays in Cultural Politics.* New York: Methuen, 1987.
Stam, Robert. *Reflexivity in Film and Literature: From Don Quixote to Jean-Luc Godard.* New York:
Columbia University Press, 1992.
———. *Subversive Pleasures: Bakhtin, Cultural Criticism, and Film.* Baltimore, Md.: Johns Hopkins
University Press, 1989.
Stratton, Jon. *Coming Out Jewish.* New York: Routledge, 2000.
Suleiman, Susan Rubin. "Problems of Memory and Factuality in Recent Holocaust Memoirs:
Wikomirski/Wiesel." *Poetics Today* 21, no. 3 (2000): 543–59.
Svigals, Alicia. "Why We Do This Anyway," *Judaism* 47, no. 1 (Winter 1998): 40–43.
Tarantino, Michael. "The Moving Eye: Notes on the Films of Chantal Akerman." In *Bordering on
Fiction: Chantal Akerman's "D'Est,"* ed. Kathy Halbreich and Bruce Jenkins. Minneapolis: Walker
Art Center, 1995.
Taubin, Amy. "The Sound and the Fury." *Village Voice,* May 12, 1998, 123.
Taussig, Michael. *Mimesis and Alterity: A Particular History of the Senses.* New York: Routledge, 1993.
———. *The Nervous System.* New York: Routledge, 1992.
Thienhaus, Ole J. "Jewish Time: Ancient Practice, Hellenistic and Modern Habits, Freud's Reclaiming."
Judaism 48, no. 4 (Fall 1999): 442–49.

Todorov, Tzvetan. *Mikhail Bakhtin: The Dialogic Principle*. Minneapolis: University of Minnesota Press, 1984.

Trinh T. Minh-ha. *Framer Framed*. New York: Routledge, 1992.

———. *When the Moon Waxes Red: Representation, Gender, and Cultural Politics*. New York: Routledge, 1991.

———. *Woman, Native, Other*. Bloomington: Indiana University Press, 1989.

Varadharajan, Asha. *Exotic Parodies: Subjectivity in Adorno, Said, and Spivak*. Minneapolis: University of Minnesota Press, 1995.

Vidal-Naquet, Pierre. *The Jews: History, Memory, and the Present*. Trans. David Ames Curtis. New York: Columbia University Press, 1996.

Waldrop, Rosemarie. "Lavish Absence: Recalling and Rereading Edmond Jabès." *Judaism* 52 no. 3–4 (Summer–Fall 2003): 161–76.

Walker, Janet. *Trauma Cinema: Documenting Incest and the Holocaust*. Berkeley and Los Angeles: University of California Press, 2005.

Wallace, Michele. *Invisibility Blues: From Pop to Theory*. London: Verso, 1990.

Warner, Michael. *Fear of a Queer Planet*. Minneapolis: University of Minnesota Press, 1993.

Weininger, Otto. *Sex and Character*. 6th ed. New York: G. P. Putnam's Sons, 1906. Reprint, Bloomington: Indiana University Press, 2005.

White, Hayden. *Tropics of Discourse: Essays in Cultural Criticism*. Baltimore, Md.: Johns Hopkins University Press, 1978.

Wickberg, Daniel. "Homophobia: On the Cultural History of an Idea." *Critical Inquiry* 27, no. 1 (Autumn 2000): 42–57.

Williams, Linda. "Mirrors without Memories: Truth, History, and the New Documentary." *Film Quarterly* 46, no. 3 (Spring 1993): 9–21.

Williams, Raymond. *Culture and Society*. New York: Schocken, 1983.

Wright, Susan. "The Politicization of 'Culture.'" *Anthropology Today* 14, no. 1 (February 1998): 7–15.

Yerushalmi, Yosef Hayim. *Zakhor: Jewish History and Jewish Memory*. Seattle: University of Washington Press, 1996.

Zborowski, Mark, and Elizabeth Herzog. *Life Is with People: The Culture of the Shtetl*. New York: Schocken Books, 1995.

Zimmerman, Bonnie. "The Challenge of Conflicting Communities: To Be Lesbian and Jewish and a Literary Critic." In *People of the Book*, ed. Jeffrey Rubin-Dorsky and Shelley Fisher Fishkin. Madison: University of Wisconsin Press, 1996.

Žižek, Slavoj. *Looking Awry*. Boston: MIT Press, 1993.

Selected Filmography of Jewish Diasporic First Person Documentaries

Akerman, Chantal. *Chantal Akerman by Chantal Akerman* (1996, Belgium/France).

———. *D'Est* (1993, Belgium/France).

———. *News from Home* (1976, Belgium/France).

Akiba, Dan. *My Brother's Wedding* (2003, USA).

Arlyck, Ralph. An *Acquired Taste* (1981).

———. *Current Events* (1989, USA).

———. *Following Sean* (2004, USA).

Bain, Brian. *Shalom Y'All* (2002, USA).

Balass, Joe. *Nana, George, and Me* (1998, USA).

Beckermann, Ruth. *Paper Bridge* (1987, Austria).

———. *Towards Jerusalem* (1990, Austria).

Behar, Ruth. *Adio Kerida* (2002, USA).

Benstock, Jeremy. *Orders of Love* (2004, UK).

Berg, Rudolf von den. *The Alien's Place* (1977, Netherlands).

Berliner, Alan. *Intimate Stranger* (1991, USA).

———. *Nobody's Business* (1997, USA).

———. *The Sweetest Sound* (2001, USA).

———. *Wide Awake* (2006, USA).

Berman, Jonathan. *My Friend Paul* (1999, USA).

Block, Doug. *51 Birch Street* (2006, USA).

Block, Gay. *Bertha Alyce* (2001, USA).

Boganim, Michale. *Mémoires Incertaines* (2001, UK/France).

Booth, Marlene. *Yiddle in the Middle* (1999, USA).

Bordowitz, Gregg. *Fast Trip, Long Drop* (1993, USA).

———. *Habit* (2001, USA).

Caouette, Jonathan. *Tarnation* (2004, USA).

Child, Abigail. *Below the New* (1999, USA).

Chopra, Joyce, and Claudia Weill. *Joyce at 34* (1972, USA).

Citron, Michelle. *Daughter Rite* (1979, USA).

———. *Mother Right* (1983, USA).

Cohen, Maxi. *My Bubi, My Zada* (1975, USA).

Daum, Menachem, and Oren Rudovsky. *Hiding and Seeking* (2003, USA).

DuBowski, Sandi. *Tomboychik* (1993, USA).

Eisenberg, Daniel. *Cooperation of Parts* (1987, USA).

Emberling, Heidi Schmidt. *Tangled Roots* (2001, USA).

Eshaghian, Tanaz. *Love Iranian-American Style* (2005, USA).

———. *Najib* (2000, USA).

Franel, Sabine. *First of the Name* (2000, France/Switzerland).

Freedman, Rod. *Uncle Chatzkel* (1999, Australia).

Gamburg, Daniel. *Tsipa and Volf* (2001, USA).

Gimes, Miklós. *Mutter* (2002, Switzerland).

Gluck, Pearl. *Divan* (2003, USA).

Gottlieb, Amy. *In Living Memory* (1997, Canada).

Greenberg, Laurel. *94 Years and 1 Nursing Home Later* (1999, USA).

Halawani, Mary. *I Miss the Sun* (1983, USA).

Helfand, Judith. *Blue Vinyl* (2004, USA).

———. *A Healthy Baby Girl* (1996, USA).

Hershmann, Lynn. *First Person Plural* (1988–96, USA).

Hoffenberg, Esther. *The Two Lives of Eva* (2005, France).

Hoffmann, Deborah. *Complaints of a Dutiful Daughter* (1994, USA).

Hyberg, Caspar. *My Jewish Grandfather* (1993, Denmark).

Jarmel, Marcia. *The Return of Sarah's Daughters* (1997, USA).

Kogut, Sandra. *Hungarian Passport* (2001, France/Hungary/Brazil/Belgium).

Korda, Susan. *One of Us* (1999, USA).

Lebow, Alisa, and Cynthia Madansky. *Treyf* (1998, USA).

Levaco, Ron. *Round Eyes in the Middle Kingdom* (1995, USA).

Levy, Wendy. *Naomi's Legacy* (1994, USA).

Lewenz, Lisa. *A Letter without Words* (1998, USA).

Lindwer, Willy. *Goodbye Holland* (2004, Netherlands).

Lusztig, Irene. *Reconstruction* (2001, USA).

Madansky, Cynthia. *Past Perfect* (2001, USA).

Meeropol, Ivy. *Heir to an Execution: A Granddaughter's Story* (2004, USA).

———. *Driving Men* (2006, USA).

Mogul, Susan. *I Stare at You and Dream* (1997, USA).

Morder, Joseph. *Memories of a Tropical Jew* (1988, France).

Myerhoff, Barbara, and Lynne Littman. *In Her Own Time* (1985, USA).

Myers, Barbara. *The Indelible Print* (1990, Canada).

Myers, Bo. *Tiny Bubbles* (1997, Canada).

Najman, Charles. *Can Memory Be Dissolved in Spring Water* (1996, France).

Novaczek, Ruth. *Cheap Philosophy* (1992, UK).

———. *Philosopher Queen* (1995, UK).

———. *Rootless Cosmopolitans* (1990, UK).

Nussbaum, Karl. *Raw Images from the Optic Cross* (1998, USA).

———. *Thanatos and Eros: The Birth of the Holy Freak* (2002, Germany/USA).

Oberlander, Wendy. *Nothing to Be Written Here* (1996, Canada).

———. *Still* (2001, Canada).

Ostrovsky, Vivian. *Nikita Kino* (2002, France).

Oxenberg, Jan. *Thank You and Goodnight* (1991, USA).

Pimsleur, Julia. *Brother Born Again* (2000, USA).

Pollack, Chana. *Fetal Positions* (1996, USA).

———. *Revisions* (1994, USA).

Rappaport, Pola. *Family Secret* (2000, USA).

Ravett, Abraham. *Everything's for You* (1989, USA).

———. *Half Sister* (1985, USA).

———. *Lunch with Fela* (2005, USA).

———. *The March* (1999, USA).

———. *Thirty Years Later* (1974–78, USA).

———. *Toncia* (1986, USA).

Rivlin, Lilly. *Gimme a Kiss* (2000, USA).

———. *The Tribe* (1983, USA).

Rock, Marcia. *Dancing with My Father* (2002, USA).

Rosenblatt, Jay. *King of the Jews* (2000, USA).

———. *Phantom Limb* (2005, USA).

Roth, Philip. *A 25-Year-Old Gay Man Loses His Virginity to a Woman* (1990, USA).

———. *I Was a Jewish Sex Worker* (1996, USA).

Sachs, Lynn. *States of Unbelonging* (2005, USA).

Schogt, Elida. *Silent Song* (2001, Canada).

———. *The Walnut Tree* (2000, Canada).

———. *Zyklon B* (1999, Canada).

Segalov, Eileen. *My Puberty* (1987, USA).

Shamash, Jessica. *My Auntie Told Me* (1995, UK).

Shiff, Melissa. *Avant-Garde Jewish Wedding* (2004, Canada).

Shopsowitz, Karen. *My Father's Camera* (2000, Canada).

———. *My Grandparents Had a Hotel* (1989, Canada).

Silverstein, Karen. *Gefilte Fish* (1984, USA).

Simon, Jamil. *Nana: A Portrait* (1972, USA).

Stein, Darren, and Adam Shell. *Put the Camera on Me* (2004, USA).

Wanderin, November. *The Night Trotsky Came to Dinner* (2005, Germany).

Wexler, Mark. *Me and My Matchmaker* (1996, USA).

———. *Tell Them Who You Are* (2004, USA).

Wilson, Andy Abrahams. *Bubbeh Lee and Me* (1998, USA).

Wohl, Ira. *Best Boy* (1979, USA).

———. *Best Man* (1997, USA).

———. *Best Sister* (2005, USA).

Yael, B. H. *Fresh Blood* (1996, Canada).

Young, Michael J. *McJew* (1991, USA).

Zylbersztejn, Ariel. *Jai* (2004, Mexico).

Index

79–80; as palimpsest, xxix, 13–19; trauma
and, 1, 12, 29, 34, 42
Hoffmann, Deborah, 178n36; *Complaints of a
Dutiful Daughter*, xxii, xxvi, xxix, xxxi, 37, 39,
40, 43–44, 82–85, 101, 111–12, 115, 128–32,
178n38
Holocaust, xvii, xxvii, 29, 62–65; nomenclature,
18; as rupture, 1
home movies, xxv, 37, 41, 44–48, 59, 61, 169n21;
domestic pastoral in, 46; patriarchal gaze
in, 46–48
homosexuality. *See under* Jewishness
Hubley, Emily, 68
humor. *See under* Jewish affect

identity politics, xiv, 96, 116, 117. *See also* visibility: politics
In Her Own Time (Myerhoff and Littman),
xxxii–xxxiii, 149–57, 162n28, 177n25, 180n5,
181n10; authorship in, 151, 152–53, 155; Jewish
rituals in, xxxiii, 152, 155, 179n63; temporal
dissonance in, 153
insider/outsider, xxxi, 88, 93–97, 104–6, 122
Intimate Stranger (Berliner), 163n29
Israeli occupation of Palestine, xxxi, 94–95, 102,
103
Itzkovitz, Daniel, 177n26
Ivens, Joris: *Rain*, xxiii
I Was a Jewish Sex Worker (Roth), 175n2

Jarmel, Marcia: *The Return of Sarah's Daughter*,
176n16
Jeanne Dielman (Akerman), 11, 26, 164n17
Je tu il elle (Akerman), 26
Jewish affect, 77; humor, 43, 73, 77–78, 96–97, 124;
music, 102, 129, 139–40, 177n33; voice, 75, 103,
171n60, 175n36
Jewish descent, xxi, xxii, 40, 168n8, 168n12
Jewish diaspora. *See* diaspora
Jewish exceptionalism, xvii–xviii, 175n6
Jewish grandmother. *See* bobe film
Jewish Grandmothers (Kramer and Masur),
170n33
Jewish identity, xxvi–xxviii, 1, 33, 35, 84–85, 150,
157, 164n9; diasporic, 164n12; post-Holocaust,
5; queer identity and, xxx–xxxi, 113–15
Jewish moments, xxiii, 43, 72–78, 118–19, 131
Jewish mother, 41, 48, 49–51, 74–75, 84–85, 169n28
Jewishness, xvi–xvii, xxi, xxii–xxiii, 1, 40, 43, 52,
116, 119, 140–41, 157–59, 162n21; civility and,
78; disidentification from, 40, 134; food and,
40, 122, 177n20; and homosexuality as historical categories, xxxi–xxxii, 113–15, 132–33,
142, 176n9, 178n39, 180n71; legibility of, xxii,
40–41, 76–77, 101–2, 118–19, 128–31, 163n38;
masculinity and, 144, 148; physiognomy, 136–7;
race and, 133–37, 178n44, 179n47; secular,
xxvii, 77, 101–2, 122; usage, 164n9. *See also*
yidishkayt
Jewish queer representation. *See* queer Jewish
representation
Jewish tropes, xvii–xx, xxxii, 142; Jew as chameleon, 114; pathological Jew, xxxii, 118, 128,

141–48, 180n75; reappropriation of, xviii–xx,
xxxii, 142–48; Wandering Jew, 4, 180n9
Jews for Racial and Economic Justice, 95
Jolson, Al, 49
Joyce at 34 (Chopra and Weill), xxiv–xxv, 170n37
Judaism, xxi, xxxiii, 17–18, 118, 132, 150, 156–57;
homosexuality and, 121–22, 125, 144, 175n6,
176n16; usage, 162n21, 164n9

Kastner, Jamie: *Kike Like Me*, 169n15
Kazan, Elia: *Gentleman's Agreement*, 169n15
kheshbon hanefesh, 44, 59
khidush, 84–85, 158
Kike Like Me (Kastner), 169n15
Kirshenblatt-Gimblett, Barbara, xxiii, 40, 77,
178n35
Kleeblatt, Norman, 161n12
Klezmatics, 139–40, 177n33, 179n60, 179n62
klezmer, 139–40, 179n60, 179n62
Korda, Susan: *One of Us*, 69, 165n31
Kramer, Sydelle: *Jewish Grandmothers* (with
Jenny Masur), 170n33
Krausz, Michael, 40, 168n12
Kushner, Tony: *Wrestling with Zion* (with Alisa
Solomon), 95

Lacan, Jacques, 168n6, 177n27; on mirror phase,
37–38
LaCapra, Dominick, 24, 165n31
Lacis, Asja, 20, 166n64
Lanzmann, Claude: *Shoah*, 29, 165n31
Lazare, Bernard, 164n49, 180n69
Lebow, Alisa: *Treyf* (with Cynthia Madansky),
xxvi, xxx–xxxi, 37, 87–110, 111–12, 117, 121–22,
126, 127, 173n16, 175n34, 175n36, 175n42
Leopold and Loeb, 145
Letter without Words, A (Lewenz), 53, 162n27,
169n21
Let Them Eat Soup (Novaczek), 137
Lettre de Cinéaste (Akerman), 167n91
Levinas, Emanuel, xii, 23–24
Lewenz, Lisa: *A Letter without Words*, 53, 162n27,
169n21
Living with AIDS (TV show), 139; spoof of, 144
looking relations, 71–72, 83

Madansky, Cynthia: *Past Perfect*, 51. *See also*
Lebow, Alisa
Man with a Movie Camera, The (Vertov), xxiii,
163n33
March, The (Ravett), 56, 171n48
Margulies, Ivone, 11, 16, 18, 19, 22–23, 165n18,
165n26, 166n58, 167n70, 167n91
McBride, Jim: *David Holzman's Diary*, xxiv
Meeropol, Ivy: *Heir to an Execution: A Granddaughter's Story*, 170n34, 172n77
Meetings with Anna (Akerman), 4, 18, 164n11
memory: displaced, 1, 36; forgetting and,
33; heteropathic, 12, 165n28; identity and,
xxix–xxx, 43–44, 82–84, 132; indirect, 3, 19,
30–35; Jewish, xxix, 15, 17–19, 33. *See also*
postmemory
Mendelsohn, Moses, 167n87, 177n34

Miller, James: *Death in Gaza*, 181n11
Miller, Jennifer, 175n35
Miller, Nancy K., 39, 45, 46, 173n15
Minh-ha, Trinh T., xxxi, 93
Mitchell, W. J. T., 30
Moscow Diary (Benjamin), xxviii, 19–21
mourning, 32, 62, 76; Jewish rituals of, 61, 75, 77, 171–72nn61–62
Myerhoff, Barbara, 149–51, 180nn4–5, 181n20; *In Her Own Time* (with Lynne Littman), xxxii–xxxiii, 149–57, 162n28, 177n25, 179n63, 180nn4–5, 181n10; *Number Our Days*, 150, 155, 180nn4–5

names and naming, xviii–xix, 65–67, 171nn50–51; Jewish rituals of, xxxiii, 155–56, 179n63
National Foundation for Jewish Culture, 163n39
News from Home (Akerman), 164n11
New York City: Lower East Side, 107–9, 122
Nichols, Bill, 106
Nietzsche, Friedrich, 33, 90, 180n73
Nobody's Business (Berliner), xxii, xxix, 37, 39, 40, 43, 44–48, 54–55, 79–81, 181n22; kinship in, 79–80; oedipal gaze in, 45–47
nomadism. *See under* Jewish tropes
Noriega, Chon, xvi, 162n17
Novaczek, Ruth, xix, 111, 112, 119–20, 136–37, 178n44, 178n46; *Cheap Philosophy*, xix, 112, 114, 117, 119–21; editing style, 133–34; *Let Them Eat Soup*, 137; *Rootless Cosmopolitans*, xix, 37, 112, 128, 132–37, 178n41; sexuality and, 137
N'tureh Karta, 95
Number Our Days (Myerhoff and Littman), 150, 155, 180n4

Olney, James, 90
One of Us (Korda), 69, 165n31
Orders of Love (Benstock), 40, 81–82
Oxenberg, Jan, 115, 170n35; *Thank You and Goodnight*, xxix, xxxi, 39, 40, 41–43, 44, 51, 55–56, 58–59, 60, 72–78, 111, 122–23, 125, 169n28, 170n41, 171n56
Ozeki, Ruth: *Halving the Bones*, 171n44

Paper Bridge (Beckermann), 27–29, 165n31
Parkins, Zeena, 102
passing, 75, 114–15, 127, 135, 179n59
Past Perfect (Madansky), 51
Pellegrini, Ann, 171n50, 179n67
Phantom Limb (Rosenblatt), xxii, 42, 60–61
Phelan, Peggy, 127
Pollack, Chana: *Revisions*, 177n20
Portrait of a Young Girl at the End of the 1960s in Brussels (Akerman), 123–24
postmemory, xxviii, 11–13, 19, 28, 70, 81–82, 165n28
Prell, Riv-Ellen, 50–51, 169n26, 177n33
Promised Land, The (Antin), 100
Proust, Marcel, 132, 178n39
Purity (Zuria), 162n28
Put the Camera on Me (Stein and Shell), 169n18

queer identity. *See under* Jewish identity
queer Jewish representation, xxviii, xxxi–xxxii, 111–48; lesbian, 108–10, 111–12, 113–14, 120–24, 131–32, 133; tradition and, 121–26, 128

Rain (Ivens), xxiii
Ravett, Abraham, 55, 60, 61–72, 171n48, 171n54; comparison with Akerman, 62–63; *Everything's for You*, xxix, 37, 39, 42–43, 44, 56, 60, 61–72, 73, 85–86, 171n48, 171n51; *Half Sister*, 62–63, 171n54; *The March*, 56, 171n48; *Toncia*, 62–63, 67, 171n54
Renov, Michael, xii–xiii, xxxiii, 36, 38, 88, 155, 159, 161n5, 163n33, 164n44, 168n3
Renza, Louis, 173n13
repetition, 32–33, 42, 48, 63, 65–69, 164n8, 166n58, 171n54; in Jewish tradition, 32–33, 171n52
Return of Sarah's Daughters, The (Jarmel), 176n16
Revisions (Pollack), 177n20
Richter, Gerhard, 25, 31, 167n68
Rootless Cosmopolitans (Novaczek), xix, 37, 112, 128, 132–37, 178n41; race in, 134–37
Rosenberg, Ethel, 170n34, 172n77
Rosenberg, Julius, 172n77
Rosenblatt, Jay: *Phantom Limb*, xxii, 42, 60–61
Roth, Philip B.: *I Was a Jewish Sex Worker*, 175n2; *A 25-Year-Old Man Loses His Virginity to a Woman*, 175n2
Rousseau, Jacques, 90, 172n6
Russell, Catherine, xv

San Fransisco Jewish Film Festival, 128–29, 177n30
Santayana, George, 33
Schama, Simon, 8, 16
Scott, Joan, 173n14
Second Commandment, 4, 6, 7, 30–31, 34, 35, 124, 167n86, 168n102
Sedgwick, Eve Kosofsky, 176nn9–10, 176n17
Seidman, Naomi, 163n38
"Self Portrait/Autobiography: a work in progress" (Akerman), 11
self-representation, xii, xiv, xviii, 89–93, 97–98, 107, 150, 173n13, 174n32; family and, 36–37; others in, 39; temporal disjuncture in, 91–92, 173n11. *See also* autobiography; queer Jewish representation
Sephardic Jews, xxii, 163n30, 177n29
shiva. *See* mourning: Jewish rituals of
Shoah. *See* Holocaust
Shoah (Lanzmann), 29, 165n31
Sicher, Efraim, 162n13
Silverman, Kaja, 12, 165n28
Skoller, Jeffrey, 171n48
Spivak, Gayatri, 173n17
Sprinkle, Annie, 175n2
Stein, Darren: *Put the Camera on Me* (with Adam Shell), 169n18
stereotypes. *See* Jewish tropes
stock footage, 44, 61, 139
Stratton, Jon, xxiii, 77–78, 134, 136
subjectivity, xi–xvi, xviii, xxi, xxiii, xxix, xxx, xxxiii, 23–25, 37–39, 42, 71, 90–93, 97–98, 106–7, 132, 138, 150–51, 152, 158–59, 161n3, 161n6, 172n4, 172n6, 173nn9–10, 173n16, 175n42

(series page continued from ii)

ALISA S. LEBOW teaches documentary studies in the School of Arts at Brunel University. She is also a filmmaker, whose films include *For the Record: The World Tribunal on Iraq* (2007), *Treyf* (1998), and *Outlaw* (1994).